UNRAVELED

To:
Mrs. Chimamanda N. Adichie

For our common humanity,
and for all you do advocating
for a just and peaceful
world where all live
with dignity.
With gratitude —
Best,

UNRAVELED:

A Personal Journey into Conflict, War, and Diplomacy

BY DR. EMMA OSONG

Paperback ISBN: 978-1-7377924-0-6
Hardcover ISBN: 978-1-7377924-1-3

Printed in the United States of America

To Praxie with all my love.
Mom

To Rev. Bro. Norbert William Simms,
the teacher, mentor, and dad to be celebrated for all time.

Also, to my mom, Odilia Neh Ngang. Though never having achieved more than a third-grade education, you poured more knowledge into me than great scholars could possibly do in my lifetime. Mommy, your quiet, unassuming, can-do spirit remains my source of inspiration and a reminder of all the possibilities throughout these years.

CONTENTS

FOREWORD

By Patrick Lock Otieno LUMUMBA and Sébastien Nadot, PhD

Patrick Lock Otieno LUMUMBA

Thⁱhis book is a candid narration of the problems that continue to bedevil Southern Cameroon by egotistical megalomaniacs masquerading as leaders.

In 1961, when modern-day Cameroon emerged out of the two colonies, one of which had been colonized by the French and the other by the British, the joy that accompanied the creation of the federation of the two states was meant to herald peace and tranquility, but as Emma states:

The reality was not equality.

The reality was immediate assimilation.

The reality was annexation.

The reality was one of oppression.

In *Unraveled*, Emma peels the different layers that characterize the festering wound that is the conflict in Southern Cameroon. The narration reveals how tyranny can dehumanize an entire population without remorse and almost without consequence.

Although physically removed from theater of conflict, Emma demonstrates that the inhumanity engendered by the conflict defies geography and reveals the tragedy of the situation, albeit without permitting the enormity of the pain to drown her objectivity.

Emma does not allow the pathos of the moment to degenerate into the bathos of inaction, and this is captured in her own words:

> *Somewhere in here, I believe there is a warrior in each of us. A warrior when life throws us a curve ball. A warrior caught up in a battle to live or die trying. Somewhere out there, there is a couch warrior, too, fighting in the sidelines . . .*

These words found in Emma's note to the reader have a subtext to them; she tells us that we cannot afford the luxury of indifference. We cannot, like the famous Roman emperor, Nero, twiddle our thumbs as Southern Cameroon burns.

The power of Emma's narration lies in the fact that she is writing as a reporter of current events and not a historian writing post facto. Emma tells a tragic story with panache and aplomb that opens the mind's eye and invites action.

Without allowing sentimentalism to stand in the path of calm assessment of reality, Emma invokes the words of Bantu Steve Biko: "The most potent weapon of the oppressor is the mind of the oppressed."

I thus hear Emma telling the reader: don't wallow in despair; don't give up but rise up in your own way and fight a fight, a fight so mighty that the oppressor will surrender.

Emma's rendition of the situation in Southern Cameroon should stir the conscience of all persons of goodwill and animate them into liberating action.

PROF. PLO LUMUMBA, LL.D, D. Litt (hc), D.Sc (hc)
FCPS (K), FKIM, FAAS (hon)

Prof. PLO LUMUMBA is a Professor of Public Law, a holder of an LLD on the Law of the Sea from the University of Ghent, Belgium, a LLM degree, and a LLB degree from the University of Nairobi. He has been trained in Human Rights at the Institute of Advanced Legal Studies University of London, United Kingdom; Humanitarian Law at the Raoul Wallenberg Institute of the University of Lund, Sweden; and International Humanitarian Law in Geneva, Switzerland. He is an Advocate of the High Courts of Kenya and Tanganyika and a Certified Mediator. He is a former director of the defunct Kenya Anti-Corruption Commission (KACC), (now Ethics and Anti-Corruption Commission (EACC)). He is the Founding Trustee of the African Institute for Leaders and Leadership. He currently practices Law with LUMUMBA and LUMUMBA Advocates and coordinates activities under the aegis of the PLO LUMUMBA Foundation, of which he is the founder.

———

Sébastien Nadot, PhD

Unraveled: A Personal Journey into Conflict, War, and Diplomacy is a critical mirror on the individual and collective life of a people in profound crisis, conflict, war, and atrocities. Dr. Emma Osong has cast a wide net for the facts underpinning these grave conditions, which she has chronicled in this book.

These include the enduring badge of shame, humiliation, exploitation, and subordination imposed by European imperialism, colonialism, and neocolonialism on Africa. Like her ancestors, the author was born into this conflicted historical, economic, and cultural environment. This book is a personal account of the devastation of the author's Southern Cameroon's ancestral land of birth, the evisceration of her sovereign identity, the systemic crimes

3

committed against the people, and the looting of her natural resources.

This account is presented from the perspective of a victim who is also a passionate student of history, a keen observer, and a determined seeker of peace and justice for her people. Throughout this book, Dr. Emma Osong has presented truth, peace, justice advocates, victims of the crimes committed by La République du Cameroun during the annexation of Southern Cameroons, renamed Ambazonia, a platform, and a voice to bring their case to the conscience of the civilized world for an immediate solution.

The shocking prognosis of the health condition of Praxie with a verdict of "You will never walk again" occurred concurrently with the ongoing war in Southern Cameroons, in which unspeakable atrocities were committed by La République du Cameroun's soldiers, known as BIR. The magnitude of the slaughter of persons young and old, the rape of women and girls, the torching of hundreds of civilian settlements, the abductions, disappearances, and the genocide alarmed the conscience of the author and impelled her to do something to abate the carnage and the crimes. The author recounts the prognosis of her daughter, Praxie, and how Praxie's health condition mirrored the reasons advanced by Great Britain for mortgaging Southern Cameroons to France through the proxy of independence and union with La République du Cameroun in October of 1961. The verdict became a subterfuge for annexation and recolonization of Southern Cameroons for the economic exploitation by France and other Western economic interests.

At the center of the crisis is a variety of actors and a defining symbol. That symbol is Praxie, the ailing but determined daughter of the author. Every reader of this book will discover Praxie is going into some respects in their lives, their loved ones, and those of the society into which they were born or are living. Indeed, there is

Praxie in humanity at large, specifically in Southern Cameroons-Ambazonia conflict. I strongly invite everyone to get and read a copy of this book to discover for yourselves the Praxie in you, your family, and community.

Praxie was confronted by powerful adversaries: her debilitating health condition with a clinical verdict of "You will never walk again." The insurance company desired that she surrender her fate to the never-walk-again dire prediction in order to safeguard its financial interests. She chose to confront these powerful forces with self-preservation, freedom, courage, determination, resilience, and justice over fear, intimidation, and timid acquiescence. She challenged the status quo and the verdict of her health professionals. Praxie won in her search for justice, defeating the medical prediction by proving the verdict of "You will never walk again" inconclusive and nondeterminative of her fate and her life. A defining moment in the fight for health justice waged by the parents of Praxie is captured in a dramatic fashion in the book when Praxie "lifts one leg—drags it if she must—across the bare floor and then the other, one step, then another. It is a victory."

This victorious moment by Praxie mirrors that moment in September 2017. In the history of Southern Cameroons, hundreds of thousands of Southern Cameroonians defied all odds and took to the streets with peace plants, singing songs of freedom and justice after more than half a century of enslavement, humiliation, oppression, and submission to cruel systemic criminality. The critical lift of one leg toward total independence, peace, and justice was an enduring moment of unprecedented victory. It was a symbolic tonic for the freedom of victims, from fear and domination. On that occasion and subsequently, Southern Cameroonians have proved to La République du Cameroun and her colonial Francemasters that their prediction that Southern

Cameroons shall never walk toward freedom and total independence was wrong.

The author has carefully provided salient details about several actors and circumstances that have occurred in the conflict, the war, and the diplomatic efforts pursued to resolve the conflict. As a participant in these efforts, she has painstakingly described her role, those of others, and the internecine crisis encountered, as well as the policies and determination of the opponent La République du Cameroun, to cripple genuine peace efforts and address the root causes of the conflict. These include keeping the Southern Cameroon groups divided and making the peace efforts difficult to attain.

The author describes the malleability of Southern Cameroonians, among other factors, arises from years of institutional brainwashing, manipulation, intimidation, victimization, divide and rule, cajoling, and corruption. These systemic and institutionalized policies permeate all facets of the society with devastating outcomes. The educational system, religious institutions, age-old cultures and traditions, and the economic system all became instruments of oppression, indoctrination, and subjugation. All the facets of the Southern Cameroon's society and life are impacted far and wide, in all societies within and out of the homeland, wherever they attempt to come together for social causes and actions toward improving the lives of the people and students in their alma maters back home. The example of LESA, an association of ex-students of the Our Lady of Lourdes College Bamenda in the United States, is discussed in the book. It highlights one example where the never-walk-again prediction appears to regretfully succeed due to a combination of factors. Some of these factors are: the uncritical subservient education, which was inculcated in the students of Our Lady of

Lourdes Secondary School by the school administrators and teachers, the praying into submission solutions, prioritized by religious and secular leaders to serious conflicts over the truth and justice, and the extensive political tentacles of politicians within the oppressive system back home, who continue to influence and sustain the support of some individuals and associations in country and in the diaspora in their own victimization and that of their own people who are systematically exterminated through war crimes, crimes against humanity, and genocide.

The parental background of the author provides a strong ideological perspective and influence on her character and the perspicacity and profundity of the narratives in this book. These qualities are informed by developmental milestones within which the author was raised.

Her father was a professed progressive and socialist administrator during a period when the total annexation and dismantling of the sovereign structures of governance of the putative federation between Southern Cameroons and La République du Cameroun occurred. As an administrator of the poor and disaffected people, he endeared himself to the masses in these neglected rural areas. This experience, which is captured in the book through the profound sensitivity and concern of the author for victims, for justice, and for the recognition of the genuine identity of her own people, makes her a prime mover of the critical step in defiance of the dire prediction by coconspirators, that Southern Cameroons shall "never walk" to freedom and total independence. Her father left in the communities he served lasting memories of humility, community development, empowerment, and freedom. Inspired by his record of service, the people in these communities are stoically opposed to oppressive administrators who have been subjugating them to brutal annexation and humiliation through systemic violations of human rights.

The education and upkeep of the author, as well as that of her other siblings, fell on her mother when her father died. The efforts she made to provide quality education in good schools that were attended by children from affluent backgrounds mirror hundreds of thousands of exemplary Southern Cameroon women who are presented as the backbone of Southern Cameroon's identity, freedom, independence, integrity, resilience, courage, and foresight.

The book is insightful, incisive, and straightforward yet complex in some regard. There may be some readers who may be concerned with her honesty and her straightforward presentation of facts without reservations in this book. They will realize that she has not withheld the truth when presenting detailed, factual renditions of events that occurred in her own life, her family's, Praxie's, and her community's, as well as within her religion, faith, and church. The perceived refusal of her Francophone bishop friend to pick up or answer her phone calls when the war was declared against Southern Cameroons, whose invitation she engineered as a sign of brotherhood between the two political and cultural divides of Francophone and Anglophone, exposes the superficial constructs of one so-called indivisible fatherland. Even Francophone bishops and clergymen are aware of this reality, and the lies to advance personal interests and political and economic agenda of the oppressors of Southern Cameroonians. The painstaking account of the Swiss Peace Process and the frustrations the author has observed or encountered shows the extent of the awareness of the heavy responsibility she and other members of ACT involved in the process have on their shoulders. Her candid assessment of the alternative options presented by persons and groups who are opposed to the Swiss

Peace Process presents the reader with one credible conclusion: that there is no other credible alternative to the Swiss process and that ACT, although conflicted, is a strong symbol of that critical step that is defeating the dire prediction that Southern Cameroons-Ambazonia shall never walk again. ACT is a strong-standing symbol of the resolve of the people that attains peace and justice through an internationally mandated and supported mechanism and addresses the root causes of the conflict.

The book is a strong and stubborn indictment of the persevering spirit of hope as it is of injustice, hypocrisy, human rights violations, atrocities, self-deprecating complicit policies of enslavement, and the praying of wrongdoings to oblivion. It is a call to action by everyone, everyone contributing to the best of his/her capacity toward our individual and collective freedom and independence. This objective, which she strongly and strenuously asserts, is significantly important to be distracted by unjustified distractions of division and costly infantile grandstanding, which are benefiting the oppressor and delaying total victory.

Dr. Emma Osong's book is compelling bedside catechism for peace and justice seekers from oppression, atrocities, colonial rule, prejudice, exploitation, and domination worldwide. *Unraveled: A Personal Journey into Conflict, War, and Diplomacy* is an inspiring elixir of the important self-determination, freedom, and independence in the individual and collective lives of all victims of dire predictions and oppression.

By reading this book, we also learn that the power of words is an essential element of humanity.

Sébastien Nadot, PhD, is a Member of the French National Assembly, representing Haute Garonne since 2017. As a Foreign Affairs Committee member, he is a Rapporteur of the Mission on "The Democratic Refoundation of the European Union." He also serves as a Member of the Parliament's Commission of Inquiry into Obstacles to the Independence of the Judiciary and the President of the France-Quebec Parliamentary Friendship Group.

A NOTE TO THE READER

"To live is to suffer. To survive is to find meaning in life." This quote from Victor E. Frankl inspired me to believe that, though the pathway of life is through conflict, you can live conflict-inspired. I have searched long and hard to state my motivation for writing this book with transparency. I hope it sparks a conversation, as I hope others with a burning desire like me speak their truth on such an impactful issue, as a mother's grief and as war: two things unexclusive. My grief as mother was in no measure less than the grief suffered or experienced by mothers in theater of war.

For the reader, let me begin by stating that I did not set out writing a history account of the construct of Cameroon featured prominently in my narration of a fratricidal war. This book is not an account of history. It is a book on my lived experiences. A simple search on "the Cameroon Crisis" or on "history of Cameroon" should suffice as a good source for more than rudimentary history. Also, many more qualified writers have painstakingly chronicled the history of the country from ancient times through Europe's colonization to the present day. I make this full disclosure, knowing full well my attempts at situating my understanding of how I came to be Cameroonian necessitates a look at some key historical markers, and for that, I ran the risk of the proverbial imposter syndrome. Where my narration does not meet the rigors of historians, it is my hope that my story still remains of some relevance and interest to you.

Women are often taught to shy away from conflict, to function solely as peacemakers, or be concerned mainly for issues of family and societal welfare. When men start wars, women and children bear the brunt of hostilities, and as all wars eventually end when the parties sit down to resolve their differences, we often watch negotiations unfold from the sidelines, if at all. Bombarded with male images of warfare and leadership, we forget half the population that is living in conflict, the mothers and daughters who are unable to turn away from the war inside and out, women who have no choice but to embrace conflict because it is all around them. I was embroiled in conflict at a deeply personal level, in the community, and globally—in my backyard. I had few choices: wallow in my misfortunes, those of my friends and families, curse the gods for their crazy omens, anesthetize—numbing my mind and soul and carry on—or take the responsibility to be answerable to myself first and accept the responsibility to create new possibilities for all around me. Yes, such utterances ring shallow for some contemplating the enormity and consequences of deadly wars. If wars are caused by humans, then only humans can and do end wars. I believe no measure is too inconsequential if deployed in service of just peace.

In the fall of 2016, I had very stark choices when all optimism for life washed away as I cradled the limp body of my twenty-four-year-old daughter at the very moment when a war broke out steps from my childhood home, changing everything for me, my family, and the birth home I thought I knew. I needed clarity and understanding for myself and others, and I needed to find empathy for myself, those close to me, and those I may never meet in my lifetime, but for whom a genocidal war ripped us apart. The latter need is often farthest from our minds. NIMBY (not in my backyard) makes events happening thousands of miles away easier to dismiss, discount, ignore, and get on with our lives as we dare to do each day. I have penned here my personal narrative of the pathways of conflict, personal and existential that I hope can compel you to not look away, as I have penned a few critical takeaways and actionable steps that anyone can employ in the arduous task of caring for our common humanity or just caring, period.

I believe a warrior is in each of us, a warrior when life throws us a curve ball, a warrior caught in a battle to live or die trying. Somewhere, a couch warrior exists, fighting in the sidelines, in the American parlance, shooting the breeze. It unburdens the conscience but doesn't change the trajectory of anything. Somewhere among us is one who is silent, a NIMBY, unwilling or afraid to upset the apple carts that are maintenance processes, systems, or persons whose stock in trade is human suffering. For the couch warrior cozied up on the couch with a cup of tea turning these pages, conflict might seem a world away. And in a way, it is. Sadly, we have also been conditioned to ignore the plight of others, to observe at a distance—rubberneck, to be aware but not involved, to be neutral and maintain the peace. No such thing exists. For the purposes of diplomacy, there might be shades of gray. But where has diplomacy gotten us? Exploitation, greed, war—for the mutually beneficial illusion of peace. I am not here to advocate for the illusion of peace. I want justice. But I cannot do it alone.

To make a real difference, I need people to pay attention, to care, to act. I want you to care about adversity and conflict—your own and others'—and to get inspired by it—yes, to get inspired when the kitchen sink is proverbially thrown at you, and it feels like the world is conspiring to hold you down. "But how?" you ask. My one-step journey, as is often the case, contains one thousand steps by others, and through them, we learn and perfect our personal and interpersonal worlds. My hope is to harnesses and unleash your energy and passion, to make a positive difference in the world, to awaken you to the fracturing conflict of my birthplace and its people.

I offer a few call-to-actions in my story, which I hope renders useful, particularly for those new to this crisis. Some might be helpful as reference for crisis in other parts of the world. After all, peace is universal.

I hope to inspire you to face the conflict in your life head-on, to unearth hidden talents, and to overcome any conflict that comes your way. I do not want you to live conflict averse. I want you to be conflict-inspired.

Conflict is a force to drive self-reflection and difficult conversations and, ultimately, catalyze change. Conflict often shocks the conscious to disengage from ideals back to reality. In the pages below, the reality forces an awakening between who we say we are and what we do. It reminds us, as Frankl is known for, to ask if we have or are responsible for the conflict around us and for whom we are answerable and what actions we are willing to take today to enroll, engage, and transform your conflict spaces. The conflict in Cameroon drives my actions, a force that fuels my very being. After all, I cannot turn away from it; it is occurring in my own backyard. I cannot look away. It is unfolding steps from my childhood home. My story will draw your attention to the conflict we all face at one time or another, specifically that deadly war in Cameroon and the workings of peace advocacy, but don't stop there. Take what you learn about this conflict and the peace advocacy measures and apply it to your own life, spirit, and cause.

My goal is for you to apply conflict resolution and peace advocacy techniques within your life. I want you to learn how to face conflict head-on. Instead of fearing or avoiding conflict, I want you to learn to live conflict-inspired, as I have.

Let's begin.

Hugs,

Dr. Emma Osong

PRAISE FOR UNRAVELED

Reviews of *Unraveled*

———

This book provides invaluable insights to members of the international community, social justice activists, peace advocates, peace builders, seeking to transform their own communities and countries and those interested in obtaining insights into the history of the civil war in Cameroon and the prospects for peace there. The author, drawing upon her own personal and heart-wrenching challenges, shares her determination and tenacity to defy the odds and her ultimate success in obtaining the requisite health care for her daughter suffering from a debilitating illness. The lessons learned from that struggle, contemporaneously waged during the civil war in Cameroon, prepared her to move from an armchair warrior to be an ambassador and advocate for peace, justice and self-determination for her people in the Ambazonia. International activists, scholars and those involved or interested in conflict resolution in Central Africa and in Cameroon in particular alike will appreciate the valuable historical background information provided.

—Lennox S. Hinds Professor Emeritus Rutgers University Permanent United Nations Representative International Association of Democratic Lawyers

———

I am really humbled to be asked to share your inner thoughts. I cannot review what you have so eloquently penned. It is an expose of a remarkable journey, from a shy rural child in an African village to a space engineer in the midst of the USA, taking on the powers that be, to save our child...and knowing your rights and how to get them. It is the song of a quiet girl, wanting to fly with her own wings, to belong to a place she calls home, where she can be her real self in her own mother tongue. A girl, to be judged by her standards and not those that came to plunder from across the waves.

This manuscript is important. It is a masterpiece and should be read by everyone who wishes to be truly themselves. Not only does it speak to my belief that "women are not victims, we are resilient human beings," but it tells a history of colonized people, the dehumanizing effects of being ashamed to be who we really are... to be me, and that is good enough for me, and who do not like me as me, it is their problem, not mine. You yearn for the day when you can fly on your own across the river and never be afraid, in the land of your birth. The book is historical, scholarly, yet practical. It is not an on the shelf type of book, but a handbook of ideas that I can play with, think about and use in my everyday life. Congratulations and thank you.

—Pauline Elaine Riak, PhD
Deputy Vice Chancellor, Rumbek University of Science and Technology Rumbek, South Sudan
Chairperson, Board of Directors, The Sudd Institute Juba, South Sudan

———

Unraveled is a powerful, passionate account of one woman's journey through the twists and turns of violent conflict and the endless quest for peace. It intertwines the issues of injustice and unaddressed grievances across two continents in both personal and political ways. Emma Osong is an example of how regular mothers, daughters and sisters, through the trials of violence and exclusion, mobilize inner resilience, transforming themselves into great political leaders and warriors for peace. It is a testament to the day-to-day survival of those who live in violence: "Conflict was endemic to us, only we mostly saw it as 'hustling' to live. Conflict was everywhere yet concealed in its obviousness. We chose to get on with life until we couldn't carry on." And from such hustling are born those who refuse to accept that violence is a way of life, and that generational suffering can continue.

Emma Osong is one such leader. Unraveling is the song from her heart and plea to us all. Read with great care and respond with flowing compassion.

—Emma Leslie, Executive Director, Centre for Peace and Conflict Studies, Cambodia

EMMA M. OSONG, D.M.

―――

An exciting and profound story that speaks of determination and choices. The author tells two parallel events that for her represent two faces of the same existence, the journey through the pain of her daughter and the experience of war and desolation of her homeland. The leitmotif of the book is always the will to choose to act, to live in the present and decide to take charge of it to try to change it. From the acceptance of reality comes a great force that pushes the author to create new ways of interacting with the surrounding world aimed at defining a better world. Life becomes a teacher of life and a continuous opportunity to look forward and try to design a better future both in her private life and in institutional life. A dense book, to read in one breath, that leaves the reader with the hope that the world can truly become a better place. Each of us can do his own part.

—Maria De Rosa, Rome

―――

Dr. Emma Osong comes across to me as a committed woman, liberated in the genuine sense of the word: liberating her family, her community, her native land. It's precisely about her new book Unraveled, I am talking about. The book reveals a keen observer of human events and the spirit animating a writer whose one goal is to tell her personal story, as it is: an honest narrative responsive to domestic, religious and historical concerns. What is more, Unraveled propels ramifications beyond her life and family; ramifications that furnish her work a universal meaning and sets her out as vanguard writer —that feminine fecundity in African freedom fighting long expected. Her metropolitan experience (be it in Southern Cameroons or in the USA), her deep faith in God and church, her meticulous obligation to family, her scholarship, all these, have transformed her work into explorations of civilization in all its dimensions and grandeur. In this work, she has such a deep-seated disgust for oppression and injustice. Her gentle but penetrating engagement into the struggle for the independence of Southern Cameroons is unquestionable. Though American, she never forgets home, for in knowing her roots, she stands out as the brave female voice of our embattled motherland, Southern Cameroons.

Emma is a silent literary volcano that has already erupted in the genius, resplendence and creativity of Unraveled, a work I very much prize and invite all and sundry to read and enjoy.

—Fr. Gerald Jumbam Nyuykongmo, PhD, Rome

James Baldwin wrote that "people are trapped in history and history is trapped in them" (from "Stranger in the Village" in Notes of a Native Son, Beacon Press, 1955). Dr. Osong's book is about getting untrapped, confronting and taking control of the history and conflicts that shape one's identity(ies) within a family, a community and a country. With courage and eloquence, Dr. Osong describes her own journey and encourages the reader to join her (in the Calls for Action) at each step. Dr. Osong's journey is framed by the historical, political, and social context of Southern Cameroons (known as Ambazonia since 2017). She was born there, and educated under the colonial power of France, which replaced Britain in the early 1960s. She vividly describes the continuing struggles for self-determination, independence, and sovereignty in Ambazonia and details her own involvements, often as the only woman, in various diplomatic efforts and negotiations. Dr. Osong is relentless in her commitment to equality and justice; her intellectual and political openness are embedded in all of the struggles she describes. For her, the personal and political struggles are all part of the same struggle. In 2016, the protests in Southern Cameroon against President Biya's colonial rule coincided with the onset of her daughter Praxie's severe, immobilizing illness, requiring more than eighteen months of hospitalization. Dr. Osong fights for health care for her daughter, especially from the insurance company that wanted to cut off coverage. This same perseverance and focus are evident in her leadership to find solutions to the continuing war and its resulting crises in Ambazonia. Dr. Osong offers her insights on Ambazonia and Cameroun, and also on issues facing the rest of the Continent. In the Foreward, Dr. Osong tells the reader, "I believe there is a warrior in each of us." Unraveled energizes each of us to look at her or his life and begin (or continue) the process of finding and nurturing the warrior wherever we are, and in whatever we are doing.

—Beth S. Lyons

International Human Rights Lawyer, Alternate Delegate to the United Nations, International Association of Democratic Lawyers

INTRODUCTION

You Will Never Walk Again

There will come a time when you believe everything is finished.
That will be the beginning.
—Louis L'Amour, Lonely on the Mountain

The Beginning, the End

The country whose flag I carried and whose anthem I sang was not my birth country. I had been taught and told a whitewashed history, a history of convenience.

I woke up one morning, and there was a full-scale war unfolding just steps from my childhood home. It spread rapidly into the hinterland. I was, again, a child, learning the ABCs, this time of who I am. All the experts—and there would be many, their mouths stuffed with jargon and rhetoric—spoke of a country and a people. Versions of their truths stuck like baby corn to their teeth.

At the time, I was very far away. The view from room 4224 was lined with trees. The street and brick-paved sidewalks leading up to the main entrance of Johns Hopkins Hospital held little to look at, but I stared hard at the steady stream of cars turning up the circular driveway. I stared at the people, too: sober, somber, not rushed, alighted; they disappeared from view below as they entered the building. It struck me as odd the way everyone walked with the same determination. Coming or going, it didn't matter. Perhaps that is what a hospital does to people. I often looked out those windows during our time at the hospital. The scenery remained the same. But that day was different. That day, the words that refused to cede ground in my head were "You will never walk again."

Events 7,500 miles away in the country I was born in spilled onto my social media feeds. The horror of bullet-ridden bodies, exploded skulls, chopped limbs, and burned-out villages darted in and out of my mind, competing for my attention. It was November 2016. In the streets below the hospital room, the world slowed down to a crawl and faded into nothing. Praxie? Cameroon? Work. I floated, it seems, into a world of diametrically opposing scenes, both life-defining and frightening. Both irresistible and consuming. How did I get here? Like the current state of my birth country, Cameroon, I was born out of conflict. And beneath my surface hummed a hidden power, beauty unrevealed and untested. For years, I had maintained a delicate balance between my two worlds and selves. In doing so, I convinced myself I was neutral. But conflict does not allow for the in-between. You're either in or out.

I marked one particular day as my beginning, but it felt like the end at that time. Everything I held dear was set ablaze in battle. Despite the many miles between Cameroon and me, its conflict invaded my consciousness. There was no abstract distance, no objectivity that sheltered me from its suffering. I lived apart but within. My guilt and relief intertwined with anger, sadness, attachment, and empathy for a country I no longer recognize. Was my identity as fluid or in danger as Cameroon's? My answer came down like a sledgehammer. On October 30, 2016, the universe simultaneously declared war on the life I had left behind, the life I was living, and the life I grew inside of me.

After attending the tenth-anniversary celebration of the Cameroon Catholic Community in Washington D.C., I headed home feeling an overwhelming sense of satisfaction. Months of planning, hours of navigating egos, and treading carefully around delicate relationships went into my role as the chairlady of the committee. It was my responsibility to organize these celebrations, and it wasn't easy.

Our bold move to invite a French Bishop, instead of the Anglophone archbishop, to be our keynote speaker and chief celebrant for the anniversary Mass for the Cameroonian Catholic Community (CCCWDC) in Burtonsville was controversial. Before the event, I sensed the frustration of those who saw us reaching across the Mungo River to invite the bishop from the Sanaga region of Cameroon as a sellout move. But I also felt the hopefulness of those like me who believed we were doing our bit to put the long-running feud between the two sides of Cameroon, French and English, behind us.

My geography lessons in the convent college on the slopes of Bamenda Station had taught me that the Mungo River was just a large river and nothing more, not the geographic divide separating French Cameroon from English Cameroon, Francophone from Anglophone. The River Mongo was a convenient divider of one people from another. Mostly masked, the river divided the faithful, too. We were brothers of one country, each with his language, culture, and tradition—at least, that is what our Christian faith and the government-imposed curriculum has taught us, what had been drummed into our minds in primary through higher education. It was, I would later learn, an existential choice by our forefathers. We lived it and believed it, loyal to our core, as Christians often can be to a doctrine. We live it, too; though now, looking back as with the Ten Commandments, no dogma kept some of our forefathers from breaking many of the rules for which they paid dearly, some with their lives.

Much to my relief, the anniversary event was a huge success. Hundreds of parishioners crammed into the church, offerings were tallied to great applause, and speeches of gratitude flowed to and from the French Bishop. He was a natural crowd-pleaser. By the time the feasting and dancing was over, the community found a new friend in the bishop. He even insisted we call him Padre. You could say I was basking in the glow of that day. And you would be correct; I weathered the storm in a community known for its deep fractures, and I came out on the other side with clear skies. Now, with a formidable win under my belt, it was time to step back into regular life: work, home, and the occasional social outing. Sunday's spectacular night wound down with Monday's promise of a familiar routine. Success was a welcome nightcap. Drained from the buzz of the previous hectic months, I settled in for a well-deserved evening of rest. In truth, I was transitioning from one day to another, but not in the way I had expected. There would be nothing familiar and routine about Monday or life ever again.

An Unexpected Illness

The next day, my daughter, Praxie, called out to me from the living room sofa. "Mom, I don't feel well."

As a mother, I've experienced my fair share of late nights: ear infections, snotty noses, scrapes, cuts, and burns. At the moment, I wasn't concerned.

"You could stop at urgent care, but if you wait until morning, you can see your regular doctor," I suggested as I made my way from the kitchen into the living room. When I saw her, all hope of an overblown illness vanished. Her face was grim, and her eyes were vacuous. Something was wrong, really wrong.

After being admitted to the hospital, my daughter's condition worsened. By nightfall, she was having trouble raising her arms and legs. The doctors were perplexed. Up until then, she was a perfectly healthy twenty-four-year-old. Her blood work gave no clues, and she had no fever, no broken spine, and no trauma.

Suspecting muscular problems, she was medevaced from our local hospital to Johns Hopkins in Baltimore. Even with Praxie's hospital admittance, I returned home expecting that, in a few days, all would be well. How it unfolded, though, was my daughter did not return home for a long time.

Three weeks into her hospital stay, Praxie was diagnosed with myositis, a rare autoimmune disease. Her immune system had systematically destroyed the large muscles in her body, leaving her unable to walk, bathe, or perform the usual activities of daily living. This type of myositis is so uncommon that Praxie would become a subject for research at the National Institutes of Health. After the onset of her illness, she became bedbound and wheelchair-bound, but no less a social butterfly, a bubbly, loveable child, friend, and sister.

An Earth-Shattering Diagnosis

"I'm sorry, but you will never be able to walk again."

It was three long months into Praxie's hospital stay when she was given that overwhelming prognosis. It was devastating, impossible, life-changing news, whose manner of delivery did little to cushion the blow. When Praxie's doctor, a musculoskeletal therapist, uttered those words to my daughter, I was not there, and neither was her father. She was alone. I went home for a few hours for a change of clothes and a brief rest when I should have been by my daughter's side. When Praxie called from the hospital bed, she was inconsolable. I raced back to the hospital, desperate to help. But when I arrived, I felt helpless. All I could do was hold her and try to absorb her tears. What could I do to help my daughter?

As I took in this news—this strange concept that my daughter would never walk again—I stared at the doctors wide-eyed but stoic. My motherly instincts were strong: I would provide emotional space for Praxie as she came to terms with her prognosis. There was no longer doubt about my role and purpose. I would be her rock and her comfort. I was battle-ready. But not before the burn of hell seared through my body.

That night, I got home at two in the morning. Finally, the dam that I had built for my emotions broke. Collapsing onto the floor of my bedroom, I filled every corner of the house with my sorrow. When my tears were spent, I found relief in the emptiness. The space where my emotions filled was now empty, ready to take my child's pain. I packed up a toiletry bag, and Gerry, my husband, and I drove back to the hospital.

Battle-ready.

A Long Road

The days and months of therapy were long and tiring. I was there, at the hospital, always. Or that's how it felt. I helped the nurses with every transfer, every bath, and any support I could give to keep Praxie comfortable. The recliner at the foot of her bed doubled as my office, bed, and contemplative space. I stepped into yet another new role: that of stand-in nurse tech, turning Praxie every thirty- to forty-five minutes to prevent bedsores, bathing her, talking to the nurses, doctors, and therapists who streamed into her room. When I could, I sank into the recliner, opened my laptop, and caught up on the bare minimum to keep the paychecks coming. Telework was a godsend. The waiting area, the café, or spaces just off the long corridors in the hospital became my home office. I often looked out the window at Hopkins into the streets below for a distraction. My mind could not settle on the work that piled up; it would turn only to Praxie. The flesh of my flesh.

But there was another distraction disturbing me, another storm brewing. In fact, this storm made landfall in full force in my birth country, that place we call Africa in miniature—la République du Cameroun (LRC) or simply Cameroon. To think that, only a few months before, I was stressed about the implications of choosing a French versus an English bishop. A new set of grievances were emerging in Cameroon. They were spilling onto TV screens and social media platforms, threatening to erupt into a full-scale war that would ultimately engulf the English-speaking areas of the country. Meanwhile, I was 7,500 miles away, in a safe harbor I now called home.

At first, I ignored much of what was unfolding. And then my newest friend, Padre, stopped taking my calls; it didn't take long to imagine why. We were indeed divided by language, culture—the River Mongo—and now on opposite sides of a war about to shake our very existence. The longer I sat in that recliner at the foot of my daughter's bed or stood by her window looking out at the streets below, the more I realized I could not turn away from what was happening on the streets I once knew so well. Nor could I process it—blood of my blood.

Rushing Forward

Just a month before my daughter fell gravely ill, a reawakening was initiated in Cameroun. Thousands of peaceful protesters carrying only branches from trees symbolically referred to as peace plants by the locals poured out fifty-nine years of pent-up anger onto the streets of every town, village, and hamlet. Their target was the president and government of the Republic of Cameroon, a country whose past had been whitewashed, lay buried for decades in a convenient history. The epicenter of this crisis was the busy, shop-lined street called Commercial Avenue, barely miles away from my childhood home. Every other major rugged road and bush path would be filled with an awakened people.

In the almost sixty years since the country was symbolically granted independence, one part from France and then later the other part from Britain, to form the construct we know as Cameroon, only two men have held the title of president. Two men in almost sixty years. Perhaps the title "kingpin-for-life despot" might be more appropriate than president.

The 1961 independence ensured that the two former colonies would become one: a federation of two states equal in status.

The reality was not equality.

The reality was immediate assimilation.

The reality was annexation.

The reality was one of oppression.

Perhaps now you realize the trepidation—and relief—that the Anglophone community in the U.S., and I felt when our invitation to the French Bishop was deemed a success?

Breaking Point

In the fall of 2016, the so-called Anglophone problem was no longer a whisper. It was now an embryonic movement on the fast track to a full-fledged revolution. I would have to go to school to understand what Anglophone problems mean. As I sat at the foot of my daughter's bed, I could not look away. Streams of images and videos of killings by the Rapid Intervention Battalion (BIR for its French acronym)—the dreaded French-, Israeli-, and American-trained killing-machine army—now filled my WhatsApp forums daily. These raw content streams became all too familiar: gory photos and videos of crimes of atrocity, chopped-off human heads impaled on sticks by the roadside or placed strategically in the middle of a road in contested territory, images of dead bodies strewn about in city corners or in the open fields where the army gunned them down, piles of bodies—mostly of young boys—shot at close range, men with guns drawn at their temples, shovel in hand, digging the grave into which they would ultimately fall once dug deep enough. And then, there were images of villages burned to the ground, charred bodies visible in ruins, wailing friends of relatives, and those whose stance told the whole story of defeat or surrender to the circumstance. It was not long after that the videos, pictures, and audios poured in of whole villagers fleeing across the border into neighboring Nigeria, across the Mungo into French Cameroon, and into the immediate safety of the forest. All this was happening steps from my childhood home, from my grandpa's villages, and in the streets all over Cameroon's Anglophone northwest and southwest regions, now simply NOSO. A people without a name are called by any name convenient to the oppressor.

Each successive image defied human comprehension. By the BIR's admission, they needed to send a clear message to those "terrorists" and silence the young men and women in NOSO who, by now, called themselves the Amba Boys (because they are part of Ambazonia, the self-declared state) into total submission. It was also said that the Amba Boys carried out similar forms of atrocities to deter the BIRs from reentering their villages to kill, raid their homes, or burn down their villages. Only those who ran into the bushes got out alive and can testify to that. As the atrocity crimes increased, it is said that members of Biya's government created rival militias to go against the Amba Boys. They, too, claim to be Amba Boys.

In that hospital room, 7,500 miles away, I did not know what felt worse: the trauma of seeing death as no one should or the pain of a mother grappling with a sick child. My mind was clouded with questions.

How do you ignore a war so senseless?

How do you support a child with an illness rare enough to study?

How do you de-escalate a conflict nearly 8,000 miles away?

How do you help your daughter when the doctors in front of you can't?

As my inaction paralyzed me, the march went on. The conflict escalated. Support erupted stateside. Southern Cameroonians of all shades and some Francophones in the diaspora began demonstrating all over Washington, D.C., and at the United Nations in New York.

From my recliner in the hospital, I followed the growing rallies in dozens of cities around the world. I wanted so much to be in the crowds in front of the UN, at the French Embassy in Washington, D.C., and on the steps of the Capitol. I was trapped. My daughter needed me.

My brothers, sisters, mothers, aunts, and uncles, young and old, rose from beneath the crushing indignities of the brutal regime of Yaoundé. The gunship helicopters that killed the peaceful protesters did little to stem the floodgates of protests. If tear gas cannons cleared the streets, it served only to strengthen the resolve of the now growing sentiment that sixty years as a *seconde classe* was enough. Was it, indeed, Ambazonia rising? The people had a name.

The pull of the cause flooded me with guilt. I was helpless, unable to fix the gaping wounds in my loved ones. The killings became more brazen and frequent. The floodgates of hell were now opened. Was my daughter's life not the most important thing to me now?

Was I missing a once-in-a-lifetime opportunity to take part in the making of history? It was disorientating and bewildering. I had a foot in both worlds, stretching my limbs forward for balance, but the ground was just beyond my reach. These were the questions, the conundrums, the agonies of this time.

Combat Begins

After nearly six months, Praxie was discharged to a nursing home. Her health quickly deteriorated. After five days, she returned to the hospital only to find that she was being discharged again. "To where?" we asked. "And why?" In their view, she had plateaued. The administration staff handed me a manila envelope and announced that, as of two weeks before, Praxie was a self-paying client. She reached her lifetime maximum, and if she stayed, her room and bedside nursing would cost $1,100 per day, and her specialty care would total almost $2,000 per day. Astonished, I accepted the envelope and started at its overwhelming contents: twenty pages of itemized rolling services totaling $180,000 and increasing every day. Praxie was devastated. To her, there was only one way to read the situation: she was being sent home to die. My daughter gave me power of attorney, and I buckled up. I promised to fight this next fight for her with every bit of grit and determination I had because I was fighting for my baby's life.

In April 2017, I wrote to my congressman and representative detailing how my daughter was being asked to go home to die because the insurance company claimed she was making no progress and had reached her lifetime maximum for health care. In my letter, I explained how, unlike the insurance company's judgment, Praxie showed marked improvement with continued acute rehabilitation and treatment. I wrote that if they stopped payment now, they would be rationing care for my daughter and reversing the gains she had made. It was not an option for me to take her home at this stage, nor could she afford the cost of her care. I pleaded to this congressman as a mother asking for assistance so that Praxie could continue receiving the much-needed acute rehabilitative care to recover from the effects of her disease fully. I sent the letter, and I prayed.

Donning my suit of armor, I addressed the hospital administration and staff. I barred them from Praxie's room and directed all communication through the mail. The pressure for us to discharge her was intense, and every week, a new summary of services and bills was left for me on the windowsill in Praxie's room. I never opened another after the first. I made the mental calculations: $186,000 + $3,000 per day = blank. I couldn't change the hand I was dealt, but I could change what and how I felt. I held off the bean counters at the hospital for months, and gradually, Praxie showed some improvements.

Court Case

The insurance company's thirst for money and failure to approve the lifesaving therapies and treatment caused the rapid decline in Praxie's health. The judge ruled in our favor. I insisted on a letter stating that Praxie was not liable for any bill she incurred while in the hospital. I got it.

And then on June 13, 2017, eight months since she was admitted to the hospital, Praxie came home—at her request. It's odd to admit that I was conflicted. I was immune to my surroundings and became accustomed to being in the hospital. The nurses were attentive. They offered me a cot at the base of Praxie's bed and a mini fridge, and I brought in a tiny Crockpot. I washed and bathed in the hospital, slept in the hospital, and occasionally came home for a change.

Gerald, her dad, ran the errands, chauffeured, and would sit in the corner of the room for as long as it took by his daughter. As I look back, it must have been too much for him to bear seeing Praxie in her state of health. I would look around, and he would not be in the seat at the corner, and often, I would find him in the waiting room, in the hallway, or back in the car, just sitting. My "job" in the hospital gave me a newfound purpose. At the onset of Praxie's illness, when she was a "complete deadweight," it required Gerald and me to turn her from side to side. As time went by, I had mastered the trick to move Praxie with much ease: to give her a full bath on the bed without making a mess of everything. In hindsight, Gerald might have felt he was not needed as much and that simply looking on was too much to bear; he would stay awhile and return to the waiting room or just sit in the car to catch a nap.

We were all sleep-deprived during the worst six-month stretch. Praxie was unable to fall asleep for longer than one or two hours. On account of her full-body paralysis, she had developed a heart condition and was also in a state of full panic, afraid as she tearfully cried out to me of being unable to move her body and of suffocating. I watched helplessly as she clung to the call button in one hand and her cell phone in the other. Even as I sat at the foot of her bed, she would call out, "Mommy, Mommy." She simultaneously pushed the red panic call button. "Please, Mommy, can you move my leg just a few inches to the left, to the right? No, please, Mommy, a little higher. Thank you." It would be all of ten minutes when she would say, "Mommy, I am in too much pain. Can you help me sit up?"

I recall the slight looks of bravery when I announced I would leave to go home for a change or that of fear as she clung to her lifelines—the red button and the phone—for she could sink and suffocate if only a pillow moved to the wrong place. I was not a nurse, but a mother never runs out of her inventions to help a child. The words, "Good night, Praxie" or "Praxie, I will see you shortly," came out of my mouth with all the care and bravery I could summon. Then, on the days I would go home for a change of clothes, as I made my final look around her bed, tucking here or there around, placing the bedside table just at the right height close by, checking and re-checking that Praxie could summon help if she needed, I dimmed some of the lights and walked out into the corridor, pushing back every tear to its place.

For months, I had watched for any change in the level of care Praxie received, stepping in to provide it myself when required. Gerry's presence was regular and quiet; though it was, of course, easier for me to take care of Praxie's personal care. I learned how best to make her bed while she was in it, I'd get medical supplies when they were needed, and I'd put her in her wheelchair to take her outside or to the bathroom. Giving her a long, slow bath became second nature. I did not mind; I dared anyone to stop me.

When Praxie was up to it, I used bathing as therapy. With the nurse tech's help, we strapped her into a bathing wheelchair. I waved Sharon off, letting her know I would call if I needed help. I will not call for up to two hours, holed in a bathroom, bathing my daughter as one would a child, lovingly conjuring her body back to health. I gathered what was now my special healing oils, bathing essentials, hospital towels, and washcloths and wheeled us both into the bathroom down the long hospital corridor. The first-day bath, not a bed bath, was deliberate, long, one only a mother could give an adult child. When Sharon rushed into the bathroom, the look on her face said it all. You are both still here? I was followed by, "Girl, it smells so good in here. What is that you have all over my girl?"

She had taken to calling Praxie "my girl." After months of no use, her feet were covered in layers of dead skin. Her condition made her body flake. I anointed Praxie's body in lavender, orange, and almond oils from the top to the bottom of her feet after scrubbing off months of dead cells all over her body.

Our next stage entered with both joy and sadness. What was I to do with her at home? I did not have the physical environment she could live in without becoming a prisoner in one room. But she wanted to come home. I sprang into action.

Come Home

With the help of Cathy, Praxie's social worker, a plan came together. We would need professionals: doctors to visit her at home, a daily nurse, a nurse tech, a specialty nurse for her infusions, and a personal aide. We would need in-home therapies, physical, recreational, and psychological. Praxie would need the same level of—or as close as possible—medical-grade equipment and supplies: a sit-to-stand lift, hospital beds, and hospital supplies. I added that my home must not be a firetrap for my daughter; I would need to be able to get her in and out of the house in the event of a fire and for recreation. I would need a ramp, an ADA-compliant bathroom, doors, and a chairlift. I wanted Praxie to join the rest of the family from the basement room that would be hers.

Cathy was incredible. She called all the departments responsible for setting up transitional in-home care. The next day, the staff, nurses, and doctors called for a discharge planning meeting. I told Cathy it could only happen when I had all Praxie's services entered into the system and the delivery and start dates, along with contact information of the vendors, nurse agencies, and doctors listed and given to me. This would take another five weeks.

By the time we took Praxie home, some of my anger at how the insurance company had treated us had dissipated. For the staff of Johns Hopkins, I penned a letter addressed to Cathy to be shared with all who cared for Praxie. I described my joy that she would be coming home and my thankfulness for their presence and care. During Praxie's time at the hospital, I had come to appreciate what love looks like in the faces of her nurses, doctors, family and friends, some of whom I didn't know and would never meet again. I shed tears that came from a place of joy, relief, and gratitude.

I received this reply:

> *Dearest Emma,*
>
> *What a beautiful note. There are not enough words to describe the most profound admiration and respect I have for you. The love you have shown for your daughter and the lengths to which you and your husband have gone to advocate for her are awe-inspiring. It is because of you and your family and Praxie's will that she has come so far and will continue to flourish. I do not doubt that Praxie will have a full and beautiful life. You are an extraordinary family, and I will forever be grateful for the lessons I have learned from you. I will never forget you.*
>
> *With deepest affection,*
> *Cathy*

"Mom, take me home."

On the day Praxie left the hospital, our spirits were high. Praxie smiled for my camera, though I knew she was hesitant about being photographed or filmed. I also knew that behind her smile was fear;

I felt that fear, too. It had settled deep into my heart. But the truth is, as a family, we were tired, tired of the hospital, tired of dealing with not only our challenges but also those of other patients, each with their own tragedies, their own battles. It was time to be home. Some nurses were excited; others cried. Here was Valerie, who was also from Cameroon and felt a kinship to Praxie and would do what she could to be scheduled to work in her wing. Valerie lingered a bit longer long after her nurse activities were finished. She, like many others, had come to form a special bond with their longest-staying patient. They had all lived these months with us, with Praxie as a consistent, joyful presence in their daily routine. Though she was immobile from her neck down, Praxie smiled from her neck up. She lit the room for whoever came by to take care of her during those long months in the hospital. I knew some nurses switched patients to have her on their schedule; her room was the fun place to be.

Two months after Praxie came home, I received a call from Johns Hopkins asking me to do a written testimonial or video on Praxie's care at the hospital. They read the beautiful note I sent and wanted my daughter's experience to be featured on their marketing site. I put the idea to Praxie. She was conflicted. I didn't blame her. I cannot speak about her acceptance of her situation. I know, for me, I arrived at a peaceful place.

I believe that it would have been a gift for others to hear about Praxie's strength, courage, and joy as she lived through pain and suffering—a legacy of sorts. But I trusted her decision to keep her suffering and recovery as it was, a family journey. Praxie is recovering and remains effervescent with an uplifting and occasionally chatty spirit.

Our new normal is now routine, and she is blooming where God has planted her, complete with friends and interests. I no longer sleep on a cot at the foot of her bed.

Whenever I encounter people who show too much sadness upon hearing about her illness, I remind them that my daughter is whole, perfect, and complete. Her illness is no different from diabetes or cancer. She gives me more courage and joy than those around me who jump and dance. No one leaves Praxie's room uninspired by her courage, her smiles through her pain. I am the only one who sees the tears when everyone else has left. I am the only one who knows the terror as her heart threatens to jump out of her chest or when her stomach aches from the concoction of therapies and medicines. I saw a broken child only once, and that was when the doctor told her unceremoniously that she would never walk again. When I arrived by her bedside and saw the swollen face and eyes, I knew I had to cradle her in my hands until the strong and resilient child emerged. And she did emerge and continues to sail through her challenges.

After seeing my daughter struggle, break, fight, and heal, I know that, in each of us, there is a wellspring of power, strength, and courage into which we could each tap. Praxie reached inward and demonstrated courage and strength where I would have crumbled and remained. I made a conscious choice to tap into my power. Within the wreckage of my previous life, I connected with something bigger than myself: a cause. There was another broken loved one that needed my support, even though I couldn't imagine how to gather the strength: my beloved Cameroon, or so I had been conditioned to believe.

Praxie, her siblings, and parents watched as she learned first to reach and lift. I began to learn who I was.

CHAPTER 1:

IMAGINARY NATION TWICE BORN

The most potent weapon of the oppressor is the mind of the oppressed.
—Steve Biko

I t's human nature to want to belong. But can you belong without knowing who you are? As I cared for Praxie, I knew who I was: mother, caregiver, wellness champion, financial litigator, confidante, and cheerleader. Those identities were clear-cut and welcome in the steady rhythms of daily life.

However, as I witnessed the atrocities on my people, the lines blurred. How was I supposed to wade through lineage, political boundaries, religion, geographical-shifting sands, and a victor's narrative of my own history? And since I left for economic and educational reasons and returned for short family vacations, was it even my fight? In my heart, I knew it was. Just as I fought to see my daughter be able to blossom and thrive, I wished the same for my own people. Unpacking my complicated feelings required distance. Although I was geographically on the other side of the world and safe, my heart beat with the pulse of each injustice. The only way I knew how to rediscover my connection with a self I'd shelved was to return to the beginning and to relearn my own history so that I could tell the world.

Cognitive Dissonance

I am awakened to stories reminiscent of countries sadly still embroiled in war. But these stories, now all too present in my media feeds, are about a country I thought I knew, a country that, since my birth, I was to hold patriotically dear as my birthplace. Had I not carried its passport, sung the anthem under the bright green, red, and yellow flag stamped with two stars—or was it one star? Was it a phantom?—I will now be awakened to its whitewashed past filled with all the intricacies of a convenient history dutifully choreographed first by the West, packaged by its former colonial work hands, and later inculcated into the young, impressionable minds of successive generations of children in the myriad convent schools and public now administered by more political calculating servants. Today, a nation is in the throes of birth as another seeks to rebirth, yet again, a new version of itself as a nation through war. Cameroon, Africa in miniature, it is called.

It wasn't only that I no longer recognized the country that bore me. The reality struck much deeper within the fibers of my identity. The country I believed to be mine wasn't.

Were the chanting masses on the street real? Are the gunship helicopters and encroaching military there to protect?

The cool metal of a machine gun presses against your neck. Dust fills your mouth where your lips press the ground. With each inhale, sharp particles coat your throat, but primal fear twists sinew and bone. Blood pounds in your ears. Sweat trickles from your forehead; saline polka dots grow on the rust-colored earth beneath. Your biceps scream from the effort of being lain flat after hours of holding a picket sign. The neighbor's elbow digs into your side, clammy and unforgiving. Hope lies beside you, facedown and under arrest.

Neglected stories of a rapidly escalating crisis float aimlessly through the ether, largely ignored by most of the world. We have

not quit. I owe it to my experiences and to the members of the English-speaking peoples of southern Cameroon: Anglophones; now they call us NOSO. Perhaps if I share and own what's happened to me and countless others, it will make a difference. Stoking the embers of change is beyond the grasp on one; it is the duty of many.

When I think about introducing the country I called for decades as my country of birth, I'm slammed with churning vocabulary—disjointed, dissonance, confusion. I'm not sure how to tell a story that's unfinished, whose murkiness inflames a deep desire for resolution, for others, the cunning for continued deception. It's difficult to pinpoint what the story is when I've only recently awakened to all its conflicts, contradictions, inconveniences, and whitewashes, sometimes its differences without distinctions, and now, its war—a war in full gear just outside the steps of my childhood home. What am I to make of this? How do I describe the soul-wrenching inheritance of twisted and partial truths? It's personal—each person carries her peculiar vexations. Mine is double-spaced, like others put kin against kith, sister against brother. Inside every human is a desire to understand, to know self, society, and a greater truth. We desire meaning, both intrinsic and expressed. We're social creatures. Belonging is necessary for survival. Our identities are the very source of that belonging. When our identity changes, our attachments and loyalties are thrown into question. Identity drives bonds, loyalty, and action. Perhaps my friend, the bishop, also feels this way. Perhaps my sister, whose husband hails from across the Mungo River, is distant, fearing it is best to stay neutral. But I may never know, as we seem set on the same heaven-bound path but divergent on our earthly paths. Even in the face of oppression, turning your back on your own country changes you. And how is it turning my back when I truly want—just like all humans—a home, a place where I am not a second-class citizen, and a true nationality? It's not my country I'm opposing; it's the parasite sucking its blood. I am opposing half-truths and a repressive past. I am opposing its war of assimilation and annexation. I can never be the same; my start is not my end. My battleground—at least, for now—is an existential one. From fear to activism with ever-present danger, I bear the scars of evolution, but what person can emerge from oppression unscathed? Generations to come will bear the trauma of today, and their lives are merely a blip on the radar. Maybe it feels overwhelming to choose a place to start my story when it's always been this way.

A Stateless Spirit

Maybe I started my story with my daughter being told "You'll never walk again" because my country's journey runs parallel. Instead of the flourishing, independent nation I imagined, Southern Cameroon, rather than being led to self-rule or full independence, received the diagnosis "You cannot walk alone." Instead of treatment, Southern Cameroon received hospice. "You are impoverished, a burden to the purse strings of the British Crown and treasury." Instead of supporting a thriving Southern Cameroon, my country of birth—a former League of Nations–mandated territory, a United Nations trust territory—received conditional independence based on peace treaties and annexations that served everyone but Southern Cameroonians. It did not matter that on April 21, 1961, the UN General Assembly (UNGA) voted UN Resolution 1608 with sixty-four to twenty-three member states voting for the independence of British Southern Cameroon. What happened next was, at the dawn of our independence on October 1, 1961, French Cameroun moved its gendarmes as the British moved out their personnel and annexed our land from the coastal towns of Buea to the plateau grass fields of Bamenda. From what was to be our progressive development toward independence turned out to be recolonization, only this time, the British left, and France stayed on, taking up more territory in the process. Through the neighboring, already independent country of *la République du Cameroun* ((LRC) French Cameroun), France became the new colonizer. I can see the temptation to wither, practice acceptance, get on, and get by. But when my daughter was told to accept a future of conditional mobility and dependence, was denied helpful therapies that could even reverse her illness, and was revealed as a burden on the deep insurance pockets, we fought back because that reality was unacceptable. I couldn't accept a world that didn't embrace my daughter's resilience, healing, and autonomy. We took on Goliath, the hospital administration—the bean counters and the insurance company. Against the current, we pressed on until lifesaving concessions were won in the courts. Our rights were presented to us wrapped in a bow, a gift with strings.

I am without history or nation. Despite holding a navy-blue passport with an eagle embossed on the front, my spirit feels stateless. Words like refugee, statelessness, exile, and immigrant all have various connotations and technicalities, none of which apply to my daily life. From my house, near Washington, D.C.—a lush and vibrant metropolitan city—my situation has been far better than most. So, why do I still suffer from the effects of displacement?

The country I was born in, believing it my own, left me. It is called LRC, the Republic of Cameroon. For the world, it is simply Cameroon. I am without a birth state, and the one I thought is my own is in a state of war with an enemy so deadly and so deceitful, with powerful friends around the world. Far from the war theater, my soul bleeds. I am a victim of war. I must be a stakeholder, as I cannot afford the comfort of silence, inaction, or neutrality.

Many would ask, "But why are Blacks killing one another in Africa? Can't they just live like brothers? Can't they kick out the old dictator (someone I would rather label 'kingpin for life,' otherwise known as president in the person of Mr. Paul Biya Bi Mvondo) and bring in a new crop of leaders? And work together and prosper together?" These simplistic but sound, vexing questions are divorced from the complexities of the construct I knew as Cameroon or what is good for Africa.

According to the Office of the UN High Commissioner for Refugees (UNHCR), there are more than ten million stateless people worldwide. That means a new stateless child is born about every ten minutes. To say the politics involved with these issues are complicated will be a gross understatement. Living within the shadows, these people face hardship, little social support, and slim to no opportunities. That has not been the case in my life. However, I have suffered from the erasure of my history. I'm cut off from the place I was born, forced to watch its conflict from afar. I'm unable to return, and I've made my peace with the life I live. But I was robbed. A chance to connect with the true story of my people, ancestors, and culture was stolen from Cameroon. The history of Cameroon is being rewritten, and the longer it continues, the more likely it will never be recovered. And people like me will be forced to forge on, with pages missing from our storybooks.

Erasure: A Well-Worn Tool

Overnight, my daughter's illness rubbed out nearly twenty-three years of physical ability. Will I ever see my daughter walk again? I am standing confident in the stronger, bolder, cheerful version she is now each day. The only place we knew where to aim our energy and time was our memories, a shared history. Love, history, and memories are life's compass. Without them, we're adrift. It's a painful journey knowing what's been erased. Memories are like footprints. They mark our journey. And historical narratives are the footprints of history. Like footprints on the shore, a persistent storm, French Cameroon, threatens to wash it all away into the deep blue.

The ability to retrace history is a privilege unbeholden to many. The ability to walk, speak, assemble, and hope is taken for granted. And erasing that ability is a well-worn tool of oppressors. Without knowing where we've been, how can we find our way home? In the fight for peace, I am fighting for our rights to know our past from our own perspective and to arrive at the very essence of peace: justice. And when we get there, know it for what it is and honor it. The tools of erasure make this daunting.

Currently the battle lines are drawn in subtle and overt ways steps from my home. In the diaspora, elsewhere in the safety of our homes, workplaces, and drinking wells, the battle lines expose sixty years of pent-up anger between an ever-growing faction of Cameroonians whiplashed into war. Social media is increasingly vitriolic and threatening. The wrong word or comment results in death threats. The wrong alliance could signal trouble for you or your family in the village or abroad. The bold and hardened do not care and spew hate and threats as fast as their keyboards can type to any enemy. Our history, now told in an ever-growing new version, gets even more confusing, and the intellectually lazy among us and the world are exhausted, offering the easy way out as solutions, as they also get increasingly dismissive.

They say knowledge is the first step to wisdom. We are born unknowing and then our impressionable minds fed with bits of data and information.

Efforts to erase history to benefit an oppressor is not a new concept. Indoctrination feeds young minds to believe and live a truth not of their ancestors. They have no way of knowing or fighting back until perhaps it is too late, and they acquiesce, or the damp of deceit breaks open. In fact, forcing a version of history that benefits a certain power structure is part of the colonization toolkit. To rid an ensnared people of any connection to their history, culture, or autonomous past begets generations of oppression. There are countless examples of this practice throughout history. With each invasion of ancient Egypt, as the power shifted from Nubian rule to Roman through Islamic (Arab), Turkish, French, and British hands, the rulers in power left their mark on people for generations to come. The British and French perfected the art of colonization, leaving the fingerprints of oppression that are still visible today all across the world. If stories across the Atlantic seem too far away to be relevant, one doesn't need to look far.

In the United States, the whitewashing of history—particularly in the context of slavery and the civil rights movement—has indoctrinated generations with stories of the "White savior." They are stories of an economy built on capitalism but silent on slave capitalism. Generations of Africans were brought to this nation and given new religions, work, families, even names, while forced to work the land stolen from the slaughtered Indigenous people. Ship loads of human cargo sailed from Africa and toiled to build the wealth of nations whose benefactors today see no linkages of their dynasties to the sweat and blood of men from Africa.

The history of the construct called Cameroon—a peaceful bastion in an Africa rife with war, a miniature Africa—is a whitewashed history, a history of convenience. Stories of a one and indivisible Cameroon are touted, but no one tells you that Cameroon, an African Union (AU) member state, ratified the AU Constitutive Act on the inviolability of borders and the UN charter on territoriality. If Mr. Biya's sad display of ignorance was not pitiful and laughable, then sadly, it is now deadly.

I can only imagine countries today in the Middle East laying claim to their neighbors on account of having been part of the Ottoman Empire. What an imperialistic dream! Even those who laid claim to a large swath of Europe or far eastern lands corralled and held ethnic groups together under the banner of nationalism and saw those mammoth edifices crumble. Where the Roman empire failed, so, too, did the Soviet Union, Czechoslovakia, and Yugoslavia. Where wars were fought in Europe and Asia over communism versus capitalism, much of the Western powers fought to defeat communism even if it meant the balkanization of former countries. Funny, yes. Sadly, it is true, in the case of Cameroon. Southern Cameroons is not part of Cameroon any more than part of Central Africa is part of Cameroon. To bend the truth, war was waged. What is a person with an erased history to do? The opportunity to go back has been taken. There is only forward. But the forgotten etchings of our past will always cry out. Justice is far from peace. Unless dead, the brain will remember.

Conflict Erases an Inconvenient Truth of Cameroon Until Independence

Transition is a natural part of the life cycle on this planet. We are born, we grow, we live, we wither, and die. Change is an innate part of this structured existence. Even during these cycles, our physical, mental, and spiritual selves fluctuate. Even within the animal and plant world, transition and change are necessary. From seed to harvest, caterpillar to butterfly, and calf to cow, change is ever-present.

Within these transitions, there are consistent phases: death, dream, build, and flight. Death is the end of something. The dream phase is when you use your imagination to figure out what's next. When you are in the build phase, you're working toward a vision. And when you enter the flight phase, you spread your wings and enjoy the fruits of your toil.

When I witnessed my child's life-threatening illness, I experienced a death of self. The woman I was before the crumbling of my world no longer exists. In losing her, I gained another. A different version of myself that was previously hidden was brought to the surface. In so many ways in life, we're born and reborn many times over. We tumble, gather ourselves, put our nose to the grindstone, and rise again. My country might be in flux, but I know it can be rebuilt. We must dream.

A Matter of History

Cameroon has been birthed many times. In the years before quinine was widely available, malaria prevented a significant European settlement. Once large supplies of the drugs became readily available, an influx of the slave trade and Christian missionaries began. As a wealth of businesspeople began building infrastructure, the German government followed suit: railways, bridges, and further territory. During World War I, the British arrived. After the war, the UK and France split the colony under the League of Nations mandates (class B). German administrators remained to run plantations. Cameroon became LRC. French Cameroun was not unlike a military dictatorship. After a nationalist movement, French Cameroun gained independence on January 1, 1960.

Cameroon became LRC, the Republic of Cameroon. We will call her French Cameroun, not for having been led to independence and the reigns of sovereignty handed over to the people but not unlike a Napoleonic military dictatorship, for remaining yoked to her former colonial master. For giving her independence, General de Gaulle, French president, relegated for himself the power and privilege, and without any need for an explanation, the right to chart the political, economic, and cultural affairs. A pernicious form of more than half a century for continuous colonization took root in Cameroon as elsewhere in *Francafrique*. France, for its labor on the soil of African in the days leading to independence, would reserve the right to exploit Cameroon's resources. For good measure, France also minted its former colony's bills, the franc *Colonies françaises d'Afrique*, later changed to the politically correct and current *Communauté Financière Africaine* (CFA) franc, with French Cameroon's foreign reserves and exchange deposited and held in the central bank in Paris. Yes, the government of French Cameroun could borrow against her funds, but most pay the stipulated interest rates. France succeeded to use French Cameroun for its good. In exchange, the people of the former colony got military assistance and some investments in the country's health, agricultural, and educational systems—and us, too.

Many patriots—true nationalists who believe in real independence—would die at the hands of French military who claimed to fight the Makiza. The homes and villages of grandfathers and fathers in Southern Cameroons were where many of these brave French Cameroun patriots fending off the deadly French gendarmes would seek refuge. Many never left. Their children—now grown citizens, Anglophones, NOSO—called these parts their birthplace.

To follow the history of Cameroon is like trying to understand, in one sitting, the complexities of colonialism of the eighteenth and nineteenth centuries, the politics of the cold-war era in Africa, the rise of Bretton Woods world ideologies, twentieth-century neocolonialism, Pan-Africanism, continued pillage of *Francafrique* Francophonie, and—for added measure—echoes of nationalism, identity politics, and tribalism. Whew! No one—I mean, *no one*—

gets it. Each person picks a favorite topic or era and zeros in, content that their perspective is the most salient histories of the area worth holding.

The White man's solutions for Africa have been calamitous and continuous to be so. Take the gentleman's agreement on African boundaries reached in Berlin in 1884. Asia is, by far, a large continent both in landmass and in population with forty-eight countries. Africa boasts the highest number of countries on any of the continents with only a quarter of the population of Asia. And this is no accident. The histories of the fifty-four, fifty-five, or fifty-six countries—depending on who is counting and to what end—is rife with one fateful Western decision after another.

The Berlin Conference of 1884 gave Africa its arbitrary boundaries: "let them each have a hill and river between them," as the myth goes, in a bid to end Europe's own never-ending civil wars at home and the ensuing tribal quarrels in the rush to lay claim on the continent. History tells us that conflicts between the colonizers, England and France, were inevitable, as one colonial power attacked inland from the Mediterranean Sea and the other from the Atlantic Ocean. It was bound to occur. To end such conflict among the powers, a boundary treaty was concluded. Africa was cut up with hills and rivers, forming clear boundaries, as is the case with the river Mungo, forming a clear boundary between the French and British colonies in Cameroon in subsequent treaties.

There would be a wartime agreement to follow, as was the case from 1914 to 1918, when international law allowed territorial acquisition through conquest. So, when Germany was defeated, the victorious placed Germany under martial law and Africa on the dinner plate to be sliced up as spoils to the victorious. To each his own. So, the once-great German colony spreading from today's Congo to the east, Burkina Faso to the north, and as far west as

Togo was, again, cut up between France and England, with England retaining a sliver of territory from today's Chad to the Ambas Bay, divided by the Mungo to the east and by Nigeria's Cross River, Taraba, and Benue States to the west. My home, my land that Britain divided, will soon slice their colony into northern and southern Cameroon for ease of administration. Why keep them together when, in small chunks, they are malleable?

The UN principles of self-determination and equality of all countries meant colonies could not be administered into perpetuity.

The administering powers were mandated to lead their colonies into self-government or full independence. In Africa, this was fraught with complications. Some, like France, just never left. Others like Britain, all too happy to leave, cared less what type of arrangement their trust territories received.

Meanwhile, the Arab colonies mostly marched quickly into independent nations. History will show that Arab nations have shown their power-surged militarism in conquering territory to destroy or occupy parts of neighboring territories. This fighting ability was not lost in Europe. Japan, for instance, had demonstrated its ability to capture and occupy parts of China and later to attack and destroy Pearl Harbor, part of America. This expansion would only be stopped by the devastating blow of the atomic bomb that brought Japan to surrender, and even so, America occupied Japan only for a short period, as Germany was only occupied long enough to rebuild it and hand it over to Germans of non-Nazi influence. The Allied nations did not stay on to direct the destinies of the Germans. Like Japan, Germany was free to chart its waters as a sovereign nation. UN Resolution 1514 of 1960, granting independence to the colonies and people, held that alien subjugation, domination, and exploitation were a denial of the same right that western and later eastern nations freely claimed for their countries and people. In Africa, the colonies marched on to independence, but the conquest and foreign dominance did not end.

Africa, though with its own intertribal wars, enjoyed large military forces and great empires. Battles were largely self-contained. Africa has not shown an ability nor an affinity to conquer territory beyond its own borders. Yet, when the Europeans arrived, they occupied large parts of territory not long enough to build, rehabilitate, or pacify but in perpetuity—or so it seems. They effectively moved in, laid claim to their respective territories, raised their flags, sent in their missionaries who were told to pray, and enslaved or exported both human and resources to other faraway lands or back to their homelands to continue as slaves. Those who resisted were killed without mercy. The colonizers just never left. Old impunities are, today, clothed in politically correct approaches. Some are just rebranded as bilateral, cooperation, or partnership.

That pacification through proselytizing remains today. There is a long-held maxim that, when the White man came to Africa, they told us our religion was the wrong kind. They gave us Bibles and asked us to close our eyes and pray with them. When we opened our eyes, all that was ours, including our long-held traditions, were taken, and we were left with only the Bible in hand. In their expedition, humans were a commodity for export.

Changing Hands

Southern Cameroons are spilling—or at least we are willing to spill our blood in the rebirth of a state that came into an abortive fruition on October 1, 1961 but was robbed of its sovereignty. On October 1, 2017, it rebirthed itself and accepted the name Ambazonia. The emotions of patriotism can be felt in the masses. September 22, 2017 signaled the people's referendum on their statehood. The tide rose and is now falling. Many are silent, fearing retribution; others are conflicted, believing in the "peaceful" version of Cameroon they have known for fifty-eight years. It is too easy to revert to the comforts of what one knows: the history we know of a one and indivisible homeland. But are we people living with dignity, or is our fate dictated by another through domination, subjugation, and fear? We move from the comforts of the familiar. We enter a new reality; this time, history is unfolding, with its twists and turns written with blood.

As I've stated, history matters. It matters for our understanding of the now. History is of us and lives with us, whether documented, recalled, or used. History, they say, is often told from the vantage point of the victorious. Whenever history fails to inform our modern understandings, we wake up in constructs like Cameroon. We wake up wondering how or why an entrenched thirty-eight-year-old dictator-kingpin, also known as president—Mr. Paul Biya of Cameroon, the longest-serving head of state in the world—possibly still holds on to power in a twenty-first-century democracy. Why does a country blessed with abundant natural and human resources rank the 136th on all major indices of prosperity? History is important when the obvious question is, why does one of the world's worst offenders of human rights abuse of people remain in power and is still celebrated as a leader in polite societies around the world? Because history matters, we wake up at war, and outsiders looking in wonder why we declare war, knowing few countries win a guerrilla war? With the erasure of history, you erase more than the past. Without history, you lose hope for the future.

Erasing Personal History: Is Forgiving Like Forgetting?

We all know the phrase "forgive and forget." We're told to forgive our oppressors, not for their sake but for ourselves. It's a self-perpetuating injustice. I'm asking that you not forgive nor forget. Remember. Pain and conflict can be fuel if you learn how to channel them.

I once believed that staying peaceful at all costs and negotiating compromises would "uplift" the people of Cameroon, no matter how many policies were created to rob the country—Southern Cameroons, aka, Ambazonia—of its natural resources, deter from the development of its people, erode its cultural, social, and legal contours, and ensure that the indoctrination of a whitewashed past of the masses take hold. It began at the dawn of our "reunification," and the neocolonial ideological pervasion continues. I confess that I believed I internalized nationalist ideas about a united Cameroon—conveniently coined as one and indivisible, the miniature Africa. Being self-critical is part of growth. I'm no longer looking for peace. I want to end injustice.

Although many people will argue that those two goals are one and the same, I beg to differ. I am not for peace that is peace for peace's sake, a harmony bought at the barrel of a gun, acquiescence, or a peace born of patronage, oppression, deprivation, or scarcity. As the globe protests the deaths of George Floyd and Breonna Taylor, the institutional racism and oppression of people across the globe gets recycled and repurposed. We're all swimming against the tide of conflict and turmoil; what separates us is what we do with it. Our type of war is not sexy enough to garner international outcry. Why are brothers fighting and dying over language?" learned journalists opine over TV airwaves. I hold a certain dispassionate view so as not to get angered by their utter nonsense, lack of discernment and knowledge of the facts. "Why do they want to separate from their brothers?" others angrily state in total vexation not about the thousands murdered, maimed, or displaced by a genocidal war, but mainly at the idea of a successionist movement.

You have to hold a certain spirit of forgiveness for their naivety, for these groups of people will hardly be heard from decrying that the USSR broke out into fourteen different sovereign nations: Czechoslovakia became the Czech Republic and Slovakia, while the Yugoslavia balkanized into Bosnia and Herzegovina, Croatia, Macedonia, Montenegro, Serbia, and Slovenia.

Whether you are being colonized or are a colonizer, you're going to hold some ideals that need to be undone. You get to choose. We're all learning how to navigate this path. Know that your choices should honor people, not infantilize them. I am letting go only if the peace is just peace. I will forgive only if, in conspiring for peace, justice is achieved.

The Stubborn Facts Buried Yet Unbroken

Entire ancient civilizations have been unearthed by the slow, persistent brush of wind against the earth and rocks. Time passes by. Slowing the old, hidden, reveals itself at last. The construct that is today Cameroon, though six decades long, has revealed its hidden past. That it lain buried does not change the fact that there were once great cities that man is yet to know.

I was through Napoleonic history, the stories that shape the contours of my life, concealed, reinvented, and repackaged as one and indivisible Africa's miniature. First, I sang the anthem under a green, red, and yellow flag adorned with two stars. Later, I was told to sing the same anthem under a flag adorned with one star. Each time an edict came from those who do not see my scares nor hear my cries—those of my fathers, too. It always felt as if a big brother had his fingers firmly pressed down on our backs. In 2016, it was a knee that held us down and threatened to asphyxiate all of us. All that is, except a few Indigenous brothers and sisters willing to play house slaves to a war-mongering regime.

Cameroon achieved independence on January 1, 1960, without the British Southern Cameroons (BSC) being part of its territory. On that day, under the principle of intangibility of frontiers, its boundaries became frozen in international law. Cameroon had also undertaken in United Nations and AU instruments to confine its sovereignty to the territory she inherited at independence, which does not include Southern Cameroon.

The British Southern Cameroons—with its own international boundaries, premier, elected government, bicameral parliament, and state structures and apparatus—was a UN trust territory under the administration of Great Britain. At the time of its decolonization in 1961, the UN gave it only two choices: to achieve independence in association with Cameroon or with Nigeria. This required a UN-organized plebiscite. Before the plebiscite held on February 11, 1961, Cameroon and the BSC reached a signed agreement that, should the plebiscite go in favor of achieving independence in association with Cameroon, the two countries would form a federation of two states equal in status. The plebiscite went in favor of attaining independence in association with Cameroon. In keeping with its promise of independence to the BSC, the UNGA voted overwhelmingly in favor of BSC independence in Resolution 1608(XV) of April 21,1961 and set the date of independence to be October 1, 1961.

However, despite the fact that the plebiscite was in favor of BSC associating with Cameroon and the UNGA vote on BSC independence, the association in a federation never took place. Cameroon repudiated the signed agreements, amended its internal law, and imposed it as the federal constitution on the BSC. The people of the BSC were never given any opportunity to endorse or vote on the constitution that was going to bind them. This constitution was adopted unilaterally by French Cameroun's parliament one month before the BSC ceased to be a UN trust territory. Article 47 of the unilateral constitution prohibited a change in the federal structure of the country. In 1972, Cameroon abolished the federation, imposed a United Republic of Cameroon, and declared the two countries "one and indivisible." In 1984, Cameroon, once again, abolished the United Republic of Cameroon and renamed the two countries République du Cameroun, the name by which she obtained independence.

In the Paris Peace Forum of November 2019, Pres. Paul Biya confessed that Cameroon's policy in all these years has been the total assimilation of the peoples of Southern Cameroons. To confirm the annexation, Cameroon calls this war between the two partners its internal affair! This is the case of two countries that are supposed to be joined legally as equals, but one partner has annexed the other and denied it all possibilities of being heard.

In 2016, lawyers and teachers went on strike to protest the enforcement of assimilation that took the form of flooding their schools with French teachers who did not understand a word of English, and the courts magistrates did not practice common law. The lawyers were beaten up and their robes seized. The government convened talks with the representatives of the teachers and lawyers, but when the talks failed, their unions were banned, and they were promptly arrested, charged with secession, and thrown in jail. On October 1, 2017, the people of Southern Cameroons declared the restoration of their independence. On November 30 of the same year, Cameroon declared its war of enforcing its annexation on the people of Southern Cameroons.

CALL TO ACTION

Here are some things you can do to harness conflict in your life and to use it as fuel.

Identify your wound. We all have them. Whether you're a refugee who fled a war-torn country or a soccer mom in the suburbs (or both), you carry wounds around. They affect every aspect of your life. Put them all on the table. Write them down. Shout them into the sky. Paint them in red. Hold them close. This scar tissue is a part of you.

Stop making excuses. You do not need to defend your hurt. Whether your pain stems from a conscious oppressor or ignorant participant, your pain and conflicts are valid.

Look at the oppression and injustice around you. Whether you're in America, France, Cameroon, Ambazonia, or Saudi Arabia, systematic oppression is endemic to the human experience. Seek it out. Educate yourself. Learn multiple accounts of historical events from various sources. Learn the atrocities of your own nation. There are no innocent players here.

Confront your ideals. A quick Google search of war or conflict will yield hundreds of results. Murder, violence, suicide, rape, torture—all these acts have a cost and gain. Even if we're thousands of miles away, a butterfly's wings ripple through time and space to reach us. How could we expect to be unscathed from such atrocities? Your benefit in all this might not be obvious. The cell phone in your hand was created from exploited miners. The fuel from the oil fields of Ekindi in the Gulf of Guinea in the tank of your car was obtained from exploitation of Indigenous people's rights in Ambazonia and their resources. I bet you have never heard about these oil fields. The clothes on your back were sewn with child labor. The food you casually toss in the garbage contributes to an industry rife with mistreatment of labor workers. The woven basket that adorns your coffee table is made by women who barely subsist on $1 per day. There is the downplaying of slavery manufactured for elementary schools across North America to assuage White guilt and the placement of Native Americans in reservations for their "benefit." We all play a part in the oppression of others, whether our eyes are wide open or not.

Step into your own truth. Lincoln said, "Be sure to step into your truth and own it." Take fifteen minutes to reflect on one of the following writing prompts:

1. How many times have I enjoyed the privilege of ignoring war or conflict?

2. How does that make me feel?

3. Does that reflect the type of person I want to be?

4. Is active ignorance better or worse than passive knowledge?

5. What are my responsibilities to my fellow humans in conflict?

Champion Campaigns Against Injustice

- We're always looking for people to spread the word and help. Do you have twenty minutes to help the people of Southern Cameroons, Ambazonia?

- Write a review of this book on Amazon.

- When you're finished reading, donate the book to a public library, give it to a friend, bring it to a book club, or make any other way to spread the word.

- Purchase the book as a gift for someone else.

- Bring up the conflict during a conversation with a friend or family member.

- Teach your children about the conflict in Cameroon and the components of privilege.

- Read several blogs on living conflict-inspired or the conflict in Cameroon.

- Join Women for Permanent Peace and Justice and share our website or social accounts in your feeds: www.w4ppj. org, @W4ppj on Twitter, and Women4PermanentPeace on Facebook.

- Sign this petition here: http://chng.it/B95n8Mw27v.

- Tell a friend.

- Please email me at osongm@yahoo.com for more info on how you can help.

- Watch this video: https://bit.ly/3F1Qg0A

- Adopt the sample script below or create your own to contact lawmakers, United Nations, and AU officials calling on them to compel Mr. Biya of Cameroon to dialogue with the armed groups or support the resolution for a referendum where people can decide their destiny.

Petition

Date: _____

Dear _____,

My name is _____. I am a constituent
of _____.

I write to urge you to take concrete actions to bring
Pres. Paul Biya of Cameroon to dialogue without
conditions with the armed groups in the five-year-
long war that has killed thousands of innocent
civilians, left nearly 1 million people displaced,
destroyed almost 500 villages, and left eight out of
ten school-age children out of school. The right to
life is a fundamental human right, without which all
other rights will have no meaning. These are
principles every nation professes and defend around
the world. The need to act is now. You can bring
this senseless war to an end and save lives.

Will you stand up for the suffering masses in
Southern Cameroons and compel Mr. Biya to
engage in peace talks to end the war immediately?

Thank you for your immediate attention to my
appeal.

Concerned citizen of _____ and of the
world.

CHAPTER 2:
THE CHURCH

He who has a why in life can survive with almost any
how.

—Friedrich Nietsche

There were other battles brewing around me, some that mildly interested me, others that, in my characteristic behind-the-scenes manner, offered what help I could, and others that were too personal, or I believed too distant to hold my attention. The crisis in the churches that mushroomed in different cities in America held its own curious complexities.

The church sits at the corner of a sleepy intersection in downtown Burtonsville and overlooked the asphalt parking lot. Its gray concrete facade is punctured by trees with its bell tower rising above a steep climb of concrete steps from the parking lot. On Sundays, three masses are held here, but on the last Sunday of each month, for 10 years now, one Mass has been added, and it's held at 2:30 pm or as close to it as parishioners will allow. A steady stream of cars can be seen entering the church lot well into the 4 p.m. hours and that will not be late. Arrive early, and you might think it is confession day, as only a hand full of Mass-goers amble around the vestibule or sit idly by in the church. There are no priests, no choir, no Mass servants, and it would be that way for some time until it starts.

But for the bell tower and the ringing to signal the start of Mass, calling all Christians to church, the building is an oddity for a place of worship. It is nudged in a residential neighborhood with an industrial park-feel. A small sign board at its entrance announces it is the Church of the Resurrection. Even when church is on, the idyllic houses setback at almost the same distance from the road makes this an odd place to be. It is the least likely place to play host to the CCCWDC. Its parishioners, though somewhat of mixed race, is mainly white.

Inside its walls, it feels much the contemporary church it is. The 2:30 Mass feels very much the exception, too. For starters, the Mass would last 4 hours, and any visitor at Mass is weary to the bone by the end staying mostly only out of a sense of guilt for the person who invited him or her. Some visits, having heard about the church, curious about its African inculturation come, and they, too, see it through to its long conclusion. For the faithful, it is a Eucharistic celebration, as it is a festival of sorts: hours of singing and dancing interspersed with the Order of the Mass. Before the first reading, the lectionary procession strains your eye to the isle. If it is a major Catholic day of celebration, the Bible is carried in a bag swung over on the back of one of 6-8 women in traditional garb, *Athogu*. The leader is typically two men, sword in hand, headgear and *Athogu*, performs a war dance ahead of the women processing down the aisle in their own routine. "Hear ye, Hear ye! It's the word of God. Arise! Hear ye, Hear!" The leader brandishes his sword in battle form, rushes to the altar, where both men perform the ceremonial clash of weapons signifying friendship, then jet back to join the women who begin chanting "Whelleellele ye! Its word of God, the word of God. Alluelua aaa, Whelleellele ye! Its word of God, the word of God. Alluelua aaa" as they take small, slow steps toward the altar.

From the distance, the lectionary procession is repetitiously slow, two steps forward, one step back in dance routine. To the faithful, this animated dance signals the beginning of a day-long celebration, except, in the Catholic faith, some call it the Mass.

By offertory time, most in the pews have danced through the Gloria played to the xylophones, guitars, and drums by the choir. But offertory is particular. There will be three or five offerings, each headed by a different interest group in the community. Each group is bent on outdoing the other, not only in animation and dance, but mostly in tithes. You have to love or hate this. I mostly love offertory. It is a party, and I dance along, occasionally taking my tithe with a group with which I feel some affiliation or affinity. The announcer does his best to urge each group to make haste and gather in the vestibule so that the whole thing can proceed faster. He promises it will not take long. Each time, though, it seems the whole thing is longer than the time before. The choir knows the more festive and sing-along the songs are, the more the pews will empty out onto the aisle, people dancing to the altar to make their offering, so they play it up with one danceable rendition after another. "Eh, eh, eh, eh . . . my God is good, eh . . . everything na double double oh, na double double . . . ?" With this opening song, the aisle fills up, and the chorus grows as all answer back "Eh, eh, eh, eh . . . my God is good, eh." The tempo is festive; the singing fills the cavernous room and spills outside. Children are particularly animated at this time and can be seen running wildly throughout the church, but no one at this moment particularly minds that. The first offering is given to the Church of the Resurrection since this church that meets at 2:30 is really borrowing the church for its culturally appropriate Mass. The second collection goes to the church council to run its business. The remaining collections—one for each of the groups who are making special collections that day—goes to some fund for Mass offerings.

Like most host churches, it is as much about faith and God as it is about politics. The parishioners of CCWDC have declined over its 10-year history. The Catholic Women Association (CWA), locked in a bitter fight over dominance with another rival Mariam group, Catholic Women Organization (CWO), a gathering of faith-based women who practice the virtues of Mary, the mother of Jesus, have left, claiming they were forced out from the church. The alumni, called LESA Inc, simply, Incers, locked in a similar fight left, too, claiming the same thing. Friends of these groups in solidarity have also left the church. Within the Church Parish Council, there are rumors that some who could not hold positions of leadership left and formed their own African churches in the neighboring cities and states. It later emerged that even some priests felt they were not getting much by way of leadership, too pushed for other similar churches to be formed. In the rush to revival what was going in Burtonsville, the faithful suffered.

That there are now several Cameroonian church communities is down to no small part to the leadership who argue that God needs more places of worship, not less, and that spreading them around is better. Being God-fearing, one would agree that this is reasonable when traveling more than 30 minutes to get to church. But largely, it is no secret that personal interests and internal politicking were at play for the proliferation of many similar Cameroonian faith communities or places of worship.

The CWA was in crisis. The Chair of Cameroon Catholic Community has just died on a trip to Cameroon. LESA, the alumni organization saga that had seen two rival LESA groups embroiled in not one but two court litigations, showed no end in sight. For these groups, the Resurrection Church was their church of choice for Mass on the last Sunday of each month, and each group clung to it dearly. The church calendar reflected that, too. It showed which group held what activity, not only at Mass but outside Mass. As a new, unpopular chair took over, CWA, a branch of the main group in Cameroon, saw the sacking of its leadership. They promptly split one part, breaking off from the main group and re-branding itself the CWO. As if the resident Pastor of Resurrection Church had nothing better to do with his time, the incessant bickering and intra-group fighting that was unfolding in his satellite church, the CCCWDC, required that he stepped in and make some decisions. The priest wanted one personal to deal with, one umbrella group to interface with. Everything else, the group can handle at their level. When the new CWA leadership appointed from their head offices in Cameroon request that it be recognized instead of the leadership of the CCCWDC Pastoral Council effectively bypassing the Chair of the community, the Parish priest rejected their request. The CWA left but not before letting their supporters at home and elsewhere believe they were expelled from this church and banned from worshipping there. The LESA, Inc, too, let everyone know they have been banned from attending the church when rivalries with LESA Alumnae could not be resolved. For these groups, they would leave and seek out other churches to worship in, but in doing so, would take along every person they could convince to go with them. The church boasted a healthy vibrant membership, but it seems this was built on an unstable dwelling of competing interest groups. The pathway of life is through conflict; the Cameroonian community of faithful had its share.

If the feuding in the church was subdued by prayers, outside, at home—in Cameroon—and online, it ragged on. The church could be said to represent the "Anglophone" population of Cameroon, as mainly English-speaking Catholic Cameroonians went there to worship. Their equivalent, Silver Spring Church, was for the Presbyterians, and they, too, faced a number of splintering challenges with similar fallouts, breakoffs, and sacrificial lambs.

In the fall of 2016, the church had undergone a significant shift in membership that nearly brought the faithful to a tipping point, not only on the question of leadership of the Parish Council but on the question of which group's needs trump another in the fight for dominance. It is in 2016 that the war broke out in Cameroon, a war that largely impacted the parishioners of the CCCWDC. I would watch as the attitudes of the faithful steered along the lines of including one or two intercessory prayers during Mass and the occasional homily calling for peace. I sense a general hesitancy to take on the substantive issues of the war. The leadership feared war was too much of a divisive issue. And they were not wrong. In the community's social media platform, you risked being expelled if you posted what is considered political matters on the forum. All things would have to remain at the level of proselytizing. In America, politician campaign in faith-based communities, pastors take on the vexing issues from the pulpit, priests create videos to sensitize their followers about breaking God's 5th commandment: thou shall not kill. The worshippers are asked to vote a particular way on some issues. Religious advocacy groups inside and outside places of worship have not shied away from making their views known and campaigned for it, too. Amid an existential threat to the members of the church in Burtonsville, there is a sense, indeed, that now is the time we should think churches should keep out of politics. For me, this was frustrating. I knew many in the church whose families were victims of the war. I know they universally want peace and may not know how best to achieve that peace except through prayer. It is that frustration of prayer in the way things are, where the church should leap in feet first, that is decried. For generations, the church has been a coalescing force for people of differing ideological streams. In the church, many gather as "one body" despite holding, at times, grave differences on everyday issues. The church—particularly mine, the Catholic church—has taken a strong stance on social justice issues. After all my limited catechesis. Here in the U.S., the catholic churches are sanctuaries for those fleeing the deportation, abuse, and other forms of abuse. When the world appears hostile to the "least among us," the church becomes "politically" active—essentially not waiting to preach the Bible, rather to practice in concrete terms what the Bible teaches. No one needs to egg them on to feed the hungry, embrace immigrants fearing deportation and separation from family members, care for the wounded abuse by brutal armed forces, or shelter the good and wicked feeling abuse or retribution, respectively. The church teaches solidarity with the oppressed and tells us it is a critical institution that would not be afraid to militate against societal forces that stack the deck against God's people in any way. As an institution, the Catholic church is perhaps one of the most vibrant institutions for Cameroonians, both French and English. As a body, they would remain neutral to the war in Cameroon. All they wanted was peace to return.

CHAPTER 3:
IS CONFLICT IN OUR DNA?

Ineluctably, the insults inflicted in one war call forth new wars of retaliation, which may be waged within months of the original conflict or generations later.

—Barbara Ehrenreich

Many people would read my story and praise my strength in caring for my daughter during her illness. In reality, my daughter is the one reason why I was able to harness strength in the face of so many crushing blows. Only because of the bone-deep love for her and the lessons of her courage was I able to shake off the shackles of my programming to quarrel ad nauseam with self, don the garb of self-deprecating pity, throw in the towel or a pity party, and tap into my well of strength. When staring into a future in which my daughter could not walk, the truth arrived at my consciousness. Instead of accepting the doctor's truth blindly, I knew that questioning authority was not only the right thing to do but also necessary. Instead of accepting the status quo, I needed to rage against the machine. Resting on what's always been and what we know was no longer acceptable. If my daughter's unknown rested in my hands, a stalemate of forced peace was no longer the desired outcome. Only by leaning into the conflict and unpacking generations of instilled otherness was I able to fight for her. Had I accepted the reality I was presented, I wouldn't have rocked the boat.

We're taught to avoid being troublemakers. We're taught to believe that it's no big deal and that others know best. I'm here to tell you that you've been lied to your entire life. No matter where you are in the world, though the pathways of life are through conflict, you've been indoctrinated into false beliefs about yourself and the world around you. It's time to uncover the truth. It is time to look within and uncover why.

Least Common Denominator

Belonging to a family of alcoholics, most people submit to genetic susceptibility without question. Those born into conflict zones rarely get the same vindication. Despite all that we know about conflict breeding conflict, we tend to look at solutions piecemeal, instead of attacking root causes head-on. Whether it is conflict, colonization, or occupation, they all initiate a systematic dismantling. This sets generations up to not only experience the conflict but to also perpetuate it.

Stopping a cycle of oppression, abuse, and turmoil is bigger than one individual. Healing a nation is more than simply ceasing violence. Imagine the intricacies of a toxic waste cleanup. All facets of life are affected: air, water, soil, and body. Stopping pollution is only the first step, not the magic pill. Cleaning up a war will take the same approach. Knowing things must change isn't enough. Knowing what needs changing is the bigger challenge for all. People need to be empowered to act and have ownership of the process.

I was only able to champion my daughter's welfare because I belong to a system that allows it, though fraught with its own weaknesses. I found partners who believed in the same set of facts as I did or could show good reason why my own were faulty. Raging against the machine is possible, but it is dangerous and inefficient. And no matter where you are in the world, you are taught to fight in a way that fits the system. French Cameroun had created a system, and to fight it was to be killed; at best, your limited freedoms would be taken away.

The Anglophone problem is unfolding miles away, 7,500 miles away, to be exact. The villages I knew in and around my city dwelling are largely burned out. They exist now only as shells, mere shadows of their previous glory. In place in a home spared the scotch-earth destruction at the hands of the dreaded BIR or the infamous Amba Boys, a tree now grows, wildlife flourishes. Women abandon their farmlands. They are too afraid to stay in their homes. They leave with just the clothes on their backs, headed for the major towns or deep into the forest for safety. Youth flees, too, in droves to the Francophone territories across the river Mungo. Young men have long since fled into the bushes. My birthplace is now a theater of war. Biya's BIR is in every major town in his NOSO. BIR barracks and staging points are everywhere in the NOSO, and they are reinforced, revitalized, refurbished, and rebuilt at feverish pitch. The airport runway, hangars, and buildings sit just a few miles from Azire Street, where I grew up and hoped would one day fly into. It is now a full-fledged military camp. The governor's office in Upstation turned to a Baghdad-style green zone, the safest place in the entire city and beyond the artillery reach of the Amba Boys. On the site of the Ngarbuh massacres on February 14, 2020, a military camp now sits. From these strategic places in Biya's NOSO, the military makes excursions into surrounding villages and neighborhoods in search of Amba Boys. Give a dog a bad name, and it is all too easy to hang him.

Young girls and women flee in droves in search of safety. They are homeless. They walk the streets at night. It is bad enough that they are raped by the BIR or by sick elements of society in their homelands. Now they survive only if they can sell their bodies. Many end up as indentured servants on farms and plantations in French Cameroun or as maids and servants for the not-so-rich wanting to live as the rich do in Cameroon—a servant for every household in need. After all, what they, the displaced, need is a little bit of food and a place to lay at night, away from the elements and far from the searches—*Kale, Kale,* daily raids on homes in search of terrorist, enemies of the state. No one is safe.

Youth flees in droves into the very heart of the oppressor to be further indoctrinated with the same whitewashed history. Cameroon is one and indivisible, and the French are king in our land. The cycle continues. They might never return. They might even join "their brothers," the French, to fight their own in NOSO. Some are doing so already. They know no other truth but those of their oppressor: a classic case of Stockholm syndrome. The doors of schools shut down as a result of insecurity either from Biya's BIR army or from the Amba Boys—boys in the bushes. A generation is now at risk of illiteracy and worse.

The Convent Years

Am I fortunate or worse off for having been born to these parts of the country that failed to tell its children who they really are? I began learning about the world in a tiny all-girls college, Our Lady of Lourdes, where I spent my formative teenage years. It was an institution storied and known throughout the country for its discipline and scholarship, but its students, country, and history were an untold secret. Today, the gates of Lourdes are manned by forces to keep who away? In October 1963, fifty-six girls, aged twelve to fifteen years, were selected from the primary schools in villages and cities in throughout Cameroon to attend an all-girls secondary school. Then it was called West Cameroon. Across the Mungo, they were called East Cameroon. We were different, distinct, and believed to be an equal partner or party in a federation. The school was yet to be built on the slopes of the Bamenda plateau.

Southern Cameroons had recently become an "independent country," a state equal in status in a federation. We were not yet completely free from the clutches of French colonialism. Vestiges of European influence would linger till the present in the political, social, and educational realms of the country. Ours would be the Anglo-Saxon legal and educational systems inherited from Great Britain and cherished to date. The colonial master, Britain, mostly packed up and left the country at the conclusion of their trusteeship in 1961. Never mind that their trusteeship agreement stipulated they were to prepare and lead their trust territories to self-rule or independence. But we held on to all the master taught us for better or for worse.

So, it came as no surprise that the European Catholic missionaries, who, too, had sailed to the African continent—some to evangelize, others for human and raw resources. They would step in to provide a decent education to the masses in sticking with their traditions. The British-born Catholic priest, Father Nabben, brought along the Irish Catholic Sisters of the Holy Rosary to help start a Catholic school for girls in then northwest province of Cameroon. It was a godsend. But it, too, was insular, lacking in instilling the curiosity of the world—of one's own reality in the minds of children.

Opening a school might not seem like a lifesaving venture, but for Our Lady of Lourdes College, it surely was to our parents. Before Lourdes College, young girls in search of decent education had to make the treacherous one-week journey to Queen of the Holy Rosary School (QRC), Okoyong-Mamfe, located in the Southwest region of Biya's NOSO regions. In the years after the British handed the reins of our sovereignty to the late President Ahmadou Ahidjo of French Cameroun, he packed up and left instead of building up and strengthening existing infrastructure and institutions. The more powerful, populous, and French-influenced Cameroon leadership did nothing to build infrastructure in its NOSO. They systematically set out to dismantle our own institutions or close them altogether in a bid to centralize power and deny any autonomy we once enjoyed. Parents who could afford it sent their sons to Nigeria for a good education. Few parents had the means to send their daughters to college. Fewer parents, at the time of decolonization, were motivated to educate a daughter. From their perspective, why educate a girl child who would simply marry and become a housewife? Even those wise to the notion of an educated girl child were chilled at the idea of a life-and-death journey to QRC, even for something as important as an education.

Why So Dangerous?

A post-independent Federal Republic of Cameroon in the 1960s boasted less than five percent tarred, motorable roads. Most roads connecting villages and towns were dirt roads, making travel long, treacherous, and often deadly. The road from my hometown of Bamenda to QRC crossed over the Tikar region, favoring the less mountainous areas to the east of the Adamawa plateaus, and meandered south toward the town of Mamfe. To say the narrow dirt road was serpentine and death-defying is to state the obvious. Mondays, Wednesdays, Fridays, and Sundays were "Mamfe go down" days—all traffic set in the direction of Mamfe. The remainder of the weekdays was reserved for "Mamfe kam up." There was no possibility of a two-way traffic on the road. Only one vehicle at a time could possibly navigate the roads, as one false turn will send the vehicle tumbling down steep hillsides into deep ravines. Driving on the wrong day spelled trouble. It was often impossible for both vehicles to bypass each other. All motorists religiously adhered to these travel patterns, but many perished anyway. This alternating one-way traffic schedule did very little to curb the mortality rate for travelers.

Accidents were frequent and often deadly. In the northwest areas, the road meandered first through grassland and corn farms and then through a thick forest of palm nut trees. Steep ascent and precipitous descent marked the latter part of the journey toward the coastal areas approaching the village of Widikum to Mamfe, and then to Queen of Holy Rosary College. Why was it called a college when young teens were students? Travelers often described moments a hair's breadth away from plunging into a ravine carpeted with a greenery of a rainforest canopy. Imagine standing on the edge of a precipice and staring down into the tops of trees several stories below. Geography was a stern captor. Some parents would not put their girl children's lives at risk. A few dared and risked everything. They must learn. The lessons would be rigorous but limited and limiting. In addition to navigating through treacherous terrain, travel often involved vehicles that pushed the bounds of physics and reason. Transport vehicles squeezed in an extra passenger into every available seat. Vehicles tilted dangerously during their meanderings up steep mountainsides and down valleys; carriages piled five feet high with bags of corn, woven bamboo cages with chickens, and large brown sacks tied with raffia twist rope. When the ascent was too difficult, passengers descended and trekked on foot in the hope of lightening the weight so the vehicle could climb up the mountainous, muddy roads. A foot more of tilt on the left or right on the winding, narrow road might send the vehicle over an embankment far below. No rescue would be mounted, just a total loss of property and human lives.

The young girls, excited at leaving home for "college," would later recount stories filled with the bliss of youthful exuberance and adventure than of defying the odds to gain an education. In the

Ekindi fields, in the offshore ocean, Britain and France had laid claim to vast oil resources that would be exploited; its waste and tar would not make those death-defying, twisted dirt roads any safer for future QRC students. For that, their parents would have to drive a full day on slightly better roads that ran through several towns and villages in the Francophone area.

There were no easy ways to circumvent the irregular chain of mountains and hills or the plunging valleys that dotted the north to southwestern parts of Cameroon. We were, after all, perched on the Adamawa Plateau. It was necessary to ramble around a mountain, climbing on one part, to descend on the other side to advance your journey. There were no bridges nor overpasses connecting topologically difficult places. River crossings were fraught with danger, too. Bridges, if they did exist in rural Cameroon in the late 1960s, were large tree trunks laid across riverbanks. Heavy rains often washed them away, making the roads impassable—for some, causing lost school years. Drivers would sometimes find shallower riverbeds to make a particularly difficult crossing. During the dry seasons, the dusty roads were littered with potholes. This was almost preferred. When the rains came, thick, red mud all but rendered the roads impassable. Still, the commerce and the movement of people carried on. And some parents persevered and made the journey with their children for an Anglo-Saxon education. Whether it was an education worth dying for, some did.

In the two and equal states of the Federation Republic of Cameroon, the dominant, French-dependent regime began the process of centralizing power—economic, social, political—in Yaoundé, first under Pres. Ahmadou Ahidjo, and later, Paul Biya. The Catholic church was increasingly convinced that it needed another school for girls in the growing town of Bamenda. In 1963, less than two years after the February 11, 1961, plebiscite, the pioneer batch, began secondary education, attending classes in the old St. Joseph's Primary School while the college was being constructed few hundred yards on the base of Bamenda Station. School was in session.

That year, fifty-six young girls arrived at Lourdes from varying walks of life, impressionable and oblivious to a life that was largely orchestrated by actors far from home and across oceans. Those from the elementary schools around Bamenda would trek on foot to the college. Affluent girls traveled mainly from the Francophone cities of Douala and Yaoundé, and they came in taxis and private cars. Others from afar came with their parents in jig rigs on the back of wagons carrying food and livestock from their villages, perhaps to sell in the city for extra money to pay their tuition. Their destination was the muddy park in the old town of Bamenda, five miles from the campus. From there, each girl would carry her belongings up the slopes to the campus, sometimes making several trips. A few with extra money would hire porters (*bambe* boys) to carry larger or heavier pieces of their belongings on their heads or wheelbarrows and trekked up toward the school. Even in these formative years, and in the 1960s, it was clear there were two Cameroons, the largely rural and growing west and the somewhat affluent east. But why? Students often brought their own mattresses made of straw stuffed into a large rectangular piece of sewn fabric. There were, of course, exceptions. A few of the girls came from elite families in the towns and villages surrounding Bamenda—the Nangahs, Kilos, and Angwafos. Their parents were civil servants or an accomplished businessman or an elite. They lived in stone, zinc-roofed houses with servants and extended families. These students would arrive by private car or hired taxi. Their parents often came along to see them off. They brought gifts, too, for their friends.

Their bigger boxes signaled that all the items suggested on the prospectus had been secured—with a few other "just in case" items added. They brought cotton or foam mattresses with a couple of clean, White sheets to sleep on. Instead of a large Savon for laundry, their parents sent them to school with packets of blue Omo laundry detergent; in place of dried eucalyptus sticks, these students brought toothbrushes and toothpaste imported from Nigeria. In place of the locally made palm oil Savon for bathing, they came equipped with the more fashionable and important brand Imperial Leather or Asepso soap for bathing. The seven-year pomade cream—large enough for a family of ten for a couple of months—would be replaced by the fashionable brand Nku cream or Avon. Homemade *kimbur* and *garri* snacks were passed over in favor of luxury Cabin Biscuits imported from London and Blue Brand Margarine or chocolate cream for snacks.

A two-class system evolved and quickly took root in the culture of the school as quickly as it did in the country. In the now declassified documents, France—through its diplomatic mission in Yaoundé and a consular office in the state of West Cameroon in Buea—traded off on how best to assimilate the English-speaking Cameroonians. A select number of our parents would be groomed not only to speak in French but also to fully integrate them into the Napoleonic way of governance. They took up mostly junior positions in the Francophone system. Compared to their yet-to-be-assimilated brothers, they were affluent and part of the bourgeoisie class. If their children knew of this, it was not apparent, for they will all be tied to the same destiny as a people.

Only a few saw the dubious plan set into motion at the dawn of our "independence" for what it was: assimilate and annex. Most saw it as upward mobility and as a thing to be converted, guarded, feted, and encouraged. To be integrated into the civil service was a big deal. Many traveled to Yaoundé to "chase documents" for integration, for pay, for promotion, for transfer. The majority of the Anglophone population—and some within the French population—mostly spiraled downward on all indicators of development and social life. The full-scale assimilation that began on our achieving independence by joining the already independent French Cameroun was fully underway. It just lay concealed in its obviousness. As children, we largely only saw a world of haves and have-nots. A strive for education was a one-way ticket out of a dead-end life. We will live this divide much of our lives, accepting, assimilating, acquiescing, or at the opportune moment, when old enough, going into self-exile to greener pastures in Europe or United States for a chance at a dignified life, where we are not considered second-class citizens.

It is my first time out of the village and into the city. My mother's black and metal trunk, borrowed for the trip, contains only meager belongings. Inside, I've placed everything I own: two large, locally made Savon soaps, one for bathing and another for laundry, a large bottle of seven-year pomade body cream, chopsticks for a toothbrush, one dress, and two homemade undergarments. A large cloth bag contains homemade snacks—fried corn and peanuts (*kimbur*) and ground and fried cassava (*garri*)—and a precious packet of cube sugar. I've packed all my past to fuel the brightness of my future. With all I've risked arriving, I'm not leaving without an education.

Educating the Great Wives of Tomorrow

The story of Lourdes of fifty years ago is about the formative years of young girls during simpler times that were void of our modern-day trappings: excessive, commodious living, instantaneous communication, transnational global relations, a vast yet seemingly intimate and connected but disconnected world. The fifty-six girls who occupied classrooms A and B slept and ate together each day except for the long summer holidays for five years. Mostly, they came from east Cameroon—French Cameroun, where their parents, working class, could afford the annual tuition. Every new batch that would enter this institution over the course of fifty years mirrored almost the same pattern: learned the same and left with the same worldview. Some things would eventually change, but most things stayed the same. They were largely sheltered to learn but were also sheltered from knowing who they really were.

The assimilation was mandated even in the religious, cloistered schools. For uniforms, the girls wore green, red, and yellow before any other color, if needed. It was important that a strong sense of Cameroon-ness was instilled into young minds at every step of their education. It was not good to use education alone to instill a one and indivisible Cameroon. All artifacts, too, would become tools of assimilation. The girls were, after all, of the generation that would see the fraudulent 1972 referendum erasing any vestiges of an autonomous nation joined in a federation of equal states. In 1961, our parents alone had voted in the February 11 plebiscite to join in a federation with French Cameroun. In 1972, the French regime in Yaoundé did not bother to consult them when it dissolved the federation and instituted a united republic. I would enter that same institution—as was the tradition in my family. My older sisters had gone to Lourdes. I would enter in 1974. I was too young to fully grasp the implications of the 1972 referendum that effectively ended our autonomous and equal status.

Hindsight would suggest that the school's operating budget was meager, considering that students paid less than 50,000 CFA as tuition for a whole year, the equivalent of $100. This amount was far less in the '60s. Breakfast was fermented cornmeal, pap, and a slice of bread. When the baker, or boulangerie, as he was known, did not show up, the girls were fed rice pilaf or jollof rice cooked with crayfish. On rare occasions, the girls were treated to sardines and bread—a feast. No one would miss breakfast on those days. Lunch and dinner consisted of porridge plantains, sese plantains, huckleberry soup served with green plantains, or beans and corn (corn chaff). Corn chaff was sadly known for having as many weevils as beans.

On one occasion, frustrated by their weevil-infested corn chaff and watered-down huckleberry soup served with green plantains, the young girls staged a riot. Speaking up for strong beliefs was not one of the virtues the Holy Rosary Sisters wanted to see take root in the girls. Assertiveness and freedom of speech was largely frowned on. Indiscipline and arrogance had no place in a Catholic school. The entire school was reprimanded for their poor behavior and sternly admonished. They were reminded at morning assembly that they ought to be grateful for what they have and are given and that perseverance, humility, and obedience were the virtues of Our Lady. Each girl was expected to learn and embody these values. And so, they learned the value of simplicity and perseverance under any circumstance but were unschooled about standing up for what is right as a collective. We were unschooled about the world: the piece they called their country. There was no questioning, only whispers occasionally from parents. Our type of education, for all that was good, numbed our curiosity gene. We were to accept the world as the elders laid out or revealed to us.

In Lourdes, the notions of individuality, freedom, and independence were regularly trampled on. During morning assembly, the Holy Rosary Sisters would tell the students "We are developing young girls, decent, respectable, with Christian values who would make great wives of tomorrow." None of the girls, except a very few bold ones, could imagine speaking up or disobeying the sisters or the pecking order that students had created for themselves. Meritocracy meant deference to seniority on all matters, a reflection of the larger society. Those rules still have not changed or should not change for some who have long graduated from the school.

Rank, too, often has its privileges. The senior student could take your piece of meat at lunchtime, the single most coveted part of a young girl's meal, as meat was considered a delicacy, and there was little you could do except perhaps the occasional prank played on perpetrators. Just don't get caught. Nonetheless, if a culprit was not found, an entire dorm, class, or group of girls was punished. So, the message often was "be a nice girl, and you will have no problems." And so, the girls learned about respect, only to later step as an adult into a country that held little respect for them, a country that held them as second-class citizens. What we embodied in discipline and wholesome Catholic values, we lacked in conflict and street grit and dogged curiosity. And that was all we needed to become perfectly educated perpetrators of spoon-fed lies.

My mom, too, sent me to this college. In my case, it was a tradition that the girls went to Lourdes, so I was just following tradition. There was no choice in schools to attend. Lourdes was the first and the last choice. There was a little catch, though. *Mami*, my mom, could not afford the cost, which was roughly $200 annually for tuition and boarding. Papa, my dad, who worked for the government and was the sole provider, died, leaving Mami with eleven children, all under twenty-one years, the youngest just months old, and all needing more than a good education. Mami, with less than a third-grade education, was now a housewife left to figure out how to care for, tend to, and educate her children. For my four elder sisters, who had gone through Lourdes, that was not a problem. When our father died, my younger siblings and I would not have gone to Lourdes College were it not for the generosity of our adopted father, a Marist brother, Norbert Simms. When Mami could not pay the required deposit and tuition, he would inquire and quietly paid it up and bought the required books, ensuring that another little girl got a fighting chance.

I got into Lourdes a very introverted and highly insecure young girl. I was acutely aware of my life's circumstances. *Mami* would sell Papa's artifacts: guns, bronze collections, furniture, and any collectible items Papa acquired over time in various remote duty posts around West Cameroon—to pay the tuition. When she could not raise the money, the reverend sisters would allow us to stay in school on deferred payments.

Papa was a district officer in West Cameroon. He died disappointed that the plebiscite had gone in favor of independence by joining French Cameroun. For him, if we couldn't get outright independence from the British colonizers, then it was to better join Nigeria. The French were the proverbial death by fire. Nigeria, though, the proverbial deep blue sea that would swallow BSC into its federation, melding us into them as Igbos, offered better prospects for us. Papa believed we stood a really good chance of swimming ashore and finding solid ground someday as a state within the Federation of Nigeria.

When I walked up the hills past St. Joseph's Elementary School through the gates into Lourdes, I had just been pulled up by my bootstraps. A few like me were indigenes. The remainder were from the elite class. They drove in from Douala, Yaoundé, or other cities, mainly in east Cameroon. I am sure, out of a sense of obligation, the sisters had to have locals in the school who were not as well-to-do.

Single-Loop Learning

End of term was nerve-racking for me. I felt mortified each time the class academic placements were announced, and I did not come first in my class. I would resolve to work even harder next term. All the accolades went to the girl who was at the head of her class. Any other placement did not matter. And indeed, my study partners and I would burn the midnight oil, cramming to retain European history. I could recite every battle Napoleon fought, every treaty and celebratory landmark he reigned over. Confident in my mastery of the history, certain in my analysis of every Shakespearean scene and every formula in my chemistry textbook, certain of all anatomical functions in the human body with the attendant hubris that I could dissect a body—well, in those days, it was a frog—and having crammed most, if not all, of the basic laws of physics for the term, true to form, I would confidently regurgitate all I learned in each exam, sitting at the end of the term. But my classmates did just the same, if not more, studying and cramming, and would ultimately outsmart me yet again for the first position and even the second and third. Coming in third or fourth place felt like failing. Yet again, I failed to earn the only prize—first. Life in Cameroon revolved only around who was at the top.

This race repeated itself for the next five years of secondary school into high school. I don't recall ever being asked to demonstrate knowledge as part of a team assignment. Even team sports and dorm competitions existed, but the star player was feted more than the team after a win. It was the same for dancing or singing. The emphasis was on who was the star player, who danced the best in Rosary or Immaculate dormitories and thus brought the halo of fleeting invincibility—pride to her fellow dorm mates. She was the celebrated player in the school all throughout. Just as the first in her class, so was the best in dance or best in you-name-it.

The team came second in recognition; never mind any secondary plays, passes, or assists that led to victory. There was no room for others on the pedestal; a space the size of the tip of a pin can hold only one. And so, our educational system taught us that power lies only in the hands of the one on top, and though brought up in a collectivist culture, individualism and competitiveness reigned over teamwork.

Discovering Teamwork

Ironically, my first encounter with teamwork was not until university in the United States, an overtly individualistic society. Struggling with different personalities, hard-to-coordinate schedules, and different priorities, I first wondered if I would ever pass the English course. We were asked to collaborate on reading and presenting our reading reaction to a text. In hindsight, my American teammates did not appear fazed by the assignment, nor did they exhibit the kind of stress I felt. It was clear that I lacked the skills of teamwork, which entailed a dance of sorts with various personality types to harness our cognitive abilities and deliver on a project. I fretted more about the lack of real work than the need to storm toward harmonizing our efforts. I worked on what I believed was my fair contribution, ignoring the bickering about when, where, and how we were to work. That was not my concern; I would do my piece, turn in it to the team, and sit back and quietly observe. I found it exhausting and distracting.

That was the individualistic training I had received during those crucial formative years. I could succeed on my terms, on my merit alone. The world would celebrate my achievements, as I beat all forty-five other girls in my class for first place in the race to the top. I had become a product of fierce individualism in a collectivist culture. Lourdes gave little of the contentious, albeit collaborative, creative environment that put our burgeoning personalities to test. Within the walls of the convent, only harmony was a valued proposition, maintained and guarded always in all spheres at all cost during our young lives. It was peaceful, non-abusive, dutiful, and always in deference if not to the sisters and your seniors but to the authorities. It did nothing to prepare us for the abusive world we would enter. We were to take that harmony with us and serve as role models of harmonious living in our own families, communities, home, church, and school and the world. Excellence on one's terms was inculcated into each of us. Outside those worlds, lay a hostile world, one we were ignorant of—or mostly.

I received a D in English. It was an all-too-important prerequisite, and without a passing grade, I would never graduate. This was my first lesson in the importance of teamwork. And it had not gone well. I had never been taught the value of the time-tested adage that "there is no *I* in team," or better yet, "if you wish to go fast, go it alone. If you wish to go far, team up."

If I Win, You Lose

To say this spirit of individualism was limited to a peculiar system of a convent education is to miss the contradictions of Africa's miniature, a collectivist society with strong norms for patronizing harmony and deference to hierarchy in a police state. Assertiveness was frowned on. Africa's miniature is as collectivist as it is secularly individualistic. With a strong aversion to conflict and a highly competitive nature, in the face of turmoil, only two options ensue: win-lose or lose-lose. The two paths settle on either a rush to achieve agreement or for a less-than-optimal solution in the interest of maintaining peace and harmony, an unending quarrel, *Ny'yetteh*—let us just get along or walk away in my native tongue;

that leaves the conflict unresolved. Our education was grounded in these values of *Ny'yetteh*.

Forgiveness was for the privileged and powerful only. Accountability was their sole province. We grew up in this atmosphere of false peace and calm, lacking in scholarship about our own history, the civics of corporate citizenry, social justice, and the building blocks of winning one for the team. We limped along as citizens of Cameroon. It would take decades before Anglophones, who now prefer the term *Southern Cameroons*, tried to unmask these contradictions. It was met with fierce resistance. It is at war.

I was the product of a system that said, "If I win, you lose." There were no trophies for second, third, or fourth runners-up. The prize went only to who was at the top, who received adulation, reverence, and an almost godlike following until the shine wore off or another head honcho came along.

Who can blame the people of Southern Cameroons, who now call themselves Ambazonia and now have what seems a penchant for divisiveness? Products of the same collectivist-individualistic educational system borrowed in part from their colonial masters, they fail to team up and collaborate as the world watches them descend into hell. If, indeed, the world is watching, in just four years since self-determination broke into the consciousness of the masses, it will bear witness to the uncountable Mass of splinter groups rising from the mess of conflict. If I win, you lose had been programmed into our DNA and would play out in the war.

Conflict Lies: An Indoctrination

The stories I tell are not unique. Colonialism and oppression have reeducated millions on their own histories, cultures, and identities. Poverty and conflict are not endemic to humanity; it is created because of uneven and unjust constructs of power. Those in power use simple, taken-for-granted levers to control the masses. For us, it was our education, the legal system, the judiciary, and the religious structures designed to give us just enough knowledge to be considered educated, just enough freedoms and rights to believe we were free, just enough resources to thrive, and a healthy dose of religiosity to keep us always heavenly bound to forget we were disenfranchised, largely poor, frightened, and malleable but mostly hoping things would get better.

Even with French Cameroun holding all the levels of control—assimilation—there remained a certain stubbornness in the hearts of Southern Cameroonians or Ambazonians. In the '90s, we would fight to bring the so-called Anglophone question to be addressed. We fought and ultimately died for multi-party politics to symbolically be accepted by the Biya regime. Neither multi-party politics nor the token Anglophone prime ministerial position was the answer to the Anglophone problem.

Conflict exists because it's profitable for people in power, governments, and companies with influence. Colonialism has shaped the way we live and think. The structure of today's world maintains the status quo. It ensures power and wealth for those who have it and guarantees strife and poverty for those who don't. Colonialism is the practice of exercising full or partial political and economic control over another country, occupying it with settlers, and exploiting it economically. Long after they left, their tentacles remain planted in their former colonies. There are many components of colonialism that exist far beyond its supposed end. Let's take a look at why.

What You Need to Know

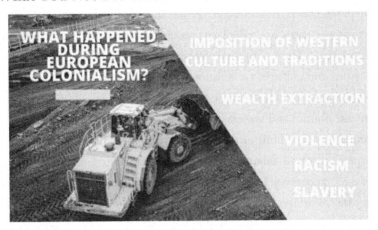

If Cameroon is a stage, every person within is an actor. Think about the impact of the various stages of colonialism on Cameroon and its people. When examining the various parties involved, ask yourself, "Did they benefit or lose out due to colonialism and the current power structure?"

HTTPS://CURTISRESEARCH.ORG/WP-CONTENT/UPLOADS/ HONEST-ACCOUNTS-REPORT-V4-WEB.PDF

It is no coincidence that Cameroon is a divided nation. Claiming independence is not enough. From the 1500s, Britain and other European nations colonized countries in Africa, including Cameroon. They imposed governance, structure, economics, religion, and culture. Generations were raised within the bounds of colonialism, including the education system. In addition to the internal politics and systems, the economics and natural resources of Cameroon were built on a foundation of exploitation. Multinational corporations and financial institutions constructed trade deals, tax systems, and risky loans that they continue to profit from to this very day. Foreign countries strip natural resources through mining, logging, and fishing, funneling billions of Africa's birthrights away. These systems are rigged but are not within public view.

If Southern Cameroon is being robbed blind, why isn't this making headlines? The very people who are profiting from Cameroon today are also responsible not only for the education systems but also for the economic and political systems in place. In addition, the globe is pacified with promises of "international development and loans." The narratives surrounding international development and aid propagate the harmful myths that outside help and European or "White saviors" are necessary for African countries to flourish. Outside influence is how the mess started.

Again, I call you to examine the profiteers of the current situation. This is not a "result of conflict." This is purposeful, systematic destruction of a people for profit.

Who Doesn't Like Swiss Chocolate? Please Raise Your Hand

Let me be categorically clear. I love dark Swiss chocolates and unapologetically will binge on them, even if I am to feel sorry later for my indiscipline. I take the polyphenols and caffeine that are good for my arteries and for my heart. If only for that, I will continue my love for the Swiss for taking our raw cocoa and turning it into decadent and delicious chocolates that we indulge in all the time.

I was born in what is today called the northwest region of Cameroon, far from the cocoa farms of Mundemba, Kumba, or Ndian. I have known all the ways our rich natural resources have been exploited by France, Britain, United States, China, Vietnam, Great Britain, and Switzerland, largely for their benefit, leaving us with nothing to show for. But excuse me for eating my chocolates at the Swiss hospitality table at the possibility that they, as interested world nations with interests, might possibly bring both the armed groups defending our homeland against a genocidal region.

I was born in and spent my formative years in the Bamenda, Biya's northwest region, now the epicenter of the war. I live in safe and comfortable harbors 7,500 miles away in a democratic country. I, like many, still could not escape the scourge of the war in Southern Cameroons. What we really can't escape are the foreign actors with interests who look the other way in Cameroon or offer obligatory statements to unburden their consciences.

Earlier in 2016, my cousin, Patrick Akuma, and my nephew by marriage Mancho Bibixy Tse, a local journalist, launched the peaceful Coffin Revolution, protesting the lack of basic things like good roads in the country. The protesters were met with live rounds of ammunitions from the army. Many were killed, hundreds injured, and hundred others summarily arrested and taken to the dreaded Secretariat d'Etat à la Défense (SED) in Yaoundé to face a military tribunal for terrorism and crimes against the state.

On January 19, 2017, Mancho Bibixy was arrested and is now serving a fifteen-year imprisonment. My cousin, Akuma, wasn't so lucky. He escaped and sought refuge in Nigeria and later died from poor medical care in April 2018. His three young sons and wife remain in Nigeria as refugees. On January 11, 2019, the villages of Alabukam and Alatoh in Bamenda, where several of my relatives live, were burned to the ground by military forces. Many of them are now part of the world's sixth largest population of displaced persons. Mr. Awasum was shot to death in his home. My story is one of hundreds of Southern Cameroonians. Sitting in with the Swiss is much more than their chocolates or cheese. It is a chance at stopping Biya's deadly machinery, a chance at negotiating a comprehensive peace, and a chance that, someday, I and my family can return to our ancestral home in peace.

The war has been raging in Africa's miniature for over five years, claiming over ten thousand lives, with staggering numbers displaced as refugees in Nigeria and internally in the country. Biya's military engaged in a scorched-earth policy, burning their way through villages, leaving a trail of death in their path. Families escape into the forest to stay alive. Boys and young men escape, joining the Amba Boys to fight the regime. Families caught in the crossfire have left whatever is left of their homes and livelihood for the major cities, mainly in the economic capital.

During the five years, the international communities remained largely silent. Since 2017, the UK, United States, and EU have issued variations of the same memos and resolutions. Each time, they called for both sides to end hostilities, for schools to resume, and for the Biya government to engage in an inclusive dialogue without conditions. The killing of civilian populations was continued by the military, who laid the blame on the Amba Boys. The Amba Boys held location advantage, having mastery of their neighborhoods, back roads, forests, and strategic locations for an attack. They would set up ambush on winding, dilapidated roads deep in the village, with nothing more than sticks and stones and a few guns or previously seized AK-47s, blowing up military trucks filled with armed military on their way to secure, defend, reinforce, or seek out the Amba Boys for the killing. A harvest of more AK-47s was the result. And another round battles, this time only deadlier on account of the new weapons, would ensue. Biya's military, through his territorial ministers, would vow an even bigger offensive to wipe out what they now described as terrorists.

For five years, with half a million refugees in Nigeria, two thousand gruesome deaths, thousands incarcerated in prison, and conditions comparable to Nazi-style concentration camps, the diaspora begged for the world to intervene and save innocent people from dying in the war. Their protests, letter-writing campaign, and online activism could buy them mostly letters from concerned congressmen to the Biya government and the Amba Boys to bring an end to the fighting and for him to call for an all-inclusive dialogue.

In the last months, as many as three NGOs—the European Institute of Peace (EIP), the Swiss Center for Humanitarian Dialogue (HD), and the British Pave the Way—have all entered into the Anglophone crisis, offering variously to be facilitators, negotiators, and capacity builders. But what exactly is their role? Many have asked how any one of these NGOs becomes the go-to mediator, facilitator, and capacity builder. In a forty-eight-hour period, the HD put out at least two versions of press releases. In one release, HD is being tasked—but by whom?—to act as mediator. In another, HD has been chosen to mediate between French Cameroun and Ambazonia. By the end of that week, HD was also a facilitator. The Swiss government and the United Nations put out their own version of press release, noting they are happy to see the start of dialogue that will return peace to Cameroon, with no mention of the fight for independence, separation, or the term *Ambazonia*.

The road to dialogue with French Cameroun has been a long and thorny one for English Cameroonians. For the past sixty years, the English Cameroonians have asked for dialogue. Southern Cameroons filed a complaint in the African Court on Human and Peoples' Rights against French Cameroun for violation of their rights of self-determination. In the '90s, when Cameroon filed to be admitted into the commonwealth, activists in Southern Cameroons opposed their admittance based on the Harare declarations and values that French Cameroun didn't have nor live up to. When the former UN secretary general Kofi Annan visited Cameroon, he was confronted with the right to self-determination for the English Cameroon, to which the secretary said the United Nation could not engage in the matter, as Cameroon was a sovereign country but called for President Biya to engage in dialogue with the English Cameroonians.

In 2009, the court upheld the territorial integrity of French Cameroun but recognized the dispute between Cameroon and the English Cameroon and called for French Cameroun to, within 180 days, enter into negotiations with English Cameroon. Cameroon did nothing, failing to respond even after requesting more time, and the courts gave them an additional three months as well as offered their good offices to mediate. Cameroon failed to respond.

Dialogue with French Cameroun has been a long-running cry. What is curious is the crop of new entrants in the form of NGOs finding it necessary to build capacity among English-speaking Cameroonians to facilitate and to negotiate. In the years leading up to 2016, when violence broke out and was continuing, no one had questioned English Cameroonians' capacity to not only lobby the international community to bring pressure on the Biya regime but also seek relief from the courts for the right to self-determination for the people. Some find the statements made by the HD to be patronizing, if not denigrating, to suggest that English Cameroonians lack the capacity to negotiate the terms for living together or for separation.

Some see the role of the NGO to make press releases as telling the world that they are beginning dialogue between the warring parties. But as a prerequisite, one party does need to lecture on what knowledge, skills, and abilities are needed to carry out effective dialogue. For that, they unilaterally determined the time, place, and date they would meet with the English Cameroonians. These very acts of picking what time is suitable for the NGO, selecting the venue, setting the agenda, and going as far as arranging for payments for the attendee are all negotiable between the two parties. In this case, as it was in 1962, in Foumban in the French Cameroun, the English Cameroonians have been brought to the negotiation table without ever offering the modicum of input. In conflict, as elsewhere where parties engage each other, who had power can be as consequential as who sits where around a table, who wields more political or economic power, and what is on the agenda.

In the Algerian War with France, which lasted more than three years, it did not end with Algeria asking for its independence from France. Why does English Cameroon find the need to negotiate its independence? In negotiations with French Cameroun, the discussions are a matter beyond independence rather than on the terms of separation. Like France did in 1961, on the eve of the Republic of Cameroon's independence, it entered into a corporation agreement with the new republic. Ostensibly direct about their purpose, France did not conceal that, as a condition for granting its colony independence, it must be repaid for all the investments done in said country till today. But knowing the nascent republic was void of any major industrialization and had an economy mostly agrarian with a few cash crops and largely peasant population subsisting on what was grown and living on less than $0.50 per day, it could never repay their purported investments, even at favorable interest rates. The fiscal wherewithal did not exist in the country. In return, the president of Cameroon signed to allow France unfettered access to any resources discovered in the country to exploit, and if they chose not to, only then can Cameroon offer the concession to another interested country.

In an even more insidious relationship-specific agreement, on their way to relinquishing control over their colony, the French instituted the colonial French franc, later dubbed the CFA monetary systems. The French would print the CFA one for its Central African colonies and another for its West African colonies, guaranteeing the CFA's convertibility to other world currencies. For this, the fourteen former French colonies shall place their national reserves into the French central bank. Each country can access up to 15% of their deposits; however, should they wish more, France shall lend the money back to the country at the going rate. If that is too much to consider as a continuation of colonialism, except, this time, through the expressed wish sealed in the form of a corporation agreement between supposedly sovereign nations, France mandated that to protect the "vast" investment in these countries, the French ambassador had the right to come to the defense of the country should the president become incapable or be killed.

Many separatists, federalists, and unionists have rushed to embrace the Swiss negotiation, facilitation, and capacity-building proposal. The UN, EU, and the United States, through its outspoken undersecretary for Africa, Tibor Nagy, have all chimed in to throw their support behind the purported Swiss-led dialogue. No one has bothered to tell the rest of English Cameroonians, those on the battleground, those in the diaspora, and those who now are ready to give anything for a return to normal in their villages and towns that there are negotiations underway—or are there? For each side of the warring factions, in secret or public, what due diligence has been carried out? What confidence-building measures have been put in place? Do both sides have clarity on what the terms of reference are? Are the Swiss through their NGO, the British, or the Belgians, as are French Cameroun, and the separatists clear on their terminologies? What do words like *terrorists, separatists, one and indivisible,* and *federalism* mean? Who defines them, and for what purpose?

What we were not taught in schools, we perfected as adults who, upon achieving the age of majority, live and breathe in a world rife with patronage, corruptions, entitlement, nepotism, and autocratic rule. We were studious and perfected the art of snatching defeat from the jaws of success. From the inception of the crisis in 2016 until present, a north-south divide emerged, and the chasm grows, giving the Biya regime great talking points that they have no one to negotiate with. Conflict was endemic to us only we mostly saw as "hustling" to live. Conflict was everywhere yet concealed in its obviousness. We chose to get on with our lives until we couldn't carry on.

Cameroon and the Colonization of Africa: A Reeducation "History is written by the victors" is a quote often associated with Winston Churchill. However, there is some debate about the origin of the saying. Whether it was Hermann Göring, Winston Churchill, or some nameless, faceless predecessor, the truth remains: those who are in power rewrite history to glorify themselves and denigrate others. Just look up the names on the great monuments adorning big capital cities in the West and East.

The history of Cameroon taught in schools is not the true history. It leaves out vital players, hides and modifies facts, and makes up others. Like most of Africa, Cameroon's people are cut off from the true stories that make up their very identities. Instead, due to intentional indoctrination, they build their lives on false narratives, painting the walls of their mind with colonialism. Add in the generational trauma from oppression, poverty, and lack of ancestral connection, and you've got a perfect cocktail of fallacies to bind and imprison the masses. If you read anything from these lines, it is that a people not captured in war is being killed and now must fight to death to break free from the shackles of another. A country with its own rights to sovereignty has ceased to exist, yet it has gained independence from its colonial masters to see itself yoked to another, France.

If Africa's miniature is a contradictory Africa, the continent is at odds with its own propositions and realities. If ever a case was ripe for negotiation, the case of the former BSC would be a good study. The continent looks elsewhere for a solution like the Swiss connection negotiation, all the while AU—like its counterpart, EU—exists to resolve continental troubles. Some historians have questioned the push for a united Africa as a sine qua non for a strong continental body. Meanwhile, within the erstwhile European Union was a formidable geopolitical and economic body made up of tiny slivers of sovereign states like Monaco and Lichtenstein, all with a few hundred citizens. The sovereign state of Nauru (population: 5,000) is a member state of the United Nations. Ambazonia has a population of 8 million.

Pan-Africanists would make the argument that the emergence of small nation-states face greater challenges in a globalized world where giants like China have smaller countries for breakfast, to coin a pun, that will not survive in a fierce global economy where countries' outputs are minuscule. If size matters, then much cannot be expected from Singapore, a country so tiny compared with China but boasts almost the same economic strength. Britain, an island, is one of the superpowers and controls the world. The continent of Europe—via EU, today—negotiates with the tiny island of Britain on Brexit. Size is not a measure of strength in the twenty-first century. Congo is bigger than Western Europe in landmass, but up until the nineteenth century was the property of the Belgian king. After finding oil, diamonds, and rare earth minerals, Congo rages war and, in spite of its riches, cannot be thought of as an economic power to negotiate favorable terms for the extraction of its resources with Belgium, Asian, and Western nations. And then if size matters, Nigeria—with a population of over 170 million, five times that of France—will be its own heavyweight and a first world country.

International bodies craft for themselves principles they must abide by, or else the raison d'être for coming together is nonexistent. As with the UN in 1946, their principles are equality and self-determination, among others. AU principles are another fallacy like those promoting a united Africa at all costs but are largely silent when it comes to the principles of human rights, freedoms, equality, and self-determination. Unity that is not entered into as free people, free nations, can only occur through coercion, conquest, economic sabotage, political manipulations, or fear. Only free persons can negotiate the terms of any engagement.

These simplistic arguments can only gain currency in Africa. Monaco, Lichtenstein, and Nauru will not stand idly by and be told they are too small and irrelevant. France must absorb Monaco while Austria or Switzerland acquire Lichtenstein as they are unable to survive economically, compete globally, or negotiate on their own terms. For a united EU, having fewer—not more—sovereign states is key. Building skills, capacity, an educated workforce, good governance, and strong institutions are what make regional and continental bodies work for their respective spheres. AU is composed of strong, weak, and failed states. At the country level, there are underpowered citizenry while education is high, and unemployment is on bubonic plague levels, reducing and wiping away any possibilities of a strong middle class or growth. Regionally, there is a war raging somewhere with the attendant consequences of loss of trade, risky flow of people and goods, and death and destruction. Each neighboring country has a different currency, making trade even more difficult. Borders are militarized for fear of the export of arms and terrorism. Economies of scope are hard to come by. Nigeria, with its naira and Cameroon's CFA, make trade difficult. There is no adoption of universally recognized treaties to lower the boundaries and facilitate movement, trade, and so on.

And to top all of the above is the proposed All Anglophone Conference III, AACIII conference to discuss, according to its proponents, the Anglophone crisis. A mix of the old and new "elites" emerges to hold a preparatory conference before a national dialogue, even as sentiments in the affected area have long since moved far from placating an entrenched, murderous dictator with tabled grievances. The press release of November 26, 2017 is but another way to arrange chairs on the deck of a sinking Titanic. Even those with staunch nationalistic tendencies believe any dialogue at this juncture must be international, as Mr. Biya and his surrogates cannot be trusted, let alone seen as a credible architect of peace in that part of Africa. It is comical to read this same litany of resolutions and appeals. Readers will naturally ask in response—if they cared enough, "Did Anglophones not have a dialogue during

AAC I, AAC II, Conclaves I, II, and many others in between? And to what end with the current regime?"

CALL TO ACTION

Building Resilience Through Critical Thinking

Before helping anyone else, you must help yourself. The first step in reeducation is to examine your own beliefs. These questions are designed to bring light and answers to highlight the status quo. Are there any realities or truths that you accept without question?

Here are some questions to get you thinking about how you view the world, response to the conflict, and your understanding of the conflict:

- How do you describe yourself? Francophone, Anglophone, Cameroonian, Southern Cameroonian, Ambazonian, NOSO, Northwesterner, Southwesterner? What, if any, does the label you give yourself bring to mind?

- Do you view the conflict as between Anglophones and Francophones, Southern Cameroons, Ambazonia, and the Cameroon government?

- Challenge yourself to create a list of foreign companies doing business in Cameroon. Begin with the energy companies and the deals signed with the government. What are the positions of these countries on the war since President Biya declared war in 2017?

- What does it mean to want peace to you? Do you see peace as between those currently fighting, and how will that happen?

- Challenge yourself to read at least one book on the history of the French and the British Cameroons.

- Who do you believe are responsible for the crisis? Are they the same people fighting?

- List three to five things that are the most vexing to you about the situation in Cameroon from your point of view.

- Do you understand the story of the two Cameroons? Write down three to five solutions that will bring about peace and justice.

- Do you believe peace can exist without justice?

- How can we use the inquiry process to reflect on and explore what we do and don't know about peace in Cameroon?

- In what ways does a dominant White (Anglo-Saxon, Francophone, etc.) culture affect your life? In what ways is it enforced?

Controversial Truths: A List of Fallacies That Lead to Complacency

Oppression and oppressive power structures rely on fallacies. They rely on fear and systematic dismantling of everything near and dear to you. Knowledge leads to wisdom. Those wise to the way of the world and people are harder to conquer, to control, and to kill. Colonialism and White supremacy receive strength and power from fallacy. Here are some fallacies that strengthen oppressive power structures.

Individualistic Fallacy

When you divide people into good and bad, south and north, or any other type of division, this is individualistic fallacy. It creates divisions between "us" and "others" and paints the picture that the people performing oppression must all be evil and that the people within the power structure are innately "good" and not contributing to the power structures that entrap them. No one wants to see themselves as their own captors. Of course, oppressors cannot be let off the hook. But a vital fact is to hold yourself accountable for the ideologies and beliefs you've absorbed from an oppressive system. We've been living in a world that was built on colonization—with some patriarchy and capitalism thrown in the mix for good measure—so, we've learned to view it through a lens that supports that reality. The entire system was built on thoughts, habits, and actions, whether intentional or not.

Legalistic Fallacy

This is the belief that, if we change the laws, everything will fall into place. Just looking at the aftermath of UN article 76 will illustrate the concept that legal precedent is only a portion of building change. Southern Cameroons, a former UN trust territory administered by Britain, was supposedly led to independence, except the reins of sovereignty were handed over to the independent French Cameroun president, Ahmadou Ahidjo, a proxy for France.

Tokenistic Fallacy

Many people point to representation as a sign of post-conflict life. Appointing figureheads from certain tribal, racial, ethnic, or religious groups to prove the system isn't inherently prejudiced without dismantling it is a common means of maintaining the status quo. Commentary regarding the Obama presidency, for example, is a perfect example of this fallacy.

Ahistorical Fallacy

This fallacy asserts that the present exists disconnected from the past. The impact of the past is alive and well. The past matters; history matters. The old adage "He who looks deep into the past can see clearly into the future" still holds and is worth taking to heart. Time tends to heal most wounds. Time never erases history. You voted in the February 11, 1961 plebiscite to join the already independent country of the Republic of Cameroon. It has been fifty-nine years since. That past is done with. The concerns now are how to implement recommendations from partisan dialogue.

Fixed Fallacy

Oppression or prejudice is something measurable and doesn't develop or change over time. Only the purifying force of violence itself overcomes systematic or institutionalized violence. Since German or British colonialism has "ended," it's been corrected. In the case of LRC, since the "reunification," it is now a one and indivisible country that nothing can or should mess with. Never mind article 47 of the federal constitution prohibiting changing the form of the state. It was unilaterally changed. Adherents ignore all historical, political, and legal precedence and contemporaneous changes.

We don't have to look far for the global north's complicity in wishing for a fixed "end" to the botched decolonization in Africa. Britain joined the European Union, but in 2016, a referendum was passed to withdraw. When conflict broke out in Africa, rather than supporting or giving the people concerned—the primary victims of the war and the claimants—a platform to speak for themselves, solutions were imposed by the oppressor and by the global north. Britain reserved the right to withdraw from a union it freely entered but denied the same rights for Southern Cameroons.

In Canada, organized referenda allow Quebec to choose whether to stay or to leave. We also see Britain allowing Scotland to decide its fate through a referendum. For Africa, countries whose colonial arrangement no longer suits one party do not have the same right to a referendum, the same means and methods other countries have used to determine the wishes of the people.

To enact effective change, we need to analyze our own thinking. This type of critical-thinking exercise is best worked through in a discussion group, since it is difficult to see within ourselves.

- Do you accept that the same international laws, principles, United Nations resolutions, and charters exercised in the independence of the UN trust territories can be used in solving the current war between the Republic of Cameroon and Southern Cameroons?

- Do you view the conflict as between Anglophones and Francophones, Southern Cameroons, Ambazonia, and the Cameroon government?

- Do you believe that the crisis is an internal affair of Cameroon, to be left for the government to work at finding solutions, or does your knowledge of the history of the country lead you to believe that it is an international conflict that needs international intervention?

If you understand the story of the two Cameroons well, are you in a position to talk about what is needed for justice to prevail?

- Do you believe peace can exist without justice?

- Could you share with us about five things that you think are needed for justice to prevail?

- What, in your opinion, are the key reasons for the present conflict?

- Do you believe that the government can solve the crisis, or does it require an outside party, like another country, to step in?

Read More

M. Desmond and M. Emirbayer, "What Is Racial Domination?" *Du Bois Review: Social Science Research on Race* 6, no. 2 (2009): 335–55, https://doi:10.1017/ S1742058X09990166.

"Colonialism and Empire ," The Abolition Project, http://abolition.e2bn.org/slavery_43.html.

"Understanding Slavery Initiative," http://www.understandingslavery. com/index.php-option=com_content&view=article&i d=307&Itemid=152.html.

Shashi Tharoor, *Inglorious Empire: What the British Did to India.*

Priyamvada Gopal, Insurgent Empire: Anticolonialism Resistance and British Dissent.

Frantz Fanon, *Wretched of the Earth.*

"The Black Curriculum Launch," The Black Curriculum, https:// youtu.be/hb3t20Nv1UY.

SAIH Norway, "Africa Corp. Radi-Aid 2.0," https://youtu.be/ HpjbkQr0JAE.

"The Truth about the British Empire," *Guardian*, https:// www.theguardian.com/tvand-radio/2020/feb/07/the-

truth-about-the-british-empire-podcasts-of-the-week
Legacies of colonialism.

Walter Rodney, *How Europe Underdeveloped Africa.*

Ava DuVernay, *13th*, https://netflix.com/ph/title/80091741.

Akala, *Natives: Race and Class in the Ruins of Empire.*

"The Racist Double Standards of International Development," Al
Jazeera, https://
www.aljazeera.com/indepth/opinion/racist-double-
standards-internationaldevelop-
ment-200707082924882.html.

The Story of Wealth (@storyofwealth), "Defining poverty and
inequality," Instagram photo.

Teva Sienicki, "We can end poverty, but this is why we haven't,"
TEDx Talks, https://youtu.be/vvlozhvQPJw.

Global Justice Now, podcast, https://open.spotify.com/
show/6FP8QiVZGomoIyVRBV9YrH.

Oxfam, "What is inequality," https://youtu.be/9FYEvfcuvy.

Health Poverty Action, "Changing Track: Putting People
before Corporations."

————, "Honest Accounts 2017: How the World Profits from
Africa's Wealth."

Tax Justice Network, https://www.taxjustice.net/. Trade Justice
Movement, https://www.tjm.org.uk/. Jubilee Debt
Campaign, https://jubileedebt.org.uk/.

Jason Hickel, *The Divide: A Brief Guide to Global Inequality and Its
Solutions.*

The Big Short, https://www.netflix.com/dz-en/title/80075560.

Laundromat, https://www.netflix.com/ph/title/80994011. Health
Poverty Action, "A Practical Guide for Communicating
Global Justice and Solidarity."

————, "The Alternatives—Approaches toward a Life in Full."

"Time for a New Narrative: Alternatives to the Language of Aid, Charity, and So-Called 'International Development,'" Development Compass, https://developmentcompass.org/blog/campaigning/time-for-a-new-narrative-alternatives-tothe-language-of-aidcharity-and-so-called-international-development.

William Easterly, *The White Man's Burden.*

Linsey McGoey, *No Such Thing as a Free Gift: The Gates Foundation and the Price of Philanthropy.*

Mark Engler and Paul Engler, *This Is an Uprising.*

Jane McAlevey and Bob Ostertag, *Raising Expectations (and Raising Hell): My Decade Fighting for the Labor Movement.*

Organeyez.co (@organeyez.co), https://www.instagram.com/organeyez.co/.

Fill in the Blanks @fillintheblanks, https://www.instagram.com/fillintheblanksuk/

Black Curriculum (@theblackcuricurriculum), https://www.instagram.com/theblackcurriculum/

The History Corridor (@thehistorycorridor), https://www.instagram.com/thehistorycorridor/

Decolonising Contraception and Health (@decolonisingcontraception), https://www.instagram.com/decolonisingcontraception/.

BBC Bitesize, "Decolonizing the Curriculum," https://www.bbc.co.uk/bitesize/articles/z7g66v4

CHAPTER 4:
TOXIC CULTURES

Toxic Positivity (Noun)—The overgeneralization of a happy, optimistic state that results in the denial, minimization, and invalidation of the authentic human emotional experience.
—The Psychology Group, Fort Lauderdale

I t's okay to not be okay. Of course, this is something I've only recently learned. In every stage of my life, I was taught that I should be grateful for my circumstances. Gratitude was equated with grace and ladylike behavior. I was taught to feel lucky to go to school, to have food in my belly, to be from Cameroon. When I came to the United States, I was "such a lucky girl" to be "welcomed with open arms" into my new home, to have "escaped" my homeland, to be where I was. As a black female engineer, I was made to feel lucky for my position at work. When my daughter, Praxie, was told she would never walk again, I was to feel "lucky that it wasn't worse." At the time that conflict erupted in Southern Cameroons, I was to feel "lucky I was so far away."

Toxic positivity makes you grateful for crumbs and forces you to ignore your trauma, identity, and true emotions. Instead of focusing on healing or creating a path to move forward, you're weighed down by guilt and shame. Gratitude practices are often referred to as the self-care golden standard: thank your way to happiness. It might be controversial, but I think most of these so-called experts take that advice out of context and way too far.

The practice of gratitude isn't about forcing yourself to feel happy about the things you "should" feel good about. It's about learning what you have positive feelings about in your life so that you can gravitate toward it. Generalizing and blanket statements telling traumatized, miserable, or ill people that they should "feel lucky," "blessed," or "grateful" for anything they are unhappy about are abusive. I experienced this on an individual level during my daughter's illness, as well as on a cultural level in my childhood. Southern Cameroons are experiencing it as a weapon of colonization.

What Does Toxic Positivity Look Like?

If you've ever struggled with a debilitating illness or tragedy, you've most likely experienced toxic positivity.

Just have faith.

Think positive.

It'll all work out.

God has a plan.

There are an unlimited number of ways to minimize someone in a crisis. Unfortunately, this idealization of positivity has soaked deep into the consciousness of modern society. When we're faced with suffering, the last thing we need to be told is that our anguish is invalid or immoral. Positivity needs to be knocked off the pedestal. In some cases, something greater than ignorance drives toxic positivity. It's weaponized. Often, the powerful polarize the oppressed with blaming narratives. "It could be worse. You've got it easy. You've got to be patient. Change takes time."

The Webster's Dictionary defines a *patriot* as "a person who vigorously supports their country and is prepared to defend it against enemies or detractors." The key to understanding this definition is understanding how to define an enemy. Is an enemy a masked robber that sneaks into the house late at night and cuts your throat? Or is the enemy the faceless manufacturer of the knives that arms the robbers with all they need to take your house and home? It's a common tactic to other a minority group and then to villainize them. Look at the viewpoint on Mexican immigrants in the United States. Even though the Mexicans share DNA with the Indigenous people, who have more rights and claims to the land than anyone else on it, they've been othered and villainized as enemies of a certain way of life. Otherness has been spun and PR-packaged into "true patriotism." If you drink the Kool-Aid, you'll believe that your way of life is in danger. Immigrants are coming to steal your jobs and throw you out of your homes. Beware of the other. Packaging nationalism with prejudice is a potent tool, weaponizing fear and enslaving the masses into maintaining the status quo.

So, who is the enemy in this case? Is it the Mexican "immigrant" to the United States, migrating from one place to another for a better life, or is it corporate greed hell-bent on keeping working wages low for maximum profit? Is the enemy the corrupt politicians capitalizing on your fear to get elected, manufacturing crisis after crisis, and then spoon-feeding you the resolution?

Unfortunately, parallels to this game of thrones run throughout every corner of the globe. What I was taught no longer coincides with what I believe. Patriotism is not only fighting the enemy. It's having the wisdom to know who the real enemy is. It is denying them the narrative to say, "it could be worse."

Nationalism Gone Wrong Through History

Nationalism or patriotism are not inherently evil. Any system that unites people under one cause can be a force for good. The problem lies with certain brands of nationalism and patriotism. The unwavering, unquestioning nature of blind patriotism or nationalism is dangerous. Patriotism/nationalism shouldn't be hostile, divisive, and uninformed. To do what is right by our country, we need to enter with our eyes wide open. Toxic cultures rob adherents of the ability to see clearly through the muck and fog. Breaking out of toxicity is the first step in realigning your actions for the better. It is the first step to accepting responsibility and knowing you have the power, agency, and control over what is going on.

Here's the problem. Any tradition has a definite history and can be redefined to fit a certain narrative. The history of slaughtering Native Americans became a holiday for breaking bread and sharing traditions. The day Southern Cameroons, the autonomous self-governing state voted to associate with a federation with its already independent neighbor, the Republic of Cameroon, became a youth day for playing sports and all sorts of games. Any mention of this violent past is considered "unpatriotic." This misunderstanding of history is not accidental. Redefining and rewriting history allows those in power to control the narrative, identity, and future of the ones they subjugate.

Nationalism is not the same as nationality. It's not the same thing as respect for a nation or desire for good. Modern nationalism began during the French Revolution. Napoleon's nationalism sparked the rise of nationalism all over Europe. The collective hatred of French invaders helped develop a national consciousness. The rise of Nazi Germany was fueled by nationalistic fervor. The blind patriotism stemming from September 11 are all rooted in the othering of a group eventually culminating with Make America Great Again (MAGA), and later QAnon under former Pres. Donald Trump. Fear-mongering, blaming, and groupthink are vital aspects of keeping this way of life sustained. Groupthink thrives on toxic cultures.

One of the most difficult lessons in my life was that I was a victim of nationalism. And if I was no longer who I was told before, who was I? If my nationality has changed, can I still be a nationalist at heart? The threads that bind me—could it all simply be propaganda? Yes and no.

Cursing the Ten Commandments

Part of being Catholic makes you feel guilty about almost everything—that is, except those things that lead to happiness in this life. Notice how the truly happy people are those who go about their lives "breaking" all the rules. No doubt they subscribe wholly to books like *Nice Girls Finish Last, Never Eat Lunch Alone, First, Break All the Rules,* or other best sellers that celebrate the likes of Trump, Rupert Murdoch, and yes, even Oprah for their feel good, steely, uncompromising, unwavering, and sometimes uncanny character. No one who picks up any of their unabashedly self-written, ghostwritten autobiographies winces once as they study these people to learn what makes them great.

How do I know this? Because my doctoral dissertation adviser told me in no uncertain terms what was in store for me as I struggled through my research. Her words continue to haunt me to this day. She said in bold red ink, on my most recent submission, "Emma, I worry for you, as you will have it hard in life with this kind of timidity—walking on eggshells. You can't go through life being nice." She was speaking of how I crafted my sentences and carried out an analysis. "Take the bull by the horn and stop playing nice with your words. I see this all the time, and it gets you nowhere. Your goal is to impress your audience, and sometimes, that means stretching the truth a bit."

As shocked and stunned as I was that my very own adviser will see such doom and gloom in my future, and all I was doing was staying within the confines of what I thought were the facts, avoiding deceitful, artfully crafted logic that would not stand scrutiny, it left me in tears. Of course, I knew what she meant: your story—in my case, my reason for researching a particular subject—must be compelling, convincing, and captivating enough to get through the approval process. I was not sensational enough to be captivating using those "soft" words, and I was not stretching the reader's mind enough to be captivating with pronouncements like "there is a dearth of xyz in the field of social sciences."

But my lesson on how I was doomed to be a failure by being nice came much earlier in life. By age twelve, neatly settled in a convent, I just began my indoctrination of the many ways of being nice: break no laws—those lain by the reverend sisters at your boarding school—and buy as many friends as you can with all your assets. I know which of the two I was. Following the rules set by the school meant I studied hard, stayed clear of any trouble with the girls, and went to confession when asked to. What I did not do was get friends on my side. I had not learned, then, how to impress my audience, stretch the truth, play nice, or be captivating. I naively thought that if I was a good student, worked hard, did not break any rules, watched my p's and q's, spoke up only when spoken to, and gave only what I could, everyone would fall in love with me.

Am I to believe, then, at the young impressionable age of twelve, as I do in my ripe old age, that I am destined for failure unless I screw everybody and everything in my path or that I brownnose or kiss ass and—for that matter—kick ass to succeed? What kind of sorry, slack imbecile I must be to continue to hedge when I can be more surgical, to be me when there are at least half a dozen personalities I could have assumed all these years—

circumstances permitting, to tell a convenient lie when the truth gets me nowhere, or to fake it till I made it? My life lay unadorned in front of me, void of any remarkableness, of any high points when I plunged into the deep, unafraid, unconcerned, and uninhibited. And so, I cursed those Ten Commandments.

How Our Happiness Culture Masks Deep Fissures

When I read James Alison's *The Joy of Being Wrong*, I loved the title and the central message in his book, which I narrowly interpreted to mean that, in the Catholic tradition, there is redemption for every sinner, so sinners should rejoice for having sin. I tried hard not to question how being wrong and being happy go hand in hand. How was I to suddenly feel joy breaking the commandments? I must make something wrong—nothing more, nothing less. I'd give my word, stand for it, and move on.

All living systems, when faced with a threat, react to restore equilibrium. We must understand that equilibrium means we are not resorting to returning to the same state we were in. Any system that reacts in this fashion, in the world of social scientists, is considered maladaptive. As Ronald Heifetz puts it, "There is nothing seductive or good about seeking a state of equilibrium. Being adaptive requires sustained periods of disequilibrium."

A microcosm of toxic culture abounds. Take the saga of my own alumni association called Lourdes Ex-Students Association (LESA), boasting 50 years of existence. The problem with LESA is its inability to deal with sustained periods of stress in its well-established machinery. Old, tried-and-true ways of dealing with stress worked well when everyone knew the problem and when the solutions were easy to implement. Here, we have stresses we don't quite understand, whose solutions or responses cannot be found in our repertoire. The recent acrimony, infighting, backstabbing, public exposé, and disrespect require a new and bold response. The threat to LESA goes beyond infighting or disrespect. It is a conflict of values that the current systems are ill equipped to deal with. Our ethos of praying our way into a conflict resolution needs to be recast. Our conflict-adverse stance does not serve LESA nor its members.

LESAns are meticulous about being happy, and happiness means getting rid of conflict the moment it rears its ugly head. Happiness also means making some noise about life-affirming moments like births, graduation, promotions, a new house, a new husband, a party event, and even the purchase of a new car. The LESAn culture, if it can definitively be defined, is one of happiness where members socialize to defer to authority—one way to maintain harmony, hold fast to traditions, and conform.

For some, happiness equates to a life of faith in their Catholic tradition that does not judge and shows mercy to all, leaving the job of conflict resolution and justice to God. For such adherents, the words of Mathew 7, *Judge not lest you are not judge* and leaving mercy and justice to God's providence offer a path out of vexing situations and into a real good chance at happiness. LESA manifests an equally indicting culture, devising intricate ways to implicate one another at the drop of a hat. Equally, the culture of LESA is one of victimization as its proclamations of immunity. Such cultures are, in the words of Bethke Elshtain, "awash in exculpatory strategies . . . fascinating ways to let ourselves and others off the hook." Equally both victim and those claiming innocence show a great capacity to be an inclusive group demonstrating a prodigal-son tendency—an enormous capacity to will forgiveness or force it if necessary. In the march toward reconciliation, the leadership of the organization has opened its e-groups to all ex-students, leaving some wondering if— with rights come responsibility or with responsibilities—there are privileges. In an unyielding quest for happiness, LESA remains at odds with itself, the best example of internal conflict and external contradictions. If forgiving is forgetting, then all histories, whitewashed or not, do not concern us.

Hope for Future: Hope to Walk Again

To have a healthy dialogue, concerns must be validated. That is not happening. The Federal Republic of Cameroon was the African experiment of what a union would look like, but even that was not to be. By President Ahidjo's own admission in his 1972 speech to his national assembly, Africa in miniature must not be allowed to walk; it needed to be a unitary state, never mind that two historically distinct cultures already had difficulties coming together. Bringing together each specific cultural, legal, and historical system's legacies was as much of a problem. The real reason was the discovery of oil in the Rio del Rey, Gulf of Guinea, just off the coast of Southern Cameroons. It was, as the former President said, "Our joy of living side-by-side as brothers that should motivate and animate all of us" to unite. And we were conditioned to believe it.

That perfect experiment—perfect example of peace, diversity, and harmony—was not to be. Underneath the peaceful veneer lurked the simmering discontent from not only the "Anglophones," who—though on paper—were an equal partner, by now were largely marginalized people within their own country. The fires lay smoldering, unnoticed by the world. Even with the ushering of a multi-party system in 1990, the main opposition party—the Social Democratic Front (SDF), led too by a sit-tight leader—was mainly fodder for the ruling Cameroon People's Democratic Movement (CPDM) to show the world it too was democratic. Adhijo capitalized on the happiness culture. Those at mid and higher economic echelons, though able to make decisions about their immediate economic viability, have little or no input in the decisions that impact their livelihood. They suffer the indignity of structural violence—not having the clear understanding nor the freedom nor influence nor voice to define the vision for themselves as they best understand it. Ideally, the middle class has the greatest interest to actively advocate for policies/processes, as well as agitate for the existence of environments conducive to its survival. After all, this is a group with the most to lose. A non-full-scale violence was taking place.

Cameroon was sine qua non, dictatorial, divisive, and patronizing. In the wake of the grand experiment—the reunification *à la Cameroun l'orient*—laid deprivation, scarcity, and downright fear. It comprised the social class, the ruling tribe's first Pres. Amadou Ahidjo, then of President Biya, and all who served them faithfully. The rest of the country worked for the government or subsisted on less than $2 per day. Cameroon lacked a vibrant middle class capable of placing checks and balances between the centralized, powerful elites at its helm and the masses at the bottom. The economy, largely third world, lacks the most basic infrastructures and institutions in the judicial, transport, health, and education sectors. In Southern Cameroons, it was not a question of lack but more of nonexistent infrastructures and institutions. For years, this part of Africa in miniature lays largely neglected, as its oil and gas resources are siphoned off and its cash crops exported while its more than six million inhabitants toil away. All the while, Cameroon's international partners forged deals and kept their own economies running. They were told it could be worse.

To say the people of Southern Cameroons, Ambazonia, will never walk is to say facts do not matter. The crisis goes beyond our resources and our identity. There are several countries around the world where strong culture identification causes clashes. It goes beyond minority complaints of marginalization. Many countries in the world have their own minority problems. It is beyond resource- or power-sharing. Power asymmetries within society mean resources or power-sharing will never be equitable. It goes beyond good governance. How the French govern themselves should be left to them. Ambazonians are not seeking a larger share of the resource pie. The resources in the territory are theirs to use and share as they wish, not to be apportioned by someone else. Neither do they seek to be the head of another country. Who leads their country and for how long and what language that person speaks are their concern. Ambazonians are rising to live in their land, an independent state with internationally recognized territorial boundaries, that has never been one and indivisible any more than parts of Chad or CAR is one and indivisible with LRC, if one accepts the contiguous area that was once German Kamerun. Ambazonians are not a minority in a majorly Francophone republic. They are a sovereign people claiming their rights back.

"You will never walk" is the mantra for those who subscribe to the convenient history that the world wants to hear. They wish to hear because anything else threatens billions in investments in the oil and gas fields in the Rio del Rey and in the cocoa, banana, rubber, timber, and mineral sectors. The crisis in Cameroon is one of two former trust territories, each with its own separate date of independence. An illegal federation of two equal states unilaterally dissolved in 1972 in favor of a unitary state in clear violation of the prevailing illegal constitution. Today, the six million people of the former trust territory that achieved independence in 1961, pursuant to UNGA Resolution 1608, are now under another colonial rule by the Republic of Cameroon. These are the fundamental issues in the Republic of Cameroon and why Southern Cameroons are being told "You will never walk again."

Conflict Diminishes

Toxic Positivity: The Dark Side of Positive Vibes

Being taught and raised to be permanently positive affected my entire life. And it's impossible to change the world when you've got your positive blinders on. When you learn that your "negative" emotions are undesirable or even wrong, you learn to suppress your true feelings, thoughts, and emotions. However, even though you aren't sharing them publicly, you still have them. Unable to deal with them, you feel ashamed and isolated. And of course, without sharing grievances, how can there be progress? Everyone sails along on a placid sea of status quo and refrains from rocking the boat. As a result, the boat sails on.

"Positive vibes only" is a toxic culture and is often ascribed with religiosity. People are told to pray away their pain, be grateful for what they have, even if it is desperately little, and thank the hands that guide them. Toxic positivity exists to keep people from vocalizing their true feelings. If you never vocalize your true feelings, you cannot find your tribe. Without your tribe, you're cut off from your power. Ask yourself, "Who benefits if I'm cut off from my power?" Pro tip: it's not you.

Individually, we excel; collectively, we remain prone to sink to new lows. Collectivism equals a failure to confront constructively. We fail to collaborate. Our coalitions are fleeting. When conflicts arise, we do not confront the conflicts with an orientation to compromise or to collaborate. What makes a senator stay in a government that commits genocide on its people? Two types of people surround the president: praise singers and those who want something from him.

Signs of Toxic Positivity

I was susceptible to a nonsensical version of history, one I didn't question until I became an adult, partly because of my conditioning. Toxic positivity means you throw on your rose-colored glasses and do your best not to see the cracks. If you're convinced that toxic positivity doesn't affect you, read on. Toxic positivity shows up in everyday life, often in ways we don't recognize. Here are some ways that you might be experiencing toxic positivity:

- Hiding your true feelings.

- Dismissing an emotion(s) without fully experiencing them. "Just get on with it" or "Just move forward."

- Feeling guilty about feelings/emotions.

- Responding to other people's experiences with "feel good" quotes or statements like "Be grateful for what you have."

- Trying to stop someone from feeling their feelings, saying, "You could have it a lot worse."

- Shaming or chastising others when they express frustration or anything other than positivity.

- Brushing off things that are bothering you by saying things like "This is my reality."

Why It Matters: Negative Effects of Toxic Positivity

Shame. Many people that engage in toxic positivity are unaware of its true nature. When our fellow humans experience pain, we want to provide comfort and alleviate the discomfort. Unfortunately, when we attempt to hurry the process, it's often damaging. Forcing people to "think positive" instead of voicing their struggles increases suffering. Shame is damaging to the soul. If you're staying silent because you are worried about what people will think or say, you're experiencing shame. Perhaps you aren't even aware of how indoctrinated into the shame culture you really are.

Hidden and Unresolved Emotions. Emotions are a part of who we are. When we deny our emotions, we're denying ourselves. Creating fake or public personas is a type of self-harm. Have you ever slapped a smile on your face even if you weren't "feeling it?" When was the last time you told someone, "It's okay," when it wasn't? When you hide yourself, you're denying the truth. All unresolved and unexpressed emotions sink in and don't let go. It's necessary to express your emotions. Honoring your emotions is a part of a healthy existence.

Isolation. When you engage in the world authentically, you attract your tribe. Your tribe is a source of wellness, inspiration, and strength. These people will uplift and support you, and together, you will rise. Inauthenticity breeds toxicity. If you cannot connect with yourself, how do you expect others to connect with you? You are not unbreakable. You are human. Humans need each other. When we fake our emotions, we attract fakeness. If you want to live outside the superficial world, you need to go deeper. Allowing others to explore all facets of themselves frees you to do the same.

What You Can Do

Changing the Narrative. Reframing how we talk about our emotions allows for acceptance and validation. We can use this adjustment in dealing with our own emotions or those of others. Here are some examples of how to reframe your thinking about negative emotions:

Toxic Positivity	Nontoxic Acceptance and Validation
"Stay positive."	"Describe what you're feeling. I'm listening."
"Don't worry, be happy."	"I see that you're really stressed. Anything I can do?"
"Failure is not an option."	"Failure is a part of growth and success."
"Everything will work out in the end."	"This is really hard. I'm thinking of you."
"Positive vibes only."	"I'm here for you in both good and bad."
"If I can do it, so can you."	"Everyone's story, abilities, limitations are different, and that's okay."
"Delete negativity."	"Suffering is a part of life. You're not alone."
"Look for the silver lining."	"I see you. I'm here for you."
"Everything happens for a reason."	"Sometimes we can draw the short straw in life. How can I support you during this hard time?"
"It could be worse."	"That sucks. I'm so sorry you're going through this."

It takes practice to change your internal narrative, but it is well within your power. Narratives can sometimes seem more powerful than what they are. In addition, they can seem like one solid structure, but in reality, they are like fabric, woven threads combined into one larger picture.

Now that you've seen your power to change the narrative of your life, I want to challenge you to work with me and so many other brave souls to change the narrative surrounding the conflict in Southern Cameroons. Help stories like mine reach the light. Here's how you can do that in one minute or less:

- Share, comment, and like my social media pages.

- Sign up for my email newsletter about my campaign for permanent peace.

- Ask your local library for a copy of my book.

- Share my speaker bio and reel with your network.

CHAPTER 5:
WINDS OF NATIONALISM: IGNORE AT YOUR PERIL

Individual rights are not subject to a public vote; a majority has no right to vote away the rights of a minority; the political function of rights is precisely to protect minorities from oppression by majorities (and the smallest minority on earth is the individual).

—Ayn Rand

I was born, raised, and taught to have pride in the country. I sang the anthem under a flag I thought was symbolic of our collective pasts, marching together toward a common future. In every country, there is national pride—national anthems, flags, songs, and historical events to glorify and praise. In itself I don't think nationalism is inherently evil, at least in a utopian society. Of course none of us reside in a utopia. While we're taught to uphold and honor our national anthem and flag, we're also taught to blur ethical lines to accept the sins of our homeland. Moral relativism at its best, most countries spout narratives that attempt to provide context for violence, oppression, or bad behavior. When we're raised with a sense of blind nationalism, atrocities become commonplace, justified, and explainable.

Even as I watched the country I called my homeland being torn apart, I felt torn. Where was my home? Was it the place I grew up in? The country where I married my husband and where my daughter was born? Or was it a place that I never set foot in? The true Southern Cameroons had yet revealed itself to me. And what of the true Cameroon?

Africa in miniature is a simmering volcano. From the pristine, lush rain forest in the coastal regions of President Biya's NOSO to the cool, dew-drenched grass fields of the Adamawa Plateau to the West, some six million people feel robbed of their sovereignty and independence. No amount of multipartyism, token heads of government conveniently rotated between NOSO, can take the sting of feeling they are second-class citizens in their own country. NOSO, the arbitrary northwest-Southwest divide of Southern Cameroons, was the former President Ahidjo's art of divide and rule, ensuring that a made-up rivalry, once maintained, can then be exploited to keep kith and kin fighting one another and not Yaoundé for having stolen their birthright and for plundering a once vibrant economy and nascent democracy. The people could barely subsist, and patronage was rife. Dissidents disappeared or at best if an up-and-coming civil servant denied promotion and sideline. Disgruntled and embattled, they acquiesced and eventually retired to a life of even more poverty, dejection, and bitterness. This is Africa in miniature.

But the winds of nationalism never cease to blow across the territory for the people of NOSO. The spirit in the Ambazonia, it seems, is unquenchable. It just lay simmering below the glossy facade of an Africa in miniature, propped up as a peaceful bastion in the Gulf of Guinea.

The 2016 protests by the lawyers and teachers are trumped up and packaged to the world as the reasons for the war in Cameroon.

Nothing could be farther from reality. The protests were just the accelerant on a smoldering fire. A fire that laid smoldering for six decades. No doubt that manifestations of marginalization awaken in some strong nationalistic feelings. It's a false narrative when the world states, "The Anglophone crisis began when the lawyers and teachers' grievances were not met." How convenient as forgotten history too often will surface in the most unlikely places. Worse, give people insufficient data and they default to negative or at worst, wrong solutions. It fits well with a convenient history saying that the crisis is the minority's complaints about marginalization, cultural identity classes over the use of civil law in common-law English-speaking areas, power between the two cultures, or the lack of alternation at Cameroon's top leadership. A bona fide Ambazonian, once awakened to her truth about who she is, can only laugh at the socio-geopolitical rhetoric about the root causes of today's fifteen thousand lost lives, four hundred villages burned down in a scorched-earth war, and nearly one million people internally displaced with at least one hundred thousand refugees in neighboring Nigeria. Minority grievances masked the deeper concerns that Ambazonians are a people with same rights to sovereignty as French Cameroon.

The young men and women now fighting are not doing just so that President Biya can appoint an Anglophone as the next president. I say this as Mr. Biya received 99.99 percent of the popular vote for the past thirty-eight years. The winds of nationalism and of restoration of sovereignty of Southern Cameroons are above all this. Everyone knows a body temperature of 102 degrees Fahrenheit means serious underlying issues. No one doubts that the 2016 lawyer and teacher protests and the government's deadly response reawakened the desire for a final, permanent solution. Ignore it at our collective peril.

Striking Against a Monster

When resolutions from a conference in May 2015 in the NOSO town of Bamenda and on February 2016 in Buea for corrective measures sent by the Cameroon Common Law Bar Association went unheeded by President Biya, in October of 2016, the lawyers called for an indefinite sit-in strike and boycott of all court attendance. In November of 2016, the lawyers staged a peaceful protest on the steps of the courts in Bamenda. They were met with antiriot gendarmes and police officers. They were also greeted with tear gas and open rounds of live ammunition. Many of the lawyers in the crowd suffered injuries. A subsequent peaceful march was staged in the NOSO city of Buea, only this time they were met with an even greater military force who had anticipated their arrival. The lawyers were brutalized and beaten, their jobs seized in the aftermath.

By the end of 2016, other groups joined in the protest. The leaders of the Anglophone Teachers Union and tradesmen joined the lawyers to devise a response to the government's position. Lawyer Felix Nghongo Balla, Mr. Wilfred Tassang for the Cameroon Teachers Trade Union, Patrick Akuma, and Mr. Mancho Bibixy, real name Conrad Tse, a journalist in Radio Abakwa, would emerge as the leaders during the early days of the revolution. Mancho Bibixy led the Coffin Revolution, so-called because he carried along a coffin and stood in to deliver speeches during the peaceful protests in the center of Commercial Avenue in Bamenda, in Biya's northwest region. The coffin was not metaphorical. Macho Bibixy knew he would be killed, and for good measure, he brought along his coffin to spare the dreaded BIR—the elite American-Israeli-trained army—any trouble finding one upon killing him.

In the weeks to come, hundreds of thousands of young men and women poured out on the streets and joined in a nonviolent revolution. Africa in miniature, touted as the bastion of peace, had eventually erupted. The people stood up and took one step and then another in the streets throughout Biya's NOSO. In Bamenda, thousands marched upstation to the governor's residence. On the steep slopes of the hill, protesters for the first time came face-to-face with BIR. Bamenda was emerging and would go on to be the hotbed of the resistance against decades of subjugation. Biya did not like such awakening and tool more aggressive military measures, deploying tens of thousands of infantry to the region. The entire area of Southern Cameroons was now engulfed in peaceful protests. For the first time in its "joined" history, NOSO launched its greatest pushback, the rupture of the simmering volcano to the surface. The peaceful facade was wiped off, and exposed for the first time were the deep fissures of a people exploited for far too long, wrong and robbed, beaten, and now battling back. But what was to come was quite uncertain and unclear. I watched images of a sea of humanity; *okada* (bike riders), old and young, peace plants in hand, flowed out into the streets throughout the territories. I listened to new battle hymns sung and old songs reworded as battle cries. Everyone with a cell phone became an instant photojournalist and captured, streamed, or posted these images online for the world to see. "But where is this Cameroon? And why can't these Black people just get along?" a few in the global north chimed in. They traveled through social media and downloaded to cell phones of Cameroonian diaspora lightning fast.

It was from my daughter's bedside at Johns Hopkins that I consumed these images, some too horrid to see. It was here that my own internal revolution would begin, ultimately leading me to step up and accept my own role in the unfolding conflict. But first I needed to acknowledge that I do not know who I am. Was this my country? Why am I called a northwesterner? First, they called it Kamerun, a League of Nations territory, British Trust Territory of Southern Cameroons, Southern Cameroon{s}, West Cameroon, northwest and southwest (NOSO). Who am I and why all these appellations? Why do I have to traverse three Francophone regions to enter the part called the Southwest? Why are we being killed by gunship helicopters for peacefully protesting? Who really am I? I would watch all these from my recliner at the foot of Praxie's hospital bed. My heart quickened and trembled at what the future held. Everything about my being Cameroonian was being questioned from that moment on. My family and friends were too awake to the real and tantalizing reality that whispers by their parents of being different and sovereign were not figments of their childhood imagination, not folklore, but indeed lamentation of a generation burdened by lost dreams. But who were they? Were we not just a day before all Cameroonians sang the same anthem, proudly carrying the national colors? Was all this truly the winds of nationalism? Which one? Nationalism for a one and indivisible Cameroon?

I would have to go back to 1884, back to when there was a German Kamerun, to learn my own history. But that too would not be enough as history is in the making, and for the construct dubbed Cameroon, it is changing fast in front of our very eyes. As it changes, the pressure to maintain a convenient history is even more consequential than it was nearly sixty years ago at the dawn of decolonization in Africa.

But whose protest, whose revolutions? What nation? Which Cameroon? Why is that I had mastered and passed European history but not given the chance during my formative years to learn the basics of who I am as a person? Who are those called variously from a trust territory of Britain, Southern Cameroonian, from the west, northwesterner, Anglophone, from the Federation Republic of Cameroon, from the United Republic of Cameroon, or simply from Cameroon—or should I write *Cameroun*?

Finally, the so-called Anglophone problem was no longer a whisper. It was now an embryonic movement on the fast track to a full-fledged revolution—some prefer "struggle" for they argue that revolutions are a change within and that we are in a struggle to free ourselves from the yoke of the French proxy, Cameroun. But whose movement? Whose revolution or struggle? Whose protests? The English-speaking people of the NOSO? The syndicate of teachers who demanded the removal of all French-speaking teachers from Biya's NOSO schools, colleges, and universities? The lawyers who wanted common-law practice in courts in Biya's NOSO? Was it a movement by tradesmen and ordinary citizens decrying a long tradition of marginalization at the hands of Francophone Cameroon? Was this a fight by the unionists bent on keeping Cameroon "one and indivisible," a unitary state, or a fight by the restorationists for a return to the 1961 autonomous state of Southern Cameroons? Is this a fight by the federalists for a return to the pre-1972 two-state federation? Was this revolution one of secession? Who are the Brigade Anti-Sardinarde (BAS) in French Cameroun fighting for? And did they speak for the NOSO cause? I wonder whose revolution and for whom the fight was for. My battle to understand the crisis I was about to enter would take me into unusual places.

After the widely circulated bungling of the lawyer's demands and peaceful protest, the government finally agreed to meet with the leaders of what was now called the Consortium of Lawyers, teachers and other organizations in NOSO. After hours behind closed doors deliberating, the government sought to force or bribe the consortium to endorse its position and give up on all its demands. They refused, and their consortium was declared an enemy of the state and banned. For this, I felt a strange sense of joy, anticipation, and fear all at once. Finally, someone is willing to take a stand. Finally! But those old enough remembered the days of the

Makiza and the gruesome massacres of the Bamileke by President Ahidjo's armed forces. My excitement at the turn of events was matched equally by my trepidation and fear at all the unknown that lurked behind every corner of all these movements and the growing vocal voices. I was filled with anticipation as I was crippled by the sadness of my daughter's diagnosis and verdict.

The street protests, by now, had grown in frequency and number. The voices on the ground grew louder each day. The protests grew bigger. I would wake up to over one thousand WhatsApp messages, videos, news, and interviews. The voices in ground zero—Southern Cameroons—in the eight other French regions, and in the diaspora were quickly taking their form. It increasingly was impossible to turn away from the unfolding events.

By January 2017, the BIR staged a raid and captured Mancho Bibixy in his home in Bamenda. His closest collaborator, my cousin, Patrick Akuma Che, escaped and ran into Nigeria. Like many Cameroonians, including those like me living in safe and comfortable harbors 7,500 miles away in a democratic country, we do not escape the scourge of the war now raging in Southern Cameroons. Akuma as we called him and Mancho Bibixy Tse, leader of the peaceful Coffin Revolution, protested the lack of basic things, like good roads, in the country. The protesters were met with live rounds of ammunition from the army. Many were killed, hundreds injured, and hundred others summarily arrested and taken to the dreaded underground torture chamber at the SED in Yaoundé. Others would be charged for acts of terrorism and crimes against the state, tried in a military tribunal in Yaoundé, and sentenced to life in jail. Those were the "fortunate" ones. Many simply "disappeared." Their plight might never be known. A family would never know what happened to their loved one—ever. University students peacefully protesting poor conditions during this period are brutalized, raped, killed, captured, and carried away, some never heard from ever again. There would be no inquiries or investigations. The civilian airport in the area is now a fortified military outpost brimming with French-speaking BIR.

Mancho Bibixy was arrested in Bamenda and transported to Yaoundé. On January 19, 2017, he was sentenced to a fifteen-year imprisonment. My cousin, Akuma Che, Bibixy's closest collaborator in staging the peaceful protests in Bamenda, escaped and sought refuge in Nigeria and later died from poor medical care in April 2018. His three young sons and wife remain in Nigeria as refugees. On January 11, 2019, the villages of Alabukam and Alatoh in Bamenda, where several of my relatives live, were burned to the ground by military forces. Thousands of families had fled their homes as the military burned down villages when it cannot capture or kill the Amba Boys. Many are now part of the world's sixth largest population with displaced persons. This scene is the same in every village in Southern Cameroons except for the heavily militarized towns in the areas.

The war has been ragging in Africa in miniature for over three years, claiming over fifteen thousand lives. Biya's military engages in a scorched-earth policy, burning their way through villages, leaving a trail of death in their path. Families caught up in the cross fire or whose homes were burned down leave everything behind and flee into the bushes or to the Francophone cities that are still oblivious to a war next door. Others join the Amba Boys to fight back the BIR. There, too, are the Amba Boys leaving a trail of revenge killings, kidnapping, and atrocity crimes in their countermeasures. For good measure, the territorial minister of one and indivisible Cameroon is said to have created his own militia alongside the Amba Boys who commit gruesome crimes—such as beheadings, school burnings, and killings of students—stream these crimes live on social media.

The Amba Boys are fast earning the reputation, as the dreaded Biya BIR, for crimes against humanity.

It can be said that had Mr. Biya, president of the Republic of Cameroon, not declared war on the people of his NOSO in November of 2016, the movement for the restoration of the once autonomous state of Southern Cameroons, equal in status to its neighbor and joined in a federation as a condition of its independence from Britain in 1961, would never had happened—perhaps. After returning from a meeting with French president Macron and other Francophone countries in Abidjan in Ivory Coast, President Biya declared war on the people in the two regions of his "country," noting that his country was "one and indivisible" and must join him in stemming all forms of extremism and terrorism. The government moved its troops into the area. And the massacre, mayhem, and extrajudicial killings began and continued into its fourth year with no end in sight.

The Trouble with Nationalism in Africa

Nationalism is good everywhere except in Africa. Nationalistic tendencies in African countries, invariably goes to "Why can't those Blacks get along?" or "If we support them in one country, we open up a pandora's boxe throughout the continent." Throughout my narrative, I have not offered a solution and that is mainly intentional. I speak of my hurt, regrets, and determination to journey through and out of my conflict now on the personal and country level. My own knowledge leaves me to state what others see that Biya cannot secure a military victory in his bid to keep the state of Southern Cameroons yoke to it. So far, those unelected members of parliament who hail from Biya's NOSO, who ostensibly speak for the 6 million they claim to represent back at home have shown no desire to quite the kangaroo parliament in solidarity with the wishes of the people. So, we can scratch that as a path to victory. Several groups and more recently, it is purported the Ambazonia Coalition Team has taken Mr. Biya and members of his government believe to orchestrate the slaughtering in the NOSO region to the International Criminal Court. So far, it is not clear that the international court of the preceding possible paths to victory, we are left with the greatest political buddy club in the world, the United Nations (UN) to put on its agenda the war and take up resolutions to end it. The UN having supported a Swiss-led peace initiative which only the armed groups have indicated their support, can put some teeth behind their support and compel Biya to engage in the process to dialogue with the armed groups without pred-conditions and find lasting solutions. For the later, Mr. Biya given the world the proverbial middle finger. What is left at the international intervention level is what has occurred in 49 countries dating back to 1944 with the break of Denmark from Iceland and as recently as 2011, with the break up of Southern Sudan from Sudan, which a referenda, is to provide a platform for the people of Southern Cameroons to declared their freely expressed wishes. The idea of referendum is not new to us. In 1961 we held a Plebiscite with choices to integration or join other already independent nations without the question of our outright choice for independence. Why can't we revisit the issue through a referendum? In 2014, the Scotland went to the poles to decide if they wish to stay withing the union in Great Britain. When the vote did go in their favor, they are planning to revisit the issue again in another referendum. Quebec, a tiny province in Canada, had held two referenda on the question of secession from Canada. Recently, Bougainville voted to break away from Paupau New Guinea.

Nationalism, be it breaking off from one contiguous country— seceding, for ethnic, political, or ideological reasons are tolerated, even encouraged in the global north. Nationalism in Africa is frowned upon by the global north even as they used force to settle the question of separation elsewhere. If Southern Cameroons was never a part of Cameroon using internationally recognized resolutions, charters, and laws, then a solution to settle the matter is to put the question to the people. 49 countries settled their dispute by putting the questions in the form of a referendum to their people.

It is time for the global north to support a UN-organized referendum for Southern Cameroonians to say what they want.

Conflict Divides, What You Need to Know, Why It Matters

At first glance a little flag waving, horn honking, and fireworks seem simply a natural part of everyday life. We're all more familiar with blind nationalism than we think, even in the United States. Think about the atmosphere surrounding "Support our troops." Is it safe to express concern with military and diplomatic action abroad in your social circle? If not, think about why that is so. Are you a subscriber to QAnon and how do you see that as nationalism?

Conservative authors such as Rich Lowry define *nationalism* as a "natural devotion to their home and to their country." In fact, most people will insist that nationalism has little to do with ethnicity, race, militarism, or fascism. Here's the thing. These rituals we've defined as "tradition" have definite history, and it might not be the history we wish—the narrative we want to propagate. And are we responsible for misunderstanding our own history? We need to hold the people who have purposefully manipulated history and redefined it to their own benefit accountable. However, we're also accountable for our ignorance. As Victor E. Frankl states, the first step in transforming your conflict is to be answerable to self and that begins by acknowledging your agency. When we offer complete acceptance without question, we allow ourselves to be manipulated. But we're talking about national pride, not nationalism. That's okay, right? Indeed, nationalism is a different beast than national pride. There is nothing wrong with having a little national pride or respect for your nation. The relationship you have with your country could be equated to a loving spousal relationship. You give and take in a balanced fashion. You're both committed to the good of each other. And sometimes you disagree on the issues, but there is enough love to see you through. And your individuality, your agency is not trampled upon. But healthy relationships allow for critical discourse, questions, and curiosity. Blind obedience is a red flag. We all want a healthy relationship with our homeland. Ours is smoldering inferno.

When you think in terms of the United States, there are certain aspects to its culture that lend to nationalism—the culture of blind patriotism that gave rise to MAGA and QAnon nationalism, the unreasonable fear of so-called socialism, and the emphasis on commodious individualism, as well as American exceptionalism, now unilateralism. All these uniquely American phenomena have whipped us into a frenzy vulnerable to nationalism. Why does this matter? Because as easy as it is to think of the rest of the world as "others," it's only your bias talking. Unraveling this bias will allow you to grow your frames of reference and your empathy for the rest of the world's problems.

What You Can Do

We pick up on prejudice early in life. We form attachments to certain groups and develop another mentality toward certain groups. It's natural for these stereotypes and prejudices to resist change. The society in which we live is responsible for perpetuating bias. We socialize to have a "dominant" group, while all others are considered subcultures. Everything throughout our lives enforces this bias, most of the time so deeply that we aren't aware of it. When we are unaware of our bias, it limits our ability to feel empathy for others who do not have similar experiences to us. We are able to other away suffering and contextualize it. For example, refuges from Syria pour into our country because of actions our country has taken, yet most people are unsure whether more immigrants should be let in.

Bias is all around you if you only have the courage to look. If you do, you can test yourself for hidden bias. Visit here: (https://www.learningforjustice.org/professional-development/test-yourselffor-hidden-bias) to take a number of quizzes on hidden bias and learn more about yourself.

CHAPTER 6:
DIFFERENCES WITHOUT DISTINCTION

Imagine if I was sitting in the hospital at my daughter's bedside when her doctor reported her treatment to be "different without distinction." It might sound good at first. Does the doctor mean that he or she treats all her patients equally? Is different without distinction how a doctor should treat their patients? I'm guessing that you will say no. You want a doctor to devote more time to your case, particularly if it is serious. Additionally, you want your doctor to fight for your case as if they are fighting for a member of their immediate family. Hospitals have a triage system to prioritize cases, but personal bias of the physician and even the hospital can manipulate circumstances. We say "differences without distinction" when we mean "I believe I'm unbiased, so that should satisfy you." When I initially came to the United States, I never imagined that my homeland's connection with this country stretched farther back than I imagined. The USA wasn't free of Cameroon and the conflict in Southern Cameroons any more than I was.

Ambazonia: Blood and War Games

In 1916, the United States of America played a key role along with Britain, France, and other European countries in ending the First World War (WWI) and bringing the German aggression to an end. At the conclusion of the Treaty of Versailles, Germany would surrender control over all its African colonies. History documents that, during the periods from 1913 to 1919, before the end of the WWI, Britain, France, and Germany scrambled for colonial domination in Africa, and we saw various boundary treaties between these countries. One was the 1916 Milner-Simon boundary treaty delineating the frontiers between the British Cameroons and French Cameroun. In 1913, Britain and Germany signed a treaty settling the frontiers between the British protectorate and Nigeria and between German Kamerun protectorates.

Since 1954, after walking out of the Eastern Regional House of Assembly, the Southern Cameroons has refused to accept that it must be subjugated under another power. A nascent and growing state, its borders indisputable, like all others with the same inalienable right to freedom and exercise of sovereignty, flees the domination and control of their affairs to Nigeria, only to land into the hands of a more powerful and determined usurper of all their rights to self-determination and exercise of sovereignty. Who achieves independence but not the fruits of independence? Is there such a thing as sovereignty without the ability to exercise control over one's affairs of state and of their borders? The flames of this conflict lay smothering in these questions.

But the French, with their mouths stuffed with high-sounding directives and decrees, preferred the more convenient truth of marginalization of the English-speaking minority by French Cameroun. Decades of institutionalized oppression combined with the government's failure to broker peace and justice have led to a volcanic eruption of violence and conflict. In addition to the thousands of people who have lost their lives to this conflict, over half a million have been displaced and several hundred villages scorched beyond repair. The president believed in the fait accompli that annexation of Southern Cameroons had long since been completed and that it, too, shall never "walk" by herself—it must remain tethered via umbilical cord to France by proxy through

Cameroon as one and indivisible, inviolable boundaries notwithstanding. They say ignorance is bliss.

The federal union in 1961, between Southern Cameroons and the Republic of Cameroon, was unilaterally rescinded via referendum in 1972, in which the majority of French Cameroun citizens voted to abolish the federation in favor of a unitary republic. Africa's great experience was Africa in miniature. LRC would finally secede in 1983, when the newly minted president Paul Biya, again, unilaterally decreed that, pursuant to law 83/01, the United Republic of Cameroon—birthed from the illegal 1972 referendum—was now the putative LRC, the state that achieved independence on January 1, 1960. Its president, Ahmadou Ahidjo, having submitted a written request, and in April 1960, the state was admitted into the UN as the 116th member state.

The assimilative and annexationist goals inched along. In the words of the famed 1960s philosopher and antiracist author Frantz Fanon, his book, *The Wretched of the Earth*, prefaced by J. P. Satre, states:

> *Not so very long ago, the earth numbered 2,000 million inhabitants, 500 million men, and 1,500 million natives. The former had the words. The other had the use of it. Between the two, there were hired kinglets overlords, and bourgeoisie shamed from beginning to end, which served as go-betweens. In the colonies, the truth stood naked, but the citizens of the mother country preferred it with clothes on.*

> *The natives had to love them. Something in the way mothers are loved. The European elite undertook to manufacture a native elite. They picked out promising*

adolescents. They branded them as with the red iron as with the principles of Western culture. They stuffed their mouths full with high-sounding phrases. Grand. Glutinous words that stock to the teeth. After a short stay in the mother country, they were sent home, whitewashed. These walking lies had nothing to say to their brothers. They only echoed.

This shoddy referendum broke the two English-speaking Cameroons that were formerly a contiguous landmass of BSC into two provinces—today the NOSO regions—not for ease of administration because all existing infrastructure, governing body, and institution were being systematically dismantled, closed, and transferred to the growing hypercentral government in Yaoundé. Castrated, anesthetized, defunded, many businesses fizzled out into the dustbin of history. In this new divide—today simply called NOSO—a growing kinglet, overlord, and bourgeoisie now serve as go-betweens.

At the dawn of independence by joining, the French—who, unlike the British, never left after granting independence to French Cameroun—set their eyes on the young people of Anglophone NOSO. There would be mandatory French classes in all educational institutions. All must be done to immerse and inculcate the principles of French culture, language, and processes into society and break down any vestiges of British influence and culture. A generation of young cadres—their mouths stuffed with high-sounding words and phrases about the bliss of "joining our French brothers," unity, fraternity, and the grand experiment of an Africa in miniature that would be the pride of all—was gradually being groomed. They went to Yaoundé to join the elite in mainly subordinate positions among their French brothers; they were the few graduates from elite professional French training institutions posted back to NOSO but never in the top leadership positions and just implemented their masters' plans. And so, a slow, deliberate erasure of any significant cultural, historical, and legal essence of the people was guaranteed.

The now declassified correspondence dated April 27, 1967, from the French ambassador in Yaoundé to his counterpart, the French consular officer, in the capital city of Buea in West Cameroon, lamented the need for more programs in the farthest reaches of West Cameroon that would ensure there were no pockets of resistance to French culturalization. Every effort must be made to entice the young men of employable age to be absorbed into the French civil service so they can, in turn, bring home the values of the French. In Frantz Fanon's view, a new crop of go-betweens needed to be groomed and their mouths stuffed with high-sounding words and deeds of the central government in Yaoundé. That effort was successful. We see Anglophones all too happy to serve in *seconde classe* positions in the Biya government, never good enough to be president. Bridesmaids, never the bride. Taken to the dance, never asked to dance.

Today, the children of the old bourgeoisie still cooperate with their overlords and remain faithful in promoting a one and indivisible history of Cameroon and are avid consumers and *promoteur* of all things fraternity and liberty. Yes, we are different, they claim. But what unites us is greater, bigger than what divides us. We are one but unequal. Some of the manufactured native elites awaken to the truth of their history, others are shocked into reluctantly accepting that truth, and many more simply prefer to keep their mouths shut—silence out of self-preservation and fear, silent for selfish reasons, not willing to bite the hand that feeds them.

For six decades, and in control for two-thirds of that period, Biya and his inner circle had a firm grip on all levers of control. Careers and livelihood stood on acquiescence, patronage, and complicity to the Biya regime. Mange in NOSO knew this all too well, and silence equated to self-perseverance. Still, the truth stood naked, concealed in plain sight. Others preferred that it be clothed in the Biya narrative that a piece of its former territory had been reunited to the motherland. Africa in miniature had run the full course of its experiment. But can it solve its multitude of problems?

Despite the escalating conflict, Cameroon's government has only offered empty and symbolic gestures. Calls for cease-fire, inclusive dialogue, or freeing of political prisoners have been avoided by the Biya government. However, they have not ignored the English-speaking region entirely. In fact, there are a privileged few among the English-speaking Cameroonians who identify as "moderates" and engage in peace discussions with the Cameroonian government. However, instead of moving toward actionable peace and justice, the government uses this elite group as fodder willing to carry out his appeasement measures and sing his praises. Elsewhere, they are called hand clappers. Look at all the peace-loving "Anglophones" in my government, in parliament, and in civil society. Those agitating are labeled terrorists, intent on destabilizing my peaceful country. Give a dog a bad name and justify its hanging.

A Grasp for Power in Africa

After Germany was defeated in World War I, the United Kingdom and France split the German protectorate of Kamerun into several territories. The French named the largest portion French Cameroun, and the British-held portions were called the British Cameroons. We were spoils of war, divided up like gold and jewels among raiding parties. In 1922, the British added the southern portion of the British Cameroons to the British protectorate of Southern Nigeria and the northern territory to the British protectorate of Northern Nigeria, sealing together their freshly won spoils. When the UN was created in 1946, promises of independence brought forth rapid constitutional changes.

When the League of Nations ceased to exist in 1946, the successive body after WWII, the UN, administered the mandated territories of the British Cameroons and French Cameroun, among others, as UN trust territories. Historically, border agreements dating back to 1913 did not change between the colonizing nations, even after the Treaty of Versailles. The old German Kamerun that included parts of today's Republic of Chad, Central African Republic, Congo, and the eastern parts of Nigeria ceased to exist. The Allied forces and associated powers through the Treaty of Versailles now laid claim and title to all German colonies in Africa, with internationally approved borders. To the winner goes the spoils. A one Kamerun ceased to exist with the defeat of Germany and the signing of the Treaty of Versailles.

The sliver of landmass known from 1919 as the trust territories of the British Cameroons, administered separately as the British Northern Cameroons and BSC, was one of the many prizes for the victorious that would emerge as nation-states in a new Africa. The British trust territory of Southern Cameroons and French Cameroun were class B mandates, the big boys' scheme to impose a greater level of administration control until such time when the colonizers felt they were ripe to be led to self-government or independence. Class A were the territories of the former Ottoman Empire.

The British protectorate of Southern Nigeria was divided physically and wholly into Western and eastern regions. Southern Cameroons was governed from the eastern region capital of Enugu. The new frontier of Southern Cameroons was shortly flooded with an Igbo-dominated workforce. In years after Southern Cameroons merged and was administered from Nigeria, the British invested very little in infrastructure, health care, education, or anything for the wellness and prosperity of Southern Cameroons' people. Poverty and illiteracy were widespread, fostering a class system of Igbo domination. A new, budding black-on-black colonialism was rapidly emerging between the Igbos and Southern Cameroonians, threatening their social, cultural, political, and economic development. An increasing dependence militated against the people's aspiration. Fear began to take hold in their hearts.

My mother would tell us that, back in the days, where they oriented west to Enugu, Nigeria, for administration, their land was awash with the industrious Igbos; the markets stalls were owned by the Igbos and their post offices ran by the Nigerian elites. They were the minority in their land. Here, they would be "bullied" to pay just the asking price in the markets, the traditional price bidding frowned on and allowed only if one had befriended the merchant. God forbid, if you spilled a tray of the Igbo seller's groundnut, you were made to buy the entire thing. And so, resentment grew as people felt a sense of unease growing, a sense that the people of Southern Cameroons were an unwanted people in Nigeria and even on their own soil. Subtle and benign, there was tension about "us versus them" growing within communities.

It wasn't until 1951 that the first few Southern Cameroonians were elected as representatives to Nigeria's Eastern Regional House of Assembly in Enugu and Nigeria's central legislature in Lagos. At the time, Southern Cameroons lacked official political parties and joined the National Council of Nigeria and the Cameroons, which was headed by Dr. Nnamdi Azikiwe. A power struggle ensued between the central government and the three regional governments. As tension brewed, the representatives were pushed from their posts, and a constitutional crisis emerged. In early 1953, supporters of Southern Cameroons in the regional Nigerian government boycotted the Eastern Regional House of Assembly. The assembly was dissolved, which paved the way for Southern Cameroons' representative to walk out, exercising their benevolent neutrality in the growing crisis in Nigeria. They sat out decisions in the assembly. Although this seemed like a huge step in the right direction, this conflict would only continue to divide Cameroon well into the next century. Nigeria gained its independence in 1960 from Britain. British Northern Cameroons voted in 1961 in a plebiscite and was integrated into the Federation of Nigeria as one of its states. The Southern Cameroons leaders, by then, had walked out of Nigeria to the capital city of Buea to set up the first of what would be a highly functional democratic government. The leaders who walked out to set up their own government in Buea, Southern Cameroons, did not all look toward the sovereignty of a people. Some tied their future in integration as a state in Nigeria. Others looked east to join French Cameroun. A small but vocal group saw a free, untethered nation-state of Southern Cameroons. This last group would not succeed.

French Cameroun gained its independence from France on January 1, 1960, with Ahmadou Ahidjo as its first president. UN archives show that on September 20, 1960, at the 864th plenary meeting, UNGA no. 1476 passed, admitting the LRC as a member state after their independence on January 1, 1960. It is worth noting here that, as this book was being written, on January 1, 2021, on the 61th year of LRC's independence, there were no celebrations anywhere in Cameroon. This is telling, if nothing else.

History notes that the administering authority, Britain, under the UN Charter article 76 (a) and (b), was entrusted with the objective, among others, of promoting the political, economic, social, and educational advancement of the inhabitants of the trust territories and progressively leading them toward self-government or independence. BSC became self-governing, autonomous states in 1954, after staging an exit from the parliament in Enugu, where it was administered, to establish its seat of government in the capital city of Buea, a mountainous city at the foot of Mount Fako in Southern Cameroons. From 1954 to 1959, BSC exercised a vibrant multi-party parliamentary system headed by a prime minister with successive peaceful transfers of power through free and fair elections. It is said that the former trust territory of BSC was the first democratic country in Africa.

Instead of preparing its trust territory for self-government or independence, the British walked away and handed over the reins of control over Southern Cameroons to the already independent LRC, under Pres. Ahmadou Ahidjo. Whereas Southern Cameroonians celebrated independence as an equal state in a federation, French Cameroun touted "reunification" and the beginning of assimilation through balkanization—divide and conquer and cancel culture. President Biya and his adherents would wish that you forget the UNGA no. 1476 passed on September 20, 1960, accepting French Cameroun as the 116th member, or that at its independence from France on January 1, 1960, it signed the UN and AU instruments that made its borders, inherited at independence, fixed and inviolable. Cameroon would want you to ignore AU Constitutive Act article 4(b), which states that borders inherited at independence are inviolable and sealed, and not ask on what evidence Cameroun asserts sovereignty over Southern Cameroons. A whitewashed version of the facts get promulgated. For successive generations unknowingly, the marched to a convenient version of history now all too familiar. Undoing will be the unraveling of a people.

UNGA resolution 1352 imposed the two options for BSC to obtain independence by integration with Nigeria or to join the already independent la République du Cameroon, a choice that was not the freely expressed wish of the people, who, in August 1959, met in the All People's Congress in Mamfe and had voted overwhelmingly for outright independence versus integration with Nigeria. When the UN voted resolution 1352 on the question of independence, this expressed view was replaced with two choices: (1) reunification with Cameroun or (2) integration with Nigeria. Were the rights of the partitions of German Kamerun to self-govern or independence couched by such binary choices that did not include outright independence? Was Congo given the option of reuniting with French Cameroun? Were the southern part of the Republic of Chad and Nigeria or the Central African Republic, which were former German protectorates, asked if they wished to reunite into one Kamerun with Yaoundé as its capital? These former parts of German protectorate turned trust territories achieved independence and sovereignty consistent with UN article 76 (a) and (b): "progressive development toward self-government or independence."

In the case of BSC, the people's wishes were violated, and so were the UN's own resolutions. It would be nearly one year and four months later, at the 994th plenary session, when the votes were counted, that sixty-four countries voted for the independence of the BSC; twenty-three, including the already independent Republic of Cameroun, voted against; and ten countries abstained. The date was April 21, 1961. The UN General Assembly resolution 1608 was passed. Opposing in 1961, the independence of the British trust territory of Southern Cameroons, LRC premeditated its annexation into a one and indivisible Cameroon. All it needed was the proxy federations to begin the slow but deliberate march toward total assimilation and annexation war. It will go to war to maintain its Africa in miniature facade.

Still Willing to Believe in Brotherhood and Expectation of Good Intentions

It is still a stroke of godly intervention that protests within the construct of Cameroon awakened the unquenched spirit for a free and independent land—the same privileges other erstwhile colonies now enjoy. The assimilation has been near perfect. The masses had not been willing to temper with natural ignorance of history through successive years of French assimilation. It was the key to their happiness in the one and indivisible construct of Cameroon. See, we are brothers, goes the patriotic chants. A little knowledge, nothing too laborious, was good enough. Too much of it could spell doom. Truth is like a balloon. It can't be submerged forever.

An illegally worded plebiscite failed to give the option for outright independence. The people of BSC, recalling their poor treatment at the hands of the majority Igbos while being administered from Enugu, believed a two-state federation of equal status was the better option than integration with Nigeria; and so, on February 11, 1961, they voted to gain independence by "joining" the already independent Cameroon. They would be two states of equal status, each enjoying privileges of independence federated on several areas. The plebiscite was exclusive to British Southern Cameroonians. The two states joined and became the Federal Republic of Cameroon, two states equal in status. The former trust territory of British Southern Cameroon became the contiguous part called West Cameroon—*Cameroun d'occidental* in French—and the independent Republic of Cameroon became *Cameroun d'ouest* in French or east Cameroon. The third option of outright independence was never given to the people, and while everything else was erased, the quest for freedom never died.

To date, the agreed treaty of union setting the terms of "joining" does not exist between Southern Cameroons and LRC, even though UNGA no. 1608 called for Britain, the administering authority, the government of Southern Cameroons, and LRC to enter urgent discussions with the view of finalizing before October 1, 1961, the agreed terms concerning their union. Both states were to meet to craft the union treaty that would be voted and ratified by the parliament in Buea, headed by Mr. John Ngu Foncha, for the BSC, and in the parliament in Yaoundé, headed by Pres. Ahmadou Ahidjo. This act would have singularly validated that each side understood the terms of "joining" and the terms under which each, as an autonomous state within a federation, would operate. In place of a union treaty, Pres. Ahmadou Ahidjo instituted his French-crafted constitution with one notable change in article 47, which stated that the form of the state was unchangeable.

History matters, and history forgotten is consequential. The bipartite meeting held in the French Cameroun city of Foumban in July of 1961, intended to concretize details for a two-state federation equal in status, resulted in Ahmadou Ahidjo providing his country's constitution and soon moving to have his parliament amend, ratify, and adopt it as the country's constitution without inputs from BSC representatives and without the said constitution ever having been read by, voted on, or signed by the parliament in Buea. The two newly formed states had just passed into a French-dominated, France-controlled, hyper-centralized nation tightly and dictatorially ran from Yaoundé. It would remain a federation only on paper, and that federation would last only twelve years until it was unilaterally dissolved in an illegal referendum.

On September 1, 1961—the date identified as when the British would leave their trust territory of Southern Cameroons, handing over control to the independent nation—the Union Jack was lowered. In its place, LRC's green, red, and yellow flag—with one notable change, two stars instead of one—was raised in Buea. Simultaneously, as dawn broke on October 1, 1961, in Southern Cameroons, now called West Cameroon, thousands of fully armed gendarmes moved in from the neighboring French Cameroun cities of Douala and Koutaba, taking up positions in barracks and intersections, notably at the boundary villages. This heavy military presence exists till today, still serving as border checkpoint, complete with laissez-passer (travel paper) control for immigration, customs control, and searches. Who travels in a contiguous state and is subject to immigration, emigration, and border controls? A difference without clear distinctions. The coastal regions and the highland grass fields of Southern Cameroons are now effectively French-occupied territory.

In short order, President Ahidjo—through successive decrees—abolished the West Cameroon House of Assembly. He systematically closed entirely or moved all existing structures and institutions built over the years and transferred wholesale, the assets, and employees to the capital city of Yaoundé in French Cameroun. Once a vibrant, growing economy, with its own air transport, robust banking sector, flourishing agriculture, deep natural seaport, emerging hydroelectric production facility, and vibrant businesses and trade with neighboring Nigeria, it was systematically abolished in favor of a hyper-centralized government in Yaoundé. What did not get managed from Yaoundé was managed from the economic capital of Douala. All government and economic services now flowed from French Cameroun. Dissent was not an option for the militarily outmanned, British-trained West

Cameroon police officers who kept the peace using only batons and not assault weapons.

In the ensuing years after the plebiscite, the French-speaking Cameroun simply added a few amendments to its constitution to temporarily accommodate West Cameroon. The territory was partitioned into two administrative parts called northwest and southwest, today simply referred to by the French as "NOSO" to match the five existing provinces in east Cameroon. One part of a culturally, linguistically, and legally dichotomous state is now on the path toward annihilation. At the judicial level, the English-speaking NOSO practices common law. East Cameroon inhabitants speak French and practice civil law in its courts. The common-law system practiced in the NOSO region was gradually and systematically replaced by the alien civil law system. French judges appointed through presidential decree, and largely through patronage, are now in the courts in the NOSO regions. It did not matter that there were differences between the two legal systems: English-speaking indigents appearing in court must deal with judges who make no effort to speak a language they understand. The English form of education, too, was slowly degraded, replaced not only with French-trained teachers who did not speak English but also with French pedagogy—yet another assimilative move by French Cameroun to wipe out any legal Anglo-Saxon traditions in their new NOSO region.

Determined, the regime in Yaoundé has accomplished another victory in its quest for total annexation of Southern Cameroons. Younger generations becoming law students will not be any the wiser about this insidious destruction of one of the cornerstones of their legal heritage. It is also whitewashed. Any resistance or semblance of resistance is met with deadly force. At the root of the so-called Anglophone problem is this botched decolonization issue.

Stacking the Odds

The federation would last barely twelve years when Ahidjo unilaterally dissolved it in yet another illegal act in favor of an even more hyper-centralized government. President Ahidjo called for a referendum. But both the people of Southern Cameroons and the majority French Cameroun in 1972 voted in it. It was all but certain that, in a country where 80 percent believed that the other 20 percent were part of their territory, there was any chance in hell that the former would lose in a referendum. As if it was not bad enough that the Southern Cameroonians now were clearly being treated in all areas of life in this new federation as *seconde classe* or that the fraudulent French constitution forced on the people was a constant source of strife, the referendum passionately called for by Ahidjo—though violating his own constitution's article 47—was yet another move for French hegemony in West Cameroon. The ballot sheet asked the English-speaking people of West and East Cameroon to vote yes or oui in favor of abolishing the federation—yes in English and yes in French with no option for no on the ballot in the English-speaking areas. The referendum is said to have passed with 99.9 percent of the total population in favor of abolishing the two-state federation. On May 20, 1972, a unitary state emerged with Ahidjo as the strongman at its helm. He would rule from here on through emergency decrees. In the run up to the referendum, Ahidjo gave an impassioned radio address in September of 1971 detailing his reasons for calling a referendum. President Ahidjo stated that, after years of separation, Cameroonians had formed one nation, one big happy family. Again, we heard references of a one German Kamerun. This reunification, he continued, was a symbol of the spirit of one Cameroon, which would be an African experiment of African unity on the continent, stressing that forming a "one Cameroon" would economically and socially consolidate our resources, help fully integrate and harmonize our lives between the two countries of the Mungo, and as such, create a far superior and united Cameroon. The federation, he pleaded in his radio address to both countries, was a handicap to the country's rapid development. He noted his profound conviction that the moment had come to go beyond the federal structure to a unitary state, all this to a great applause at the predominantly Francophone national assembly in Yaoundé. We could walk, only if we were led by French Cameroon.

The die was already cast. The majority of French Camerounian citizens overwhelmingly voted to reverse what BSC alone voted for in their plebiscite of February 11, 1962. The form of the state, which was inviolable, according to President Ahidjo's illegal constitution, was illegally changed by another illegality.

Our destiny, again, it seemed, was in the hands of the French. There was no calculus that could favor the minority BSC, who made up about 20 percent of the total population, even if the illegality of the referendum was overlooked. A new nation, again, emerged. The United Republic of Cameroon was born. LRC, in twelve years, had passed from being a French trust territory (French Cameroun) to the independent LRC to *la République Fédérale du Cameroun* (the Federal Republic of Cameroon [east Cameroon]) to *la République Unie du Cameroun* (the United Republic of Cameroon). But under the tutelage of its master, France, it still had some ways to go.

Instead of handing over power per his own constitution to the speaker of the national assembly, Solomon Tandeng Muna, an Anglophone, Ahidjo handpicked his then prime minister, Mr. Paul Biya, as his successor. He left the country and later died in exile in Senegal. Again, even in this uneasy arrangement where the French ran the lives of those now called Anglophones, the French Cameroun heaped one insult on top of another, passing them off to the now largely timid, frightened, and marginalized Anglophones and a few handpicked bourgeoisie classes who militated to keep the masses in the bottom of the pile. The violations now piled up.

The final plan was to obliterate all traces of a separate and distinct state of Southern Cameroons. Successive acts carried through unilateral decrees aided by brute force, intimidations, extrajudicial killings, arrests and disappearances, demotions, or passed-up promotions. And if that did not work, for successive generations to come since the illegal plebiscite, the history of the people of the former trust territory of BSC would also disappear— erased. And in its place was a whitewashed, convenient history taught to generations. Students, mostly English-speaking ones, were to learn only from state-printed textbooks laden with party propaganda.

The Proverbial Straw That Broke the Camel's Back

The final straw for Southern Cameroonians was President Biya's decree of January 1, 1984, changing the name of the country from the United Republic of Cameroon to LRC, the name obtained by French Cameroun at the time of its independence. This would prove too much for the young lawyer, Fon Gorji Dinka, who declared that, by President Biya's own law, LRC had essentially seceded from the union. He automatically proclaimed the restoration and christened it Ambazonia, the former autonomous state of Southern Cameroons, and himself as its tutelar leader. In his now famous suit filed and won in the high court in Bamenda, HCB/28/92 demanded that President Biya withdraw from the territory or show proof of a union treaty between the two states. None would be produced.

But President Biya, in his infinite wisdom (dictatorship), arrested and jailed Fon Gorji Dinka and later released him on house arrest. In 1986, he fled into exile. It is said that, upon arriving in Britain, he petitioned the Crown for full citizenship, noting himself as a person emanating from a trust territory managed by Britain that had not been granted full independence and was then, and is still, a subject of the queen of England.

Fon Gorji Dinka's provisions in HCB/28/92 have been used along with a host of other international treaties, UN resolutions, AU charters, and precedents to make the case in favor of an independent nation-state of Ambazonia. Ambazonians continue to use the force of arguments to make their case; till today, arguments rely on the use of precedent, international court cases, or the law. LRC prefers the lame and false premise of a "one and indivisible Cameroon"—traced back to the period of 1887 to the early 1900s, during which the Germans had control of large colonial parts of Africa as German Kamerun—to make its case. In this convenient history, Cameroun hopes to bury references to a period when parts of German Kamerun were colonies under Great Britain and even before when these lands were the indigenous homeland of African kings and queens and their peoples. What to make of this?

Putting aside the illegal referendum, forgetting the Restorations Law 84/01, when the president left the federation, as such leaving Fon Gorji Dinka with no choice but to restore the statehood of Southern Cameroons, Africa's own constitutive act perhaps makes the most compelling case on why Fon was right and why all those now fighting and dying are also right, true, and correct in their stance. Article 4(b) states that all nations on the continent must maintain the borders as achieved at the time of their independence and that borders are inviolable and fixed. Did French Cameroun, now LRC, not achieve independence on January 1, 1961, with marked borders nearly one year and ten months before Southern Cameroons, now Ambazonia, would achieve its own independence, making its borders sealed? If the answer is yes, then the presence of LRC in Ambazonia is a continuous act of war, as many notable scholars have opined.

When historical facts are contested and the absence of treaties between sovereign states dismissed, what about international court cases? The Greentree Agreement, signed after the war between Cameroon and Nigeria, over the oil-rich region of Bakassi, ruled that both belligerents agreed to move their armed forces to their respective borders as achieved at the time of their independence. Nigeria would move west to their border with Ambazonia, and Cameroon would continue to occupy Bakassi, as it did not move its armed forces east to the river Mungo, its border with BSC at the time of independence. Another international court case, the AU Commission on Peoples' Right ruling in Banjul, Gambia, upheld that Southern Cameroons constitute a people with rights to self-determination and statehood distinct from their neighbors to the west, Nigeria, and to the east, LRC. It is worth noting that most, if not all, of the UN Security Council (UNSC) members and UN member states have as part of their mission the promotion of peace and security and the defense of human rights to self-determination and statehood. None so far has publicly come to the defense of Ambazonia; though, publicly, the UNSC has called for dialogue without conditions addressing the root causes of the conflict in the NOSO regions of Cameroon.

A British Calculated Exit

First, Britain shirked its responsibility to guide its former trust territory to self-government or independence by handing it over to be annexed and assimilated into French Cameroun, fearing an independent state would be a financial burden. The 16,364 square miles of landmass, with its own Indigenous people and demarcated borders east, west, north, and south that was the first known peaceful democratic state in all Africa was a prosperous, emerging African state with an estimated GDP in excess of $2 million in 1959–1960. It was a democratic and peaceful autonomous state. But for the war raging in neighboring French Cameroun between the Union of the Populations of Cameroon and the French Cameroun gendarmes, it looked to unfettered control of its affairs at the dawn of its impending independence. Today, it is a shadow, even of its old glory days of the 1960s, though the territory dubbed as NOSO provides nearly 65 percent of the Cameroon's GNP yet enjoys none of the benefits from its large resources like oil and natural gas, timber, cocoa, tea, banana, and minerals like cobalt, iron, and gold nor from a natural deep seaport that has been left unimproved in favor of the Douala Port in French Cameroun that must be dredged regularly to allow for large ships to come as close to shore as possible. It was independence without the benefits of an independent state.

Though not yet exploited, exploration by both the French and British as early as 1967 showed that both French Cameroun and their colonial operators had discovered large reserves of oil around Bomono and in Etinde. New Age African Global Energy, which, just in 2017 signed a multibillion-dollar oil and gas contract, wrote that the Etinde fields had been of great interest since 1967 for the discovery of hydrocarbons and how this field would be developed and monetized to deliver world-class production assets. Assets that accrue to French Cameroon. We now know that the discovery of oil dimmed the prospects for Southern Cameroons' outright independence as France, through its proxy nation, Cameroon, lobbied hard against any UN-sanctioned options for independence as evident in their UN 1608 "no" vote on the question of independence. They, along with Britain and France, propagate a convenient story of an impoverished territory that was not viable enough to become an independent state. For the French and Cameroon, an independent Southern Cameroons meant they would not have access and control over the significant resources and future revenues from their exploitation.

Conflict Distinguishes

What You Need to Know: Modern Cameroon

We have taken up a difference without any distinctions, answered to names the enemy gives, and fought to defend those names just because we can make a good argument. Even as the winds of the Arab Spring of 2011 appear to have picked up steam with its latest casualties, Algeria's Abdelaziz Bouteflika and Sudan's Omar al-Bashir, ousted in April 2019, Africa's miniature balkanized state is ill-suited to capitalize on the winds of social change and put an end to the pernicious, interminable reign of their president, Paul Biya. In the country, opposition parties have taken on some semblance of opposition to the long-ruling Beti-Bulu-Fang dynasty, at the top of which is the figurehead Paul Biya. When it appears that the opposition might gain sympathies from the larger population that, so far, shows no desire to capitalize on the successes of Mass protests in Zimbabwe, Tunisia, Sudan, Libya, and Algeria, the Biya machinery co-opts, coerces, threatens, and brings the errant opposition back into line. Because the opposition never takes on a grassroots approach, it is limited only to party bigwigs and a few loyalists complaining; they are easily silenced or simply bought over, lured into promising, lucrative positions by LRC standards of self-aggrandizement. So, political parties are, in fact, coconspirators in the maintenance structures and ensure that the Biya hegemony has internal and international validation. Biya can proudly say, "I beat out the opposition," even when the opposition is fodder for his political games.

In 2018 after Africa's miniature held an election where one-quarter of its so-called population in its NOSO regions refused to go to the polls, the Cameroon Renaissance Movement (MRC) opposition party claimed victory, pronouncing its leader as the duly elected president. Paul Biya never conceded the elections and remained in power. After a few small public protests in the country and in Washington, Paris, and Berlin, MRC leader Maurice Kamto was promptly arrested, charged with intent to destabilize the country, and thrown in jail. These protests were short lived and timid and never gathered the type of political winds of change as did the Arab Spring and now its second coming in Algeria and Sudan.

Recent events have shown the impact of collective social power. What is different in these Arab Spring protests is the role of the students—the under-thirty cohorts who, through precedence in the 2011 uprising, now fully appreciate that power in the hands of a single individual, albeit with his attendant maintenance systems it is limited power, vulnerable power, and fleeting power. These cohort believes in democratic institutions, harmony, open borders, and power that is essentially and profoundly social. And they get out into the streets and whip up the power some more. And through that power, even if they are beaten by their country's military, tortured, or imprisoned or fled their country, by threading and building on disparate social groups and unaffiliated people, it can be mobilized into a force big enough to unseat longtime kingpins, also called presidents-for-life dictators, in Africa. That is what the Sudanese youth built on, threading together amorphous groups, unaffiliated and multi-ideological groups, and unions to mobilize the masses under a singular, powerful, higher denominator to strip al-

Bashir of power. Never mind that they did not think about who would take al-Bashir's place in the aftermath.

For the Ambazonians, their time has been spent fighting who will be their own Martin Luther King. They often forget what or why they fight. Only a few have their hands on the plow and their nose to the grindstone. Another war brews, and the guns are turned inward. The masses have splintered into groups, each with their own strongman at the helm. It is debilitating, deadly, and double deadly. Meanwhile Biya, already reluctant to end his senseless war, now has an off-ramp—he proudly lets any international community calls to dialogue by proudly asking, "Who do you want me to dialogue with?"

Why It Matters: Differences Without Distinction

The people of Southern Cameroons are no strangers to difference without a distinction and conflict born out of a history of convenience. Families divided by the revolution are innumerable.

Phoebe was an example of a woman caught in the middle during America's War of Independence. She was married to a patriot nationalist. Her brother is a Tory loyalist. Patriots and Tories engaged in a scorched-earth battle. The patriots were further split between those for full independence and those in favor of independent statehood under Great Britain. The swords were soon turned inward, brother against brother. Imagine the case of the children whose rich mother of noble class and extensive wealth married a peasant and who found out that they and their mother had lived mostly as paupers and been disinherited from the father's will, while the father enjoyed his wife's inheritance with others. Not surprisingly, they fought each other for the upper hand.

To say harmony exists in the construct called LRC is as trite as a statement can be. Africa's miniature is as divisible as an Africa divided more than a hundred years ago. Africa's miniature finds its full justification as a nation in a whitewashed history: a history of convenience hidden in plain sight from a segment of what it claims as its populace. That history has been told variously by those with power and at the barrel of guns, a history of convenience passed down successfully from parent to child. Unraveling the history proves challenging because only the oppressor's version has been recorded.

What benefits accrue to the local population from where petroleum is exploited? In Limbe, the Southwest city where the Sonara refinery is located, petroleum is more expensive than in Douala. The minister of mines and power relegates to his office-wide latitude to act as a contradiction to ourselves. One-half is content to be merely tolerated as a full citizen. The others are willing to die to assert rights to manage their own affairs. Interestingly, we are clear-eyed about two things: religion and the tribe. We are people cleared-eyed about death, but ours is a love affair, one that, if put into a business model, will make the owner wealthier than Jeff Bezos or Alibaba. We are also clear-eyed about class and bribe and a sliver of elite who tell them who they are and who run their lives. Our sensibilities run to a culture of dependency aided by the black gold curse, the French curse, and the government curse. For in each of these curses, a pool of underserved, underprivileged, undereducated people stand apart from it all and the establishment who benefits. It is these masses that fight today, each for a slightly different reason far from the root causes.

What You Can Do

We have stakeholders that are invested in every aspect of our lives. There are selfish motives and unselfish motives. For example, one unselfish motive for writing this book is to speak out against injustice and to draw attention to the conflict in Southern Cameroons. Additionally, I want to make a difference in the world and to bring lasting peace. A selfish motive might be that I want people to read my writing and make some money out of it. Stakeholders in the outcome are my friends, family, and colleagues. You have unselfish motives, people who want my success and purely desire good for me. There is also some who will have the belief that a rising tide lifts all boats. I'm also of that belief. I believe that in raising a woman of Southern Cameroonian origin, I can lift all. Please help me shout it from the rooftops.

CHAPTER 7:
COMPETING AGENDAS: HUMANITY VERSUS PROFIT

No tree has branches so foolish as to fight among themselves.

—Native American Proverb

Maybe it always seems natural to me that my country of origin is filled with contradictions because I have so many within myself. Juggling the different roles of mother, spouse, daughter, sister, and community member is the usual pull of womanhood. However, inside my identity lies equally strong and contradictory elements. I am an aerospace engineer. Conscientious, dutiful, bright, and analytical, I have thrown my energy into a career worthy of admiration to many, one that is "good enough" to justify the sacrifices of *Mami* and Norbert Simms, my adoptive father. I'm also a passionate author and speaker drawn to the spotlight, animated by social justice causes. Having been pulled up by my bootstrings, raised *Mami* who did all that she could for her children, I am all too often familiar burdened by any privilege I might enjoy as my life's circumstances changed. My upbringing informs my shame, guilt, and modesty to a fault. A good girl isn't seen. To be a good girl, you do what you're told. But inside, my soul stirs the desire to break bad.

Accepting the status quo of my ancestors is hard to swallow. Seeing how hyperfragmented successive generations have become stirs anger and frustration. And I believe that, to shake things up, there is noise to be made. In the late U.S. representative John

Lewis's take, "We need to get into a little bit of good trouble." Influencing a wave of change strong enough to stop a persecution of an entire people isn't something that can be done quietly from the shadows. It isn't something to be done alone. It's something that must be done in the light. All my life, I've been told that I don't have the wealth of personality required to be a star, to make a difference. All the while, my gifts hover below the surface, waiting to be uncovered. I'm not unlike Southern Cameroons in that regard, a piece of land rich beyond imagination, stirring the spirit within. It's the world that's keeping us enslaved with scarcity, attempting to break the will within. In breaking bad, as per John Lewis, a Southern Cameroonian, Ambazonian, negotiates treacherous waters filled with super predators, each intent on being the big fish in the proverbial small pond.

Wealth of Cameroon

Peace is hard to keep when conflict is profitable. How can war be profitable? Conflict allows natural resources to be pillaged by foreign entities and sold with no benefit to the people. It allows a distraction to cloak behind-the-scenes dealings and decisions. Conflict invites millions of dollars of aid from Western countries that want to wash their hands of guilt while effecting little change. Peace will mean that the people of Cameroon, French Cameroun, will have the capacity to hold government officials accountable for war. So far, *those* people, equally indoctrinated and frenchified, play within the strict contours of their politics. It's more profitable to keep war, not peace. Helping a "poor African country" is a whitewashed version of history most likely because an "immensely wealthy African nation dismantled from years of White colonization and de-education" doesn't have the right ring to it. And Southern Cameroons has wealth beyond imagination.

Cameroon is often referred to as Africa in miniature. Flip the map, and—voilà!—you get a miniature map of the continent of Africa. It's a narrative of the perfect, peaceful experiment of what a united Africa—an Africa united in its full diversity—looks like. It's the perfect metaphor that fuels intense nostalgia. Situated in the Gulf of Guinea, it is a collage of many things, real and made up. Africa in miniature is a contradiction of sorts. It is neither fully at war nor fully at peace throughout its territories. One part in a full-scale war, the other oblivious to the destruction and death. A concatenation of sorts, one side cries genocide, the other says they have a crisis with no two agendas to find a solution cohering. If Africa in miniature is not what it seems, if not of its altered past, even in times without war or crisis, the fragmentation along all possible lines of division will make it a basket case.

This dream of a united Africa, a perfectly packaged Cameroon, is a dream. Nothing is wrong with this dream except Africa in miniature is far from a lush, green, peaceful nation. Africa in miniature is a country just slightly larger than the state of California or the United Kingdom. It is a culturally, ethnically, religiously, and geographically diverse land. If Africa has eight geographic regions (the Sahara, the Sahel region, the Ethiopian highlands, the savanna, the rain forest, the African Great Lakes, the Swahili Coast, and Southern Africa), Africa's miniature boasts more than half of these physical distinctions than any other country on the continent. It boasts tropical grasslands, rain forests, highlands, and the savanna. Its northernmost parts straddle the semiarid, dry, and mostly barren Sahel landmass that sits between the more arable land to its south and the Sahara Desert to the north. It boasts the second highest peak in Africa, Mount Fako, in Southern Cameroons.

The country is endowed with vast riches such as oil, natural gas, cocoa, bananas, tea, copper, bauxite, and gold. Despite its wealth,

Cameroon ranks in the bottom third of all countries in terms of its gross domestic product (GDP) and still participates in the IMF's Heavily Indebted Poor Countries initiative for debt relief. In addition to being rich in minerals, it has a dwindling tropical rain forest that is continuously exploited for export with its rich wildlife and species under risk of extinction. A report in 2020 pointed the finger at Vietnam, who is the number one exporter of timber from Cameroon, a majority of which was illegally logged and shipped out, making Vietnam the largest exporter of timber in Africa, Cameroon precisely. It is believed the ancient woods hulled are meant to refurbish their temples. Beyond the devastating impacts on the environment from illegal logging and deforestation, rather than improve on its GDP as Africa's foremost producer of timber, Cameroon continues to lag behind countries with few natural and human resources on most key indicators of economic growth.

Africa in miniature touts itself as a democratic nation with a vibrant, diverse political landscape. Upon a closer look, since its independence, two presidents have ruled. The current president, Paul Biya, eighty-eight years old, has clung to power since 1982 and, today, holds the dubious distinction as the world longest-serving president on the continent and in the world, barring queens and kings. To be kind, his tenure as the head of Cameroon dates back to 1975 as prime minister under Pres. Ahmadou Ahidjo, who ruled the country from 1960 to his resignation in November 1982. Africa's miniature is as linguistically diverse as it is culturally hyperdiverse. Like Canada, it is bilingual, French and English, but here is where the similarity ends. Africa in miniature has 250 different ethnic groups and over a thousand different indigenous dialects. Every ten kilometers is enough to find separate identities, slightly different indigenous languages and dialects, a chief or Fon for good measure, and an "other" group with its specific cultural norms of differentiation. Africa in miniature's hyperdiversity, language, creed, and norms creates increasing layers of "us versus them" at every level of society. Biya understood these layers well. Africa's miniature was made up of two former trust territories. After the 1961 plebiscite, it became a federal republic with a West and East Cameroon designation, which lasted until May 1972. Not content to preserve the historical, legal, cultural, and linguistic specificities of West Cameroon—Anglophones—Ahmadou Ahidjo decried the financial burden of the federal structure placed on the government and so ordered a referendum on May 20. The question was not put for West Cameroon alone to decide but also to Francophones, who made up 75 percent of the total population. The die was cast. Anglophones went to the polls and voted in ballots with yes and *oui* (French for "yes") on both questions for and against the end of the federation. In other words, BSC and West Cameroon are the shared histories of a people, land, and government who were once colonized by the British. For the French Cameroon, a singular agenda must be pursued.

Dutiful Kinglet in Service of Masters in Faraway Places

Less than twelve years into perfecting the African experiment, the assimilation of Anglophones needed speeding up. West Cameroon was balkanized into Ahidjo's NOSO provinces alongside the five existing provinces of east Cameroon. For each province, the president decreed a governor from a distant land to sit as lord and master over the masses. Kinglets were dutiful, and obedience was needed for the assimilative agenda to work. They came to reside in brick homes in capitals in the provinces. Their wives, like them, were foreigners to the people they would govern. Their children went to school back at home or elsewhere and did not walk the dusty streets with their classmates nor played *tabala* or skipped rope on the sidewalks. They did not invest in the local economies or build homes. If they owned land, it was purely transactional. For these governors, they were political appointees with a mandate from Yaoundé and with another decree could be sent packing. They held no interest in the people, nor did the people hold much hope in them. One thing they achieved was to ensure that the new northwest-Southwest divide held political winds for those who played along with the politics of the day. Through the new breed of kinglets, Yaoundé's agenda went largely unchallenged. For the locals, the enemy was not those in Yaoundé; it was a brother from the northwest or Southwest. A difference was implanted into a people without distinction and exploited by Yaoundé to keep fear, mistrust, and acquiescence in the hearts of the people. We all bought the divide hook, line, and sinker and, to date, feed on it in our own local politics.

It has been said that Cameroon is the only place on the earth to eschew cardinal points. The cardinal directions orient humans and are used for spatial orientation and for navigation. To the west of Biya NOSO lies Nigeria, while to the east lies the Western Province, now Western region in Biya's NOSO. Southern Cameroons is Biya's region. The southwestern town of Victoria, founded by the English missionary Alfred Saker, was renamed Limbe. It was just another erasure for Africa in miniature's Anglophones on the way to total assimilation.

"Africa in miniature" is a description fit for the greatest of public relations campaigns, but it is a figment of global imagination. It neither resides in West Africa, geopolitically the Economic Community of West African States, nor in Central Africa (Central African Economic and Monetary Community region).

A predominantly Francophone country, it is a member of the commonwealth.

Africa in miniature is said to be a resource-rich country yet highly indebted and impoverished. Where do the profits from the riches in oil, gas, minerals, and cash crops like cocoa, tea, banana, and cashews go? Cameroon ranks 153 out of 188 countries in corruption index. In 2017, eight months after declaring war in the oil-rich Anglophone region of NOSO, President Biya's government signed a £1.5 billion contract with the London-based New Age African Global Energy for the mining and gas company's refinery in the Etinde gas field. It also has oil concessions with Swiss-based Glencore, Russian Lukoil, and Scotland's oil and gas company Bowleven. Billion-dollar contracts were executed, while the country remains an impoverished state that is highly indebted. A few decades ago, the world said "never again" after the holocaust. In 1994, those words were, again, uttered in the international circles not before nearly 1 million Rwandans had been killed and twice as many fled, only to die in refugee camps in Congo and elsewhere. As the war enters its fifth year in Cameroon, calls to world leaders, including the church, have largely fell on deaf ears. In the hall of power, in distant world capitals, leaders prefer to issue statements or offer their thoughts and prayers as the death toll increases.

Reports point that both the French and British knew that large reserves of oil existed around Bomono and in Etinde as early as in the late '50s to early '60s. New Age African Global Energy wrote that the Etinde fields had been of great interest since 1967 for the discovery of hydrocarbons, noting on their website how this field would be developed and monetized to deliver world-class production assets. We now know that the discovery of oil dimmed the prospects for Southern Cameroons' outright independence. France needed access to the oil and gas fields. It had the perfect vehicle, and that was its proxy former colony, the malleable and coachable leaders of LRC. It is believed absent Francafrique's resources and national deposits, France will plummet into a third world country on the GDP scale. As written earlier, France lobbied hard against any UN options for outright independence, casting a "no" vote for UNGA no. 1608.

Hindsight suggests that, at the time of the UNGA vote of April 21, 1961, it was all too easy for Britain to propagate a convenient story of an impoverished state of Southern Cameroons being a burden on the queen's purse—if given outright independence. An independent Southern Cameroons, while dependent on Britain for its every breath, also meant France would lose out on having unfettered access and control over the significant resources and future revenues from their exploration. A story of impoverished, helpless, and dependent people took root in the years leading up to the plebiscite. This story was, again, used in 1972, when President Ahidjo argued that the federal system was a drain on the federal government and cannot be sustained. To resolve the question, the entire country was asked to vote in the referendum of May 20 to abolish the federation in favor of a unitary in the famous *oui* and yes ballots, even if the federal constitution prohibited any action that would change the form of the state. There were no points of intersection between the West's agenda and the will of the people.

The Contradictions of Cameroon: Africa in Miniature

Africa's miniature, LRC, is characterized as a state in the Gulf of Guinea and is a collage of contradictions—contradictions that have taken a turn for the worse, and that, too, depends on who you ask. Those in NOSO experience war. The rest of the country is essentially peaceful. The global north sees it as a bilateral partner in the fight against Boko Haram, conveniently rebranded ISIS of West

Africa, fighting in the Sahel region. The global east—China and Vietnam—a bit late to the continent, pillages for raw material, and there's plenty to be exploited and hauled away. For their trouble, an infrastructure project here and there, loans, and concessions are often concluded between Biya's innermost circle of personalities and Asian countries. In return, Cameroon is a guaranteed vote for China, even if its own human rights abuses are to be sanctioned. The two countries shared the same values and agree broadly on holding each other's backs, even in an inequalitarian relationship. China is a threat to Cameroon, as France is believed to be still its colonizer. Africa in miniature's spinning winds of contradiction gathers strength in the west, east, north, and south of this small piece of Africa.

Beyond contradictions, Africa in miniature displays a stunning amnesia of itself, a convenient history of sorts of Germanic, French, British origins; no one quite agrees on any one set of facts, real or made up. Africa's miniature cannot tell its authentic self from its make-believe self. It is like the Puebloan shopkeepers of South America in Charles Mann's book, *1493*, who worried that an invasion of counterfeit porcelain from China would destroy the local brand, but no one who left could tell the imitation from the original. Africa's miniature represents a Chinese imitation of a Chinese-made Mexican imitation of a Chinese original. Few care enough to figure out the original from the imitation. They are happy to go with the story told. Southern Cameroons wants the world to know what the counterfeit is. For that, thousands are dying. This will be a great beginning except it is deceptively simple to speak of a metaphoric representation of what Africa offers.

Africa in miniature, like other countries forged out of colonial legacies, has a history. Its history has been wiped out and replaced by a convenient truth. History matters. It matters for our understanding of the now. History is of us and lives with us but does not make us necessarily. Whenever history fails to inform our modern understanding, we wake up in a construct that, today, is Cameroon, Cameroun, the Republic of Cameroon, or LRC. When history is forgotten, a country wakes up engulfed in a war that knows no end.

But for the Berlin Conference of 1884, which still lives in infamy for having imposed arbitrary divisions on the continent, perhaps German Kamerun will be another country as large as the Central African Republic (CAR). Cameroon, la République, is not Kamerun. It wants you to believe this at all costs.

Africa's miniature finds its full justification as a nation in a whitewashed history—a history of convenience hidden in plain sight from its populace. That history has been told variously by those who hold the power and mostly at the barrel of guns, a history of convenience passed down successfully from parent to child. Southern Cameroons is tapped into a deep-seated resentment about their status in the construct called Cameroon, Africa in miniature. They have always felt it, and how could they not?

For nearly six decades, they wandered into a union that saw their inheritance swindled, their cultural identify annihilated, and their people labeled as dogs, rats, *seconde classe*, *les Biafras*, or Anglofools. Now they just call us NOSO. Never good enough to be president, they are relegated to patronage, a ministerial post of prime minister ostensibly without power, alternated for good measure between the NOSO elites with the inevitable power tussle among a people who now see themselves as divided as described by their oppressor. Many are resentful but largely silent, as the state runs a tight, brutal, and deadly ship. They went from a "free" colonized people—first as a free, autonomous, self-governing state administered by proxy by the British from Enugu in Nigeria and then as a free, peaceful, democratic, self-governing state with headquarters in Buea—to an equal state in a federation, only to see its instruments of union unilaterally passed from the queen into the hands of the president of another equal state, French Cameroun. Just as quickly, NOSO was back to being a unitary state, Republic of Cameroon. Largely seen as second-class citizens in a French-dominated nation, a quarter of the people in Africa in miniature largely suffered indignities in their own land: no jobs, no infrastructures and health care, and little or no institutions. For that, they must travel across the river Mungo into the French territories. In Africa in miniature, the Anglophone problem—though mostly a whisper—loomed large in the fabric of society. There are always whispers of rights to self-determination.

As with all histories, convenient or not, they tend to repeat. A new generation and their parents realize there is no shortage of Africa in miniature's history. But which is theirs to hold and to pass on with fidelity?

For starters, the name of the country has changed so many times, and many historians have trouble keeping track. This is nothing new, as most African colonies have shed their names after independence as a way of breaking with their colonial past. And so, Rhodesia, becomes Zimbabwe, shedding its colonial past as an independent country, and Gold Coast becomes the independent nation of Ghana. A change from Kamerun to Cameroon will align with the shedding of colonial baggage—except this was not the case. Before independence, there was BSC and French Cameroun. After independence, BSC became part of the Federal Republic of Cameroon, referred to as West Cameroon. This would later change to the United Republic of Cameroon and back again to the Republic of Cameroon. To many, it is simply Cameroon or Cameroun. All these names would not matter if in each of the name changes did not lie an inconvenient history promoted and protected, even at the cost of war.

After the dissolution of the federation, the appellation of the territory of Southern Cameroons, called West Cameroon, was quickly set aside. To any possible dissidents, President Ahidjo set out to break west Cameroons into two provinces, NOSO provinces. To the west of these two provinces is the Federal Republic of Nigeria. In what confused all cartographers, Ahidjo named the province to the east of the two regions the Western Province, *L'eoest* in French. The southernmost parts of Cameroon would be named the southern province. All references to a former Southern Cameroons or West Cameroon, the successive names of BSC, were removed. It would not feature in the general lexicon—children born after the decree to break up and rename the territory would not learn what happened in their history lessons.

Africa in miniature does not celebrate January 1, the independence date of the Republic of Cameroon, and October 1, the Independence Day of BSC. The date of the plebiscite, February 11, is celebrated as youth day with no references to its historical significance. The country does not celebrate its independence, rather a national day on May 20, the date in 1972 when the final act to annex Southern Cameroons was completed. It took the form of an illegal dissolution of the federal state. It is said that this date is the birthday of President Ahidjo's wife, and a nation must celebrate its first lady.

For this piece of Africa, no harmony exists. Southern Cameroonians have woken up to a period of hyperpartisanship. They are embroiled, embattled, and fully immersed in a full-scale war. The only problem debated outside the battlefields that has spread to every distant village is about the people and little about the actions. The underlying issues go largely unresolved. The number of deaths climbs each day as is the number fleeing into neighboring Nigeria, and more are packing up what meager earthly possessions are spared by the scorched-earth strategy of Biya's army and fleeing into the bushes or to French Cameroun.

The country finds its full justification as a nation in itself first. It finds its justification next in its storied history with another nation. That history has been told variously by those with the power of the purse and at the barrel of guns. Biya declares that his country is "one and indivisible" and that nothing will ever change that. It is, he claims, enshrined in the constitution and imbued in the history and origins of the people. Cameroon is as divisible as four is divisible by two and along every conceivable epistemological construct imaginable. Only through intellectual dishonesty—and to a large extent, intellectual laziness—can this fact be obfuscated.

Africa in miniature is divided along education lines. The French pedagogy is different from the English. Today, the French have six years of elementary preparation; the English have seven. Africa in miniature is divided along judicial lines. The French practice civil law, where one is guilty and must be proved innocent; the English practice common law. It is divided along linguistic lines, French and English. Sixty-five percent of its resources come from the English region, but less than 10 percent is returned to the region in terms of investments. According to government census, Anglophones occupy less than 3 percent of the top-level jobs in the nation. As if the division is not stark enough, when the Anglophones protested beginning in October 2016, the internet was cut in the region for ninety-four days to stymie protests. The restive populace is held together by an artful, selective-style dictatorship, divide and rule, patronage, and an assembly of willing "Mbindong" saluting collaborators and octogenarian military brass. It is divided by internationally recognized border treaties. It is divided by its settled populations and governments.

Africa's miniature contradictions go back to the old, defunct one, Kamerun of Germanic era, laying claim to sixteen thousand square miles of land that happens to be endowed with rich natural resources. All other parts of German Kamerun are not claimed to be part of LRC's one and indivisible country, just Southern Cameroons.

Multinational interests remain just beyond the full grasp of the masses. They are the real power players and the member states. Is this an abortive second, third, fourth birth? I see the concept of an Africa in miniature looming large for all its contradictions and militating to frustrate any rebirth.

Competing Agendas

"Leaders do not need followers, but all great leaders have followers." There is a saying that if you don't know where you are going, all roads will lead you there. Amid turmoil, this statement rings true for the Anglophone crisis. To write about the competing agendas will take an eternity. I cannot help but say here that, if anyone's agenda aligns with mine, then it is on the right path. For Southern Cameroonians, we can't even agree that we are second class in a country that 75 percent believe they own the rights to determine the future of 25 percent of the population and have created and promoted a history—a convenient one that we have bought into—that we are indeed part of the citizenry and that the land under our feet a reclaimed piece of land.

Cameroon is sliding into a genocidal war. The world cannot again afford to be silent. There is an uneasy silence within the international communities about the root causes. Each principal actor has its own agenda. It is, after all, the Anglophone crisis with

strong hints at minority population grievances. Throw enough aid—
and for good measure, military assistance, and the masses will soon
be appeased. The universe seems to conspire not to do a root cause
analysis, which we are often taught is the best approach at finding
solutions. For to do so means to fully understand the situation,
delve beneath to reveal the system of causes contributing to the
current civil unrest, define the problem that needs to be solved, and
solve it.

Perhaps the international community wants LRC to see for itself
the universe of contradictions it represents. Perhaps in knowing the
roots of the problem, they wish to give a rope to the separatists to
hang themselves in or time to coalesce and give those willing to help
a lever to hang on to. Perhaps in carrying out a root cause analysis,
LRC cannot dismiss the obvious, potent problem it will uncover
that it cannot continue in its one and indivisible mantra and must
fess up to its checkered past and neocolonist stance.

But for now, the rush is not to perform the difficult task or visit
the devils of past lies. What is expedient is that the leaders huddle
together to craft yet another policy position or edict designed to
fool or appease the masses. When any is upheld, they are cosmetics
at best. These leaders have too much to lose in an independent
Ambazonia. Even in an autonomous Ambazonia, these leaders fear
the loss of patronage, power, and pride they now enjoy.

History is our guide in matters of conflict. In the aftermath of
the Holocaust, the world searched for answers on why such untold
brutality and deaths were met with silence for so long. We now
know lives could have been saved had leaders had the moral courage
to intervene when faced with irrefutable evidence of Nazi death
matches, Mass graves, and Mass murders. Credible reports point
out Mass killings in Cameroon. Readers can see for themselves by
logging into the genocide library in the links provided. It was only in

the aftermath that the world rose to strongly condemn the atrocities, vowed retribution, and resolved to bring an end to killings. That was in 1946. Barely fifty years later, in 1994, the world, again, stood in silence as nearly one million were killed in Rwanda before the UN intervened with peacekeeping troops to end the hostilities. This was only a few years before the genocide in the former Republic of Yugoslavia claimed hundreds of lives. In the aftermath of the Rwanda genocide, world leaders, again, made a commitment to "never again" be silent and to prevent such crimes from ever occurring anywhere in world.

A Growing Number of Frontline Groups and Purported Leaders

If we can all agree that the pathways of life is through conflict, then all that is left is for us to work at transforming each conflict situation as best we can. When I struggled daily, frightened as my daughter was that she was being asked to go home or to a nursing home to live out the rest of her life because she has maximized what the insurance companies considered a lifetime maximum health cost, it is easy to fall into the pity spiral self-loathing trap or its equally pernicious cousins: hatred and resignation. My limited research into healthcare agenda thought me to take a different approach. First, there are those focused on patient agendas that prioritize patient empathy, support and those whose focus largely lies in prioritizing cost-effectiveness sometimes at the expense of patient service and care. I lived that and navigated all the often contradictory and sometimes overlapping gaps in the healthcare delivery arena, from the bean counters in the hospitals to those at the insurance companies. I came away bruised at times, but my faith was restored in those as Dr. Elena, Nurse Valerie, Praxie nurse, Cathy, her social worker coordinator, or in her nurse tech, individuals whose professional skills performed in came along daily with deep-empathy and emotional support for my daughter. I came to understand, also, that behind the computers in the big insurance companies lay another set of motivations. My job was to find the gaps and bridge them in my daughter's favor and hope for the best. It was easy to form strong alliances with Praxie's medical team to see how the insurance agenda to save money could be bridged through engagement to save my daughter.

That there is value in bringing conflict parties together to see if the gap between different agendas can be closed is nothing new in conflict resolution. In the war in my homeland, all techniques available to coax collaboration among Southern Cameroonians appears to fail. There is the same hyper-divisiveness in those hoping for their country as it is in the country they want to separate from. First, there was the consortium, a hastily brought up amalgamation of teachers and lawyers. Before they burst onto the national consciousness as something of consequence, many could only speak of political parties, such as the party of Bulu-Beti-Fang Biya dynasty with its heart in Southern Cameroons—the real southern Cameroon in the geographic south—and the SDF of another sit-tight leader, Ni John Fru Ndi, whose stronghold was in the restive NOSO region of Bamenda and, today, a mere shadow of its former self. In Biya's parliament, nine out of the ten regions are controlled by Biya Cameroon Peoples' Democratic Party (CPDM). Mr. Ndi had taken a page out of Biya's political book to hold on to his power, intending to stay on for as long as there is breath in his chest. In later years, the Bamileke—the Indigenous peoples in Biya's Western Province—would marshal behind one of their own, Mauruice Kamto, as leader of Cameroon Renaissance Movement. Like Ni John in 1992, Kamto, too, would win the presidential elections in 2018, but neither men nor their parties were strong enough to

187

dislodge the grand master of Etoudi, Biya. Biya would consolidate his seventh national election victory, going on to be the world's longest-serving dictator.

As the war in Southern Cameroons continued unabated, by 2020, the full crop of armed groups had emerged. There was the Ambazonia Defense Forces (ADF), The British Sothern Cameroons Restorations Forces—the only group lead by a woman, BSCRF, Southern Cameroons Defense Forces, Red Dragons, Seven Katas, Sword of Ambazonia, Ambazonia Restoration Forces, Ambazonia Restoration Army, and the list of ground forces grew each day. To counter these forces of Amba Boys militia, the minister of territorial administration would create a parallel force. The path was set for brother-on-brother killings. It was rumored that, with a few hundred dollars, one could get their own militia on ground zero. I know this because I have received offers from anonymous men asking if I could adopt and support them to build an armed group to prosecute the war against us. With a little more of the going price, you could even buy any one of these existing groups. A flurry of non-armed groups grew mainly in the diaspora. Theory goes like this: If I am not satisfied with what I find in a group I belong in, I leave in disgust, kick up a storm, and set up a parallel group. I take care to cultivate my own lapdogs, and when the time is right, as I leave, they are sure to follow me and parrot every grievance that I utter. Once uttered, my minions will go to bat for me. Now there are more town halls than in all the United States. Every weekend, there is one holding at some time or the other. Every evening, there is telecom or the other by groups. Each group decries the injustices not only of LRC but also of a rival group. A torrid mess of intra-group fighting fills up the social media. Those who claim neutrality point to this acrimonious state among those fighting for their homeland as reason why they stay out. The international community say it is reason enough, as they see another South Sudan in the making. What they fail to acknowledge is, though South Sudan went through periods of brother-on-brother killings, today, it is well on its way to crafting a constitution for a peaceful, independent nation where all stakeholders play a role.

If there was ever a place on the earth where leadership is decried, Africa would be the epicenter. Perhaps the balkanization of Africa's miniature correlates positively with its crisis of leadership. Though most will readily explain good leadership, the masses have an uncanny tolerance for bad ones. Where clearly bad and good leadership is evident, Cameroonians gravitate to bad form of leadership, preferring mainly a divide and rule strongman tendencies.

The masses hold a misguided conception of their leaders as the only ones capable of solving the country's problems. Leaders are purely a function of tribal affiliation. In fact, it is the president's sole prerogative to pick and choose not only his cabinet ministers to head various agencies but also the associates, directors, assistants, governors, and down to the regional delegates and local department heads. Even if we tout our Anglo-Saxon culture of debate and meritocracy, in practice, we are the product of French Napoleonic processes. Leaders as individuals are so revered; they believe they are above everyone else. They take on a demigod status to their kin and kith. For this penchant, the strongman, Biy, imposed on us a special status decreeing into existence every aspect of our political life. Rather can jointly confront, pushback, and deny the latest neocolonization tactic, we busy ourselves in our own rush to divide.

The Ambazonia Coalition Team (ACT)—set up in 2019 as a politico-military structure representing Ambazonian movements, organizations, self-defense groups, and independent people—held out hope for the people. The ACT is made up of ten frontline groups: the Ambazonia International Policy Center (AIPC), Ambazonia Peoples' Liberation Movement, Federation of Southern Cameroon Women, Movement for the Restoration of Southern Cameroon (MoRISC), the Interim Government (IG), Southern Cameroons Restoration Movement, Southern Cameroons Peoples' Organization, Southern Cameroon National Conference, Republic of Ambazonia (RoA), Republic of Ambazonia National, and Civil Society (two independents). Per their bylaws, the ACT is committed to finding lasting and a just, permanent peace in the war in Ambazonia through a negotiated settlement with LRC. The ACT reserves the right to explore, exploit, and prosecute her engagement to return the former UN trust territory of Southern Cameroons, aka Ambazonia, to sovereignty and to its place as a nation of the free world. It's a laudable mission. In July 2019, it signed up and gave its mandate to Switzerland to act as a mediator in the conflict between factions of its armed groups and Biya's government. President Biya, for his part, had not given a written mandate. The ACT, it seemed, had the people's mandate to participate in mediations, build technical teams, identify its negotiator(s), and eventually enter negotiations with LRC. It was supposed to be the people's platform where all the groups melded into a coherent, cohesive, collaborative body to fight as a common front. ACT would be the cure of the hyperfragmentation. The ACT was to build the bridge while crossing to Buea by walking the circuitous road between war and negotiated peace. For two years and counting, the ACT remains stuck in the not-so-small matter of calling a crisis of leadership while confronting not only the competition for coalition and platforms but also the "never Swissers" an ardent block of other frontline groups hell-bent against the Swiss mediators. For that body of Ambazonians, anything Swiss, let alone as a mediator, is sacrilegious. For supporters of the Swiss, why throw the bird in hand when its wings are broken or not strong enough to flap?

The ACT is a rudderless ship struggling with the winds of war and adrift because of its own internal wars. It has sought help but does not take the medicine. It struggles. The people continue to hope. The fighting and killing is now on two fronts: the BIR in our villages. The brother-on-brother killings in the fight to be the strongman.

The ACT is fragile. ACT is failing and falling fast out of its place as the last best hope for the people. The world waits and watches. The Swiss needs it. Without ACT, there is no Swiss Peace Process. The ACT needs to advance the priority of the people it purports to lead and do so from a position of strength and unity, if not with the critical Mass. Six decades of divide and rule, privilege, decadence, exploitation, bribery, corruption, nepotism, and other vices leave many naturally suspicious of those in the leadership. Cameroonians have experienced the same type of leadership for nearly six decades, ruling by decrees. We have seen high school dropouts, felons, and unqualified people with the reading comprehension of a first grader become the top ministers in Biya's government. They wield enormous power. They not only control large budgets, they now deploy the military to ride their country of terrorists. That leadership deficit permeates all levels, even among the more experienced, educated, and seasoned people and groups.

The Coalition for Dialogue and Negotiations (CDN)

The CDN broke into the scene stealthily and fully. One of the directors called me with the marketing pitch. When I was contacted by an old friend, I was elated. Finally, civil society was taking on a greater role and engaging in the crisis. The civil society in Cameroon operate in a lion's den. They play the safe middle road, preferring prudently not to ruffle feathers in Etoudi. Many are mostly concerned about welfare issues. A safe space to operate. CDN claims they want to accelerate the process of getting to negotiations.

The CDN is an NGO organizing an international conference with the goal of mobilizing to end the war and create a dialogue and negotiation platform and bringing together technical experts for postconstruction. How do we change the perception, the narrative? The international community does not see us Southern Cameroonians as people with a plan for solving the conflict or plans post-conflict, they claim. The lack of plan is harming our cause, and we are not being taken seriously. We are not organized. For the CDN, the fragmentation within the groups fighting for independence gave them a great opening to bring others who did not care for the Swiss Peace Process, breakaway groups, and many in the country whose positions are considered moderate in a coalition. My friend announced to me that we would end up with federation as a solution. We were not equipped and organized to deal with what this outcome would mean for Anglophones. The CDN, he told me, had engaged the reputed, retired secretary of state for Africa Herman Cohen. To ease my fears, my friend announced that they, on the CDN team, took great care to separate their individual views from that of the coalition—right to self-determination versus right to self-defense are not questioned. The CDN, I was told, was neutral on the arguments on federation, secession, or status quo.

The second call came in after a dear friend and relative whose wife is related to Kamto reached out to me, urging me to attend and participate in the CDN. His reasons were benign, as they were suspect. I lived close to Georgetown University, where the conference would be held; as one who attended the Boston conference in 2019, I could bring back valuable information to the team, which was now preparing for another high-profile gathering of top-notch participants at the Chatham House in London. Information out of the CDN, I was told, would help shape the agenda for Chatham House.

The pleas for all hands on deck for the CDN was up to a fever pitch. There was urgency to merge all the fragmented pieces of the revolution on the platform to come up with a comprehensive, common position. Who could argue with that? I had always advocated for coherency, coordination, and collaboration.

The CDN would hold seven thematic groups on the judiciary: education, health and humanity, reconstruction, governance and peace, mediation, and negotiation. This, they argue, was the best way to bring together the stakeholders of Southern Cameroons, not partisan groups, to talk to one another, and participation was open to all. Participants in each of these groups would come up with recommendations. These recommendations would then be taken up in an open plenary session and the majority position voted, forming the blueprint for our future. Some like me believe ours is not a problem of nominal solutions but rather a truth of who we are: a state equal in status. The proposed CDN exercise was no different from what Biya tried with his Grand National Dialogue (GND), essentially guaranteeing in every context, our singular issue becomes a minority issue in the universe of minority grievances in the entire Cameroon. I differ with them on the fact.

The GND

"Let them each have a commission among themselves and bring me your recommendation," declared President Biya. "From there, I will decree into law all that is good for the people of NOSO." And so, it was for the launch of the GND among Biya's CPDM bigwigs and a few handpicked favorites. On September 30 to October 4, 2019, President Biya held the GND with mainly the ruling party adherents. The security climate precluded participation of the separatists and diaspora groups. It was held in Yaounde, the agenda set by Biya alone, participants picked by him, were enough to keep Southern Cameroonians hoping to deal as two states equal in status out if not for good measure, clearly that just a few months earlier, ten of the IG members under Sisiku Julius AyukTabe had to be arrested at the Nera Hotel in Abuja Nigeria, forcibly returned to Yaoundé and today are serving 15 years to life in Biya's Kondengui prison.

By September 2019, the war showed no signs of abating. President Biya delivered on September 10 an address to the nation via TV to announce that he had appointed his Anglophone prime minister, Dion Ngute, to hastily convene the GND. The speech infuriated me even further. While the world called for a dialogue without pre-conditions that addresses the root causes of the Anglophone problem, in a crackly, hoarse voice, he explained how his decision to call for a grand dialogue would help in examining the problems in his country, particularly in the restive NOSO regions. The war that he declared two years to the date of his speech, he told us, was unfortunately based on secessionist propaganda. For Mr. Biya, there was a so-called marginalization of Anglophones by the French-speaking majority. By his terms, his government had always been willing to dialogue to end a war that he declared. In the figment of our imagination, Mr. Biya reminded us in his rare TV appearance—recall that this was a president who spent most of his time out of Cameroon at the InterContinental Hotel in Geneva, where he was a frequent guest and known to take an entire entourage with him—that he was fighting not only the ISIS of West Africa, formerly known as Boko Haram, but also a new breed of deadly terrorists in the NOSO regions of his beloved country. And for good measure, all the armaments and military dutifully funded and trained by the United States and Israel had been deployed in those regions to protect lives and secure the public good. For the eight million people of the NOSO of Biya's country, who had now taken to social media—Twitter, WhatsApp, and Facebook—and to the streets to protest in major capital cities with cries of genocide, all these were secessionist propaganda. Our brothers of the NOSO handpicked, offered menial stipends, would flock to Yaoundé even as they know nothing would come out of their efforts except more decrees from on high.

The sit-tight president for thirty-nine years announced to the world, "As for dialogue itself, the question has been asked, with whom?" Our destinies, he insisted, was to remain *un et indivisible*, one and indivisible. Had Biya just forgotten the history of his country and how we came to be?

They say that to hang a dog, all that is required is to give it a bad name. By juxtaposing the war in the NOSO to the internationally supported fight against the spread of ISIS, this time of West Africa, Biya had successfully garnered sympathy for his actions—after all, terrorism here or there is a threat to our common humanity. As another clever tactic, all the old man in Etoudi did was to call for sympathy from the 75 percent majority, the French-speaking citizens, in his speech. They are out to get us! The problems faced in his northwest-Southwest regions are like *nos compatriots* in all the other regions of our dear country. Who is oblivious to the fact that many sub-Saharan countries suffer from poor governance and experience marginalization within their minority populations? Which country is immune to minority grievances or issues dealing with regional balanced programs? The media was inundated with pundits taking on the merits for a GND and how this was a good first step in the right direction. And the international community followed in lockstep to lend their support for Biya's statesmanship in moving forward with a dialogue. It was predicted to fail, for how does a party to a conflict relegate for himself alone the conditions for dialogue? Many would argue Biya can do as he chooses. He is the state party, and the Amba Boys are non-state actors.

The international community had just forgotten that, just months ago, it endorsed something called the Swiss-led process, where they called for Mr. Biya to engage in dialogue with separatist groups without re-condition, addressing the root causes to find permanent solutions to the crisis. As soon as the GND was launched, Biya was applauded. The outcome was already predetermined. The dialogue was with conditions.

When the massacres continued, now described by the Norwegian Refugee Council (NRC), as another Rwanda in slow motion and falling under an avalanche of complaints from Cameroonian Americans, nine congressional members of the foreign affairs committee headed by Karen Bass issued a two-page letter condemning the ongoing killings by the dreaded BIR and citing the failed GND. The international community followed suit, declaring the GND a failure for not including all stakeholders and not going far to address the root causes. But had they not just praised it for its great success, with all the world eagerly awaiting the implementation of the recommendations from the eight notorious committees? The GND was widely judged as a failure. I and many saw it as a charade intended to wade off the increasing pressure the international community was finally putting on the regime in Yaoundé. It seemed, for some, that Biya was tone deaf. He could afford deafness. France threw its full weight behind Biya and his outings. That has and continue to embolden the sit-tight-dictator to hold on to the reins of power and to refuse to dialogue with those he calls secessionists. For this, thousands will die and continue to die.

When the Anglophones agitated for elected mayors to run their city affairs, Biya appointed through patronage government delegates who oversaw the mayors to ensure the party's interests were strictly followed in the English-speaking regions. When the Anglophones protested, staged marches, and called for school boycott for English-speaking teachers, the government decreed a few *appeley a d'autre function*, redeploying a handful of French-speaking teachers back to French Cameroun and vice versa. And so, when ten thousand Anglophones had been slaughtered by Biya's BIR army, nearly one million displaced, and one hundred thousand made into refugees, a dialogue was convened not to speak about the Anglophone "grievances," as Biya described it, but to dialogue about all the problems facing his failed thirty-nine-year rule. How convenient and saintly to die addressing a problem another did not ask for or complain about. Again, the interest of the Anglophones was put aside for 75 percent of the people content to live under the dictatorship and regressive policies of a government.

I was beyond furious learning that our hopes, dreams, and needs—in short, our destiny—were supplanted and buried in the destinies of a majority who neither cared to voice theirs nor fixed our problems. We were, indeed, *seconde classe*. The deck continued to be stacked against us. I asked simply, "Will you take a risk knowing from the get-go that your chances of winning are 75 percent against you?" It is difficult for me to grapple with the ideas our Anglophone brothers and sisters who flocked to the GND thought about this probability. Mind you, I did not bother to discount the almost 10 percent of the Anglophone minority who derived their livelihood from Biya's patronage and who were the ruling party's lapdogs and often sent to do his bidding, bribing, coercing, and—when the former did not work—killing their brothers and sisters to maintain the octogenarian, sit-tight strongman of Etoudi. Who can blame them? They had known no other way of earning a living except as a government employee.

What *Status Speciale* Is Not

For fighting and dying, the price will be *status speciale*, special status. We already had a status: it was independence in 1961 as two states with equal status. What happened? How do you obtain independence without the benefit of being independent? Biya continued to arrogate for himself the right to name, gerrymander, and bestow favors on his NOSO.

At the conclusion of five days of who is who at the Palais de Congress de Yaoundé, the ruling party picks and paid participants flown in from the diaspora, plus a handful of young boys claiming they had surrendered and now repentant for having taken up arms against their beloved country, LRC, convened to find solutions to the crisis not in the NOSO but in all Cameroon. First, participants were to dialogue only on eight keys areas, of which they were forbidden to discuss the nature or form of the state. Then the separatists were to drop their arms if they wish to participate, and at the conclusion, Biya would consider their recommendations for actions.

One key recommendation out of the GND was giving the NOSO a special status on account of its linguistic, cultural, and political heritage. They could elect regional councillors, hold regional assemblies, and have their favored house of chiefs. For good measure, Biya would appoint a secretary general for each region to handle the business of the region, but the regional council president would serve as his closest aide. Interpretation: we maintain control. For good measure, the NOSO could convene their regional meetings, but such a meeting could not be held unless the government-appointed regional overseer was present. Any actions taken in such a meeting would not be binding on the people of NOSO or the government. In the same span of time, Biya called for a GND, decreed a special status, called for elections, and pursued a genocidal war on the people he hoped to appease. On December 13, 2019, the national assembly convened an emergency session and passed the law on special status for the two regions of NOSO, a step the international community had, again, noted as too little too late.

The people of the NOSO held mixed reactions, which predictably followed ideological lines. The special status was pouring old wine into new bottles—the more things appeared to have changed, the more they were the same. Was this yet another act of aggression, an instrument of neocolonialism? The NOSO people were tired of seeing their children die and all too eager to accept benevolence from Yaoundé and some peace in the streets of their towns and villages.

The special status merely delegated powers to the NOSO with limited control over self-government. If those who hurdled in Yaoundé in a one-sided discussion believed they had snatched a small victory for the people of Ambazonia, they merely heaped more insults onto old ones. In this new ruse, Yaoundé retained even more sovereignty. The special status could only be described politely as an amorphous construct lacking in definition—insidious at best.

I found this to be yet another attempt by the Biya regime, now on life support, to continue to control the destiny of Ambazonia and keep a firm grip on our resources. Through the civil protest called Ghost Town Day, where the entire NOSO comes to a screeching halt with zero activities, the Biya economy had taken a major hit and was bleeding cash. After all, what was a country to do with

Glencore, Perenco, and all the ten- to twenty-year oil and gas concessions? How about the tentacles of not only France—people looked mainly at France as the bad cop in the neighborhood—but also of Switzerland's Glencore, Russia's Lukoil, UK's British Gas, Norwegian Oil, and the United States' Cameroon-Chad Exxon pipeline? Control over key resources in the Rio del Rey cannot be turned over to the Anglophones; worse, what was going to happen to all these deals that pumped millions into the pockets of shareholders in the West? We should not forget that countries do not have friends; countries have only interests. GND was the West's hope to put the genie back into the bottle. It was too late. The Amba Boys new to their true history—though many still do not know it, want nothing less than recognition of their once stolen independence. They feel intoxicated and emboldened.

The special status did not merely fall flat as a new government initiative to help end the war. It was yet another insult on the people of Ambazonia, a new act of terrorism against us if accepted; it further legitimized Biya's continued assimilation and annexation of Southern Cameroons. Handed down in the form of Biya's unending litany of decrees from Yaoundé, this time the special status was particularly as it was designed—to asphyxiate and decapitate the Anglophones, put an end to any form of dissent, and enslave us further. After the decree, the license to enforce the genocidal war was now renewed and carried out. With the special status, powers remained with Biya. He won in his "one and indivisible" mantra.

That Kamto sought this form of status throughout his world tour and meetings with key world leaders and that some Anglophones took to the airwaves to support, applaud, and beg Biya to kindly and quickly implement the key elements of the special status was particularly sickening. The special status was a mere semblance of devolution of powers from the highly centralized Biya mafia to his NOSO regions. No one in the NOSO was consulted on what this special status was to be. It was another insult to the people. Where were the freely expressed wishes of the people? Did Cardinal Christian Tumi fail to relate that, in his survey of Anglophones, 69 percent had expressed their desire for an independent nation?

The Kamto Effect

Once, I watched a Sherlock Holmes movie, and the theme was "the dog that did not bark." There had been a murder, and Holmes stepped in to investigate. Everyone was assumed guilty until Holmes excluded him or her. One person appeared quite innocent, and all his alibis checked out. The trouble, though, was upon cross-checking with another person in the house, he confidently recalled that it was impossible for the intruder and murderer to have done so without the guard dogs barking throughout, even before they were killed. It was possible, then, that the killer was familiar and friendly and came bearing treats for the dogs.

Obviously Kamto is the dog that didn't bark in the Anglophone saga. To overlook him is to be a failed Sherlock Holmes. Holmes is yet to have an unsolved mystery. My friend Ivo and Francophone brothers, whose agendas are antithetical to ours, will prefer that we overlook Kamto as an innocent victim, charming us to where we hope to extricate ourselves for six decades.

When I received the call from Ivo in January, I had not spoken to him for a while. I immediately knew something was up, but the last thing I could come up with was politics. I knew him as an entrepreneur who had returned home to build a business in the construction sector. In my last conversation with him at a party, he lamented his great disappointment in the trajectory of LRC. He had sadly given up, abandoned his business, and sadly returned to the United States. He was no fan, he said, of the shocking depravity, gaffe, and tribalism endemic in LRC, and he was done. Africa and LRC were doomed. No amount of good reporting really moved the needle for the average African. Cameroon, despite being so rich in resources, was near the bottom of every index of growth.

Ivo began by asking what my position was on the Anglophone problem but hastily stated as if waiting would signal a "got you" question, "I am, just so you know, a federalist." At the conclusion of his introduction, he again noted that LRC was a German colony in 1884. Ivo reminded me that there can't be peace with secessionists unless we wanted to keep fighting. He had made an about-turn from being in favor of seceding to being a federalist, but his concern was how we can have peace and resolve the crisis for future generations. I agreed and pivoted for my burning question. "Are you for negotiations without pre-conditions called for by the UN?" Again, I asked, "What is it, in your belief, that I can offer?"

"We need a new president who can change the direction of the country and allow for a coexistence of the French and English. Biya does not want to solve the problem. Have you thought of what will happen if Biya dies in power?" "I have." I replied. And now, he eased into the real reason for his call. "I have had several conversations with the Kamto team. And I am calling to find out who the leaders are in the Anglophone side who can sit at the table with Kamto and hold a conversation for the future of LRC. Kamto is looking for people who want to hold a genuine conversation. My job is to organize."

"What does Kamto want?"

"I was told that Kamto is open for federation as a political solution." And for good measure, Ivo added that his position can evolve. He wanted to meet behind closed doors with a limited number of leaders. "And if you would like, I would add your name to that group. Have you considered that you might be used to advance Kamto's inroads into the Anglophone side? I believe Kamto has something to offer that we need today."

Kamto, after his release from Biya's Kondengui prison, had taken a whirlwind tour of the Western world's capitals from Brussels to Berlin to Paris to throngs of cheering LRC Battalion Anti-Sardinard (BAS) supporters in the diaspora. Kamto looked and sounded like the president-elect, as his supporters referred to him, and quite the leader that a country like LRC needed. His oratory skills were in full display in one TV appearance to the other. He was the only solution that LRC needed, and with the duly elected leaders whose victory was stolen, he and his closest collaborator were hurled away and locked up in Biya's dungeon for daring to protest in the streets of Douala against what he called an electoral holdup. It would take Emmanuel Macron being accosted by a BAS in Paris to promise to intervene for his release. And he did intervene, and Kamto was later released from jail. But not Sisiku and the Nera 10. Again, we were different.

The Anglophone crisis was now his to champion. Buried in the cries of *nos freres de NOSO*, yet again the Francophone relegated the right to themselves to name, label, and decide what we were to be called. Under no circumstance could he imagine letting us go. He is prepared to speak with us, unlike the "former president," Biya, who did not. For Kamto and his supporters, we were no longer Anglophones, northwest or Southwest; we were not the people of NOSO. For them, it was sexy and expedient. How infuriating and condescending. The indignities piled on.

"We are the same country. I will not let my brothers of NOSO go. We need to work together to create the conditions for dialogue, to build confidence, and to deescalate the crisis. Even if *nos freres de*

NOSO say they are Southern Cameroons, they are still Cameroonians. We are the same." These were nice and conciliatory words for Mr. Kamto.

With a captive audience of thousands, if not millions, of Francophones in the diaspora and Anglophones craving a return to normalcy, even if that meant returning to a highly centralized regime, economic and social decline, and state control, Kamto's soaring speeches were greeted as a breath of fresh air. And so, to sweeten the deal, and win over Anglophones and to be seen as their savior from the tyranny of Mr. Biya, he joined the international community to criticize Biya's GND. "I am the solution all of Cameroon has been seeking."

When Yaoundé realized there was a problem, they held a dialogue with their friends. Speaking mainly to the Francophone crowd, his message was always centered on and directed at the Anglophones and the Anglophone's problems. "We should give the secessionists a chance to be heard. You must know that those in the middle are more than the extremists. We will—I promise you—arrive at a solution."

The dog that did not bark was Kamto. His soaring speeches hit all the right conciliatory notes, appealing to both his BAS constituencies, the beleaguered and tired Francophones who had only seen their fortunes diminishing in the past fifty-eight years of the Beti-Bulu-Fang dynasty under Mr. Biya, and the people of Kamto's NOSO, now facing genocide by Biya's dreaded BIR army. All these groups were for anything other than the status quo. And so, Mr. Kamto was not put under any scrutiny. He was received by Tibor Nagy and, secretly, by other heads of states. For the Ambazonians, he was the dog that did not bark. He jumped over the fence—a known quality to not only his BAS supporters, French Cameroun, but also his NOSO, who also saw him as a victim of the same regime. His victory as the next legitimate president of LRC was stolen in 2018, as was Ni John Fru Nid of SDF in 1992 by the dictator, who was killing people in the NOSO. What better friend in war than the enemy of your enemy?

Kamto had been described as more dangerous than Mr. Biya. A product of Biyaism, Mr. Kamto was the architect of the constitution that saw the end of federalism during his stint as a junior minister of foreign affairs. In the '90s, when the Anglophone problems reared its stubborn head, Mr. Kamto proudly reminded Anglophones that he was the architect of the *status speciale*. The people of the NOSO should be grateful and welcome him as the solution for Biya's failed policies and as the only one capable of bringing an end to the crisis and building a bigger, better, and one and indivisible Cameroon.

Africa's Perceived Weakness

The Berlin Conference of 1884 gave Africa its arbitrary boundaries in a bid to end Europe's civil wars at home and the ensuing tribal quarrels in a rush to lay claim on the continent. To end such a conflict among the powers, a boundary treaty was concluded, and Africa was cut up, with hills and rivers forming clear boundaries, as was the case of the river Mungo, forming a clear boundary between the French and British colonies in Cameroon in subsequent treaties. There would be wartime agreement to follow, as was the case from 1914 to 1918, a time when international law allowed territorial acquisition through conquest. So, when Germany was defeated, the victorious placed Germany under martial law and Africa on the dinner plate to be sliced up; to each his own. So, the once great German colony spreading from today's Congo to the east, Burkina Faso to the north, and as far west as Togo, was again cut up between France and England, with the latter retaining a sliver of territory from today's Chad to the Ambas Bay, divided by the Mungo to the east and by Nigeria's Cross River, Taraba, and Benue States to the west. Britain divided their colony into a northern and southern Cameroon for ease of administration.

The UN principles of self-determination and equality of all countries meant colonies could not be administered into perpetuity. The administering powers were mandated to lead their colonies into self-government or full independence. In Africa, this was fraught with complications. Some, like France, just never left. Others like Britain, all too happy to leave, could not care less what type of arrangement their trust territories received.

Meanwhile, for the Arab colonies, they mostly marched quickly into independent nations. History would show that Arab nations had shown their powers militaristically in conquering territory to destroy or occupy parts of neighboring territories. This fighting ability was not lost on Europe. Japan, for instance, had demonstrated its ability to capture and occupy parts of China and later to attack and destroy Pearl Harbor, part of America. They took the fight even to those they feared militaristically. This expansion would only be stopped by the devastating blow of the atomic bomb that brought Japan to surrender, and even so, America occupied Japan for a short period, as Germany was only occupied long enough to rebuild it and hand it over to Germans of non-Nazi influence. Why is France still in Francafrique? Could be on account of their perceiving weaker states. At the writing of this book, France will be served to sit up. A sea change appears to be taking rook in the countries still yoked to France. On June 9, 2021, Mailians could be seen chanting "rentrez chez vous," which means "go back to your country" in front of French tanker, bomber, and other military artillery deployed into the capital of the city, Bamako. Like the push from the women and youths in Sudan that oust Ormar Bashir's long, unsettling grip, it appears, finally, that France might be dislodged. But that hope will have to spring eternally long in Africa.

Africa, though with its own intertribal wars, enjoyed large military forces and great empires. Battles were largely self-contained. Africa had not shown an ability nor affinity to conquer territory beyond its own borders. Yet when the Europeans arrived, they occupied large parts of territory not long enough to build, rehabilitate, or pacify but in perpetuity—or so it seemed. They effectively moved in, laid claim to their respective territories, raised their flags, sent in their missionaries, and enslaved or exported both human and resources to other faraway lands or to their homelands. France hopes this arrangement remains overtly as in the continuous use of its CFA currency or subtly in their support for the like of the sit-tight 39-year dictator in Cameroon.

That pacification through proselytizing remains to date. There is a long-held maxim that, when the whites came to Africa, they told us our religion was the wrong kind. They gave us Bibles and asked us to close our eyes and pray with them. When we opened our eyes, all that was ours, including our long-held traditions, were taken, and we were left with only the Bible in hand. In their expedition, humans were a commodity for export. When humans agitate, they are killed.

Cameroon's Competing Agendas and Contradictions

The war is extremely complex and has a lot of moving parts. That is mainly due to the interest parties who stand to lose much in a settled war. If you've had some trouble keeping up with all the subtleties of the conflict, here is a fact sheet of the competing agendas. Competing agendas are on LRC, as they are on our side. The ever-growing crop of purported leaders is a sign that we don't know what we want, a sign that we fall prey to LRC propaganda, and a sign that our egos are bigger than the war. LRC has its fixed political realities it stops at nothing to maintain. The armed groups show little coherence on their demands. Who can blame them? Many like me, today, question everything we knew as truths about our country.

Competing agendas are on multiple levels:

- Foreign nations and their multinational corporations pillaging our resources

- LRC citizens and political parties like MRC of Kamto capitalizing on the war to advance their objectives that they are a better alternative to "save" Cameroon from Boko Haram and from the Anglophone crisis

- Political pundits, lobbyists, and other state actors (Herman Cohen, Tibor Nagy, the Africa Forum) who change their positions as the tides of war change

- The federation's flavors of the day: CDN, civil society actors (Agbor Balla, Munzu, women's groups, and others forming each day)

- Ultimately, LRC's ever-growing creative ideas in search of a solution like offering us *status speciale*

- Lately, engaging some of the Nera 10 and Macho Bibixy in a parallel dialogue, just as the world mounts pressure for LRC to come to peace talks in Geneva

- Biya talk among his CPDM bigwigs on things that have nothing to do with the root causes of the war in Southern

Cameroon and trumpeters of commissions on bilingualism, diaspora engagement, education, decentralization, or cultural integration as vehicles for addressing the question of Southern Cameroons' statehood

- Separatists, restorationists, secessionist, and independentists for whom there is no common agreed to narrative

EMMA M. OSONG, D.M.

CALL TO ACTION

Staggering Cost of Wars

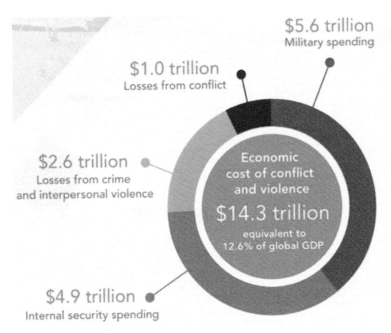

$5.6 trillion
Military spending

$1.0 trillion
Losses from conflict

$2.6 trillion
Losses from crime
and interpersonal violence

Economic
cost of conflict
and violence
$14.3 trillion
equivalent to
12.6% of global GDP

$4.9 trillion
Internal security spending

Image: World Humanitarian Data and Trends report

Read this article: (https://www.academia.edu/39769652/THE_ IMPACT_OF_THE_ANGLOPHONE_CRISIS_ON_THE_ECON OMIC_DEVELOPMENT_OF_CAMEROON) about some of the economic costs to Cameroon and about its future. This article is more conflict quantified.

I want you to imagine that you are in a normal, everyday issue. Let's say a car accident. What can you quantify in economic terms about the accident?

- Damage to your car

- Damage to the other car

- Hospital bills

- Time off work

Let's say that, all in, this car accident costs you $1,400 and the other person $1,800. We've quantified the economic impact of this car accident. Are we done?

- Could you tell who had a worse experience?

- Can you quantify psychological damage or trauma?

- Is there a way to quantify a loss in monetary terms?

Many lawyers spend their days quantifying things like that. But I ask you: is equivalence ever truly possible?

You will never get the time wasted back. And if you lost your life or a passenger's, it's game over. There are many ways to attempt to quantify a conflict in economic terms, but it is not the only part of the tale. The conflict in Southern Cameroons costs parties on both sides billions, but can there ever be a price put on human life? I think not.

Think about the items you have in your purse or pocket. Cell phone? Rewards credit card? Driver's license? Will any of that be worth killing for? But people die every day for resources just the same: gold, diamonds, oil, minerals, things Cameroon has in spades. Are you sure that you haven't already put a price on another human life? Your material comfort? This topic is uncomfortable, but it must be said. You are a consumer of news, content, food, utilities, technology, fashion, and everything else on the planet. Your choices dictate the demand. No thirst, no blood.

CHAPTER 8:
LEVERS OF CONTROL PRESSED INTO SERVICE

Colonialism deprives you of your self-esteem and to get it back, you have to fight to redress the balance.

—Imran Khan

Colonizers want a nation that secures their freedom to oppress and to dismantle cultures, families, and individuals. They demean, silence, and kill resistance. Exploitation brings poverty, downtrodden people, and a lack of hope. Slowly, the oppressed forget the riches that have been stolen and the culture and language dismantled, new ones imposed, imbued, and a new way of life creeps in. Time spawns generations completely oblivious to their enslavement. The only freedom that exists is for the colonizer.

The colonization, or should I say the destruction, of Africa is too profitable to resist for the nations that have built their fortunes on exploitation. And the reality of colonization is so expertly woven into the fabric of society that even its residents don't fully understand it. I myself would have vocalized my identity as an American Cameroonian several years ago. And now, I have changed this nomenclature to an American of Southern Cameroonian origin. If you imagine colonization as a tree, it's not enough to chop it down. Roots have spread through the soil. Digging them up and sifting through debris is the only way to rise above. It's hard work but possible. And possibility is all that's needed for hope.

In Service to the French, the P5, Nigeria, and International Organizations

COVID-19 had come to aggravate the war in NOSO. As if we needed one more enemy, the pandemic had come to make life worse for the people. Largely, they did not heed the calls for preventive measures to curb the spread but, rather, had opened up even more leeway for LRC to fortify its military presence in NOSO. When the UN called for a global cease-fire to fight the pandemic and open up the corridors for humanitarian assistance, LRC's BIR invaded Bafut in the northwest, killing, raping, and burning villages. They said they captured Amba fighters and had brought peace to the area. The villagers had escaped to the bushes, and there would be no farming nor harvesting in the months to come. The UN called for LRC to get to the negotiating table. If the UN's permanent member, France, told the world they supported LRC, there should be no mediation. Who were we to believe?

As the coronavirus spread, LRC increased its hostilities. The international community rushed, in the name of curbing the pandemic, to provide aid and reduce or cancel LRC debt but did nothing to condition their aid on the cessation of hostilities. The UN was happy to announce that it shared the concern for a global cease-fire but did nothing to actually silence the guns. Different wars, different solutions is an understandable geopolitics given contextual differences or difficulties. As the war rages in NOSO, with the attendant devastation, the same international community reacts to the war in Yemen. In 2020, a special envoy is sent to Yemen, and confidence-building measures are taken up to reach a political settlement and engage in broad dialogue and consultations. In Cameroon, the once touted Swiss Peace Process by some of the UN member states is barely being mentioned. Except for ACT, its strongest supporters—it, too, a basket case of hyperfragmentation;

the phrase the Swiss-led peace process is an anathema. Any confidence-building measure undertaken is bungled due to intra-group fighting for dominance and relevance. They forget Biya's triumphant utterance, "Who do you want me to dialogue with?" Regional countries did not play a role at all. The fighting continued despite the call to stop and fight the pandemic.

In Yemen, the UN called for all parties to engage in negotiations. All sides must stop hostilities and resume talks. In LRC, aid was provided with no assurances to end the hostilities. When it comes to the U.S.'s policy in Africa, the traditional rule book is tossed out in favor of one issue policy—funding for health-related issues or funding to fight the now rebranded ISIS of West Africa. What you hear most often are things like "we engage with regional bodies . . ." The Swiss did not speak about the Bafut massacres. How can this not be thought of as complicity? On the eve of the new year in 2021, the U.S. Senate passed Resolution 684, calling for a credible process for inclusive dialogue that includes all stakeholders. It addresses the grievances and imposes targeted sanctions. The resolution went further to call for investigations of human rights abuses and for the first time in the history of U.S./France bilateral relationships via Africa, called on France to help in finding a solution through mediation. Sadly, the resolution still placed the conflict in the realm of marginalization of Anglophone minority within the construct of Cameroon. In the case of Yemen, the UNSC members said that a solution can be achieved without recognizing the legitimate concerns of a weak state, a failing state, but one with the strongest strategic partners. How can that be? In June 2021, the U.S. did eventually put some teeth behind the resolution when the U.S. State Department issues instituted a visa ban policy for those it claims are perpetuating violence in Cameroon.

Biya's one and indivisible country was largely believed to be weak and unstable, yet it had survived Boko Haram, bottomed-out oil prices, fiscal devaluation, an alleged coup d'état by his prominent current minister of youth services, removal from African Growth and Opportunity Act (AGOA), defunding of its military, and now, four years of senseless war that he himself declared on what he called the NOSO of his country. Biya was largely embraced and caressed by his Southern Cameroon regions' son of the soil who ran his administration. He was insulated from the shock any dictator might face after nearly six decades of repression and generalized malcontent. For man and country, Biya dutifully enacted France's bidding to keep Cameroon, the bastion of Francafrique. At the height of the war, in 2019, when it appeared the majority of UN members wished to see a credible dialogue between Biya and the armed groups, France's ambassador in Yaoundé proclaimed there will be no foreign intervention in Cameroon, as the problem is of a domestic nature. Biya, it appears, is a necessary evil for the Nigeria and the multinational interests' parties, as he is and remains for France.

I have heard various pundits on the ever-ubiquitous academic discourse state that Cameroon, in its current state, is susceptible to coordinated international intervention and incremental pressure to engage in a genuine dialogue or for a cease-fire. I am afraid that coordinated intervention is either lacking in coordination or nonexistent. The White man's solutions for Africa had been calamitous. Take the gentlemen's agreement on African boundaries reached in Berlin in 1884. Today, no degree of internationally recognized partition is reason enough to forestall the amalgamation of NOSO to French Cameroon or to recognize it for what it was and is: its own people, state or country.

What Is Good for the Goose

My daughter benefited from great doctors and nurses, passionate about their patients. Some, having cared for her over extended periods, became not only vested but like family to us all. But all this did not shield her from the push and pull in health care delivery with the goal of reducing cost while sometimes skimming on the patient care. I must be clear: this was never the goal for my daughter's direct, healthier delivery team. The majority of them loved what they do. In the months to years steeped in battling a chronic and debilitating condition, it was the underlying structure that were slow to change even with the institution of the Affordable Care Act, dubbed ObamaCare. So, there was access to health care, and the elimination of lifetime maxima on health spending, yet my daughter's care was downgraded or cut because she had "maxed" out. In lieu of the recommended care, she was told to go to a nursing home or go home. She did not have a choice in the kind of care she got, how much, who provided the care or in which setting. To change this, dynamics required confronting the very structure of the system. Luckily, she had a united, dedicated team willing to speak up and act in unison and advocate forcefully for her.

LRC can claim the levers of control: judiciary, education, communication, and so on. They have used that power for extrajudicial killings, unlawful arrests, and imprisonment. They have used the lever of education to water down our education system and deny us opportunities. They have used the media to sell their propaganda, and six decades later, when the NOSO asked only that their roads be fixed or to maintain their English and common-law systems, they turned the guns on us and declared war. Indeed, not all crises are equal, yet a war is war, and only bad things happen. Between the global north, east, and south, when war broke out, there are stark political power, political influence, and economic support that are brought to bear in resolving and putting an end to the conflict.

These differences are pronounced in wars in Africa and elsewhere. Usually, the answer given to the disparities in wars elsewhere and in sub-Sahara Africa is: it is complicated.

An oppressor's tool is not often deadly. Education is often the most insidious means used to assimilate and to subjugate others. Our history books were not that of the great civilizations of Africa, the warriors or conquerors like Shaka Zulu, or the great queen of Congo, nor was it a rich history of how we came to be "attached" to a country that did not speak our language nor shared our Anglo-Saxon culture. We were to read instead European history—the wars fought by Napoleon Bonaparte, life in France, Europe's own civil wars, the rise and fall of civilians. Does the good book not say that people perish for lack of knowledge? Even in the education of "housewives," would knowledge of who we really were be hidden if not for nefarious ends? As the events of today show, we were indeed thought of as captive people with one exception—our rights were not outright yanked; they were systematically erased, taken away. The tool of erasure was education. When that could not be sustained, there would be military assault.

Conflicts in the Middle East and Europe are treated differently by the global north and, to a large extent, by the international community. Whereas the Ambazonia-Cameroon war, now entering its fifth year, has the world's sixth largest population of displaced people; it is by far the least funded humanitarian crisis. Those forced into exile in neighboring Nigeria are yet to be fully accounted for, counted, and documented by the UNHCR. Nearly four years in exile, many are yet to have their application for refugee status granted. This can only mean that the international community still treats the war as a domestic problem, a minority agitation where, given the implementation of the recommendations from the GND of September 2019, a dialogue the *big guys* called failed, the population will be sufficiently appeased, peace and calm will return, and the refugees will be encouraged to return on their own. When it comes to wars in the Middle East, for example, the international community shapes not only the narrative but also the trajectory of the war through dialogue and economic and military intervention. There is hardly the question nor hesitation about funding. When a crisis erupts, the UN is quick to appoint a mediator or send a special representative to the crisis. A contact group is formed, an international coalescing emerges—the Munich Group, of which France is the key player for the Palestinian-Israeli conflict.

Conflicts in Africa, in particular the sub-Sahara region, tend to follow a different path altogether. There are no heavy involvements from the heavyweight international actors; those from the region interested in brokering peace come hat in hand to look and beg for funding for humanitarian needs. They will tell you: if you want the international community to pay attention, you should stress mainly the humanitarian aspect of the war. The NRC has, on multiple occasions, sounded the alarm about the dire need for humanitarian funding for the nearly one million displaced people's food insecurity, health care, and so on in Southern Cameroons. To date, there has been little done in that regard, be it in upping the funding or in interventions to stop the hostilities.

The Paper Tiger of Africa

Africa Union is weak in conflict resolution because it is weak in providing substantive funding in ending conflict. AU relies on foreign powers' funding that come laden with partisan interests. Take China, believed as a whole subsidiary of the AU having not only built, but equipped the AU headquarter building in Addis

Ababa, Ethiopia. China's stranglehold on African member countries translates into their votes on matters ranging from human rights to rights for China's own abuses of its minority Urgyrs to rights to build its military bases around the world. It is no stretch of the imagination that Yaoundé, a benefactor of China's economic largesse in the form of loans and infrastructure development, will vote lock step with China against the U.S. and others each time in the UN. In turn, China is unlikely to entertain a motion in the UNSC that goes against Cameroon, even in the face of the later, committing crimes against humanity. They say he who pays the piper calls the music is clear who drives the peace agenda at the AU. AU is sluggish and bureaucratic with lifetime, sit-tight dictators with a myriad of seeming conflicts and outright wars, sitting in Addis Ababa and presiding over agendas to end conflicts in their own backyards. There is little incentive to offset "the apple carts."

Yet if AU—the fifty-four-member body of Africa who wields power in the corridors of the UN—were to take on a conflict with the intent to resolve, it naturally would amplify the conflict and make it hard to ignore by the P5 (UNSC) and other nations. Too often, it preaches a Pan-Africanism that fails to address simmering, long-standing problems, turns a blind eye to colonial pillaging in Africa, and prefers a quasi peace that advantages dictators only.

On Being Cameroonianess and the Tyranny of Control

LRC is a country with no credible past, a state run by criminal amnesia specializing in tyranny. History tells us that criminal tyrannical regimes eventually self-destruct—the evidence abounds—if not by democratization, then by the people rising and toppling the regime. LRC has demonstrated that, where it cannot hold power through democratic means, it will do so by fiat or by decrees. And when that, too, is perhaps tricky, it will use assigned positions of authority to reign with terror on the largely acquiescent populace.

Our steady slide into what Tibor Nagy terms "the Camerooianess" in every Cameroonian did not occur overnight. In fact, it happened as the clock struck midnight on October 1, 1961. As the proverbial curtain of colonial rule was being lifted to usher in a sovereign nation, albeit one of two sovereign nations equal in status, the long, pernicious colonial arm of France—and Britain— lurked in the background and would begin instituting levers of control to systematically assimilate and ultimately annihilate all vestiges of a once proud Westphalian democracy on the continent of Africa. At the dawn of its "independence by joining," the former trust territory boasted less than 2 million inhabitants, the majority of whom held less than a standard six level formal education. Though hardworking, resourceful, and endowed with countless yet untapped natural resources (recall that oil had been discovered in the Delta regions of Nigeria, and by extension, the oil fields spread as far as the Ndian region of Southern Cameroons), the population looked trustingly to its small class of elites to steer its political destiny. France, through its consular activities and with the understanding from Amadou Adhijo, sought from the very onset to inculcate in the Anglophone elites and their progenies, Frenchification.

So, it can be said that, in 2016, the awakening of a nationalistic fever was born. Another realization was that a demagogue, LRC, and its French masters had nearly completed their assimilation of Anglophones but had within their reins of control all the levers of governing and power and will kill to retain it. Theirs was a slow, sure, systematic progress to imbue "Camerooianess" into each of us. Our parents learned Yaoundé was the center of their professional and private lives. We learned that all roads led to Yaoundé as the ultimate citizen. Every resistance along the way on its own could never stand up to the power maintenance structures that undergirded these control systems. We chased "papers" in Yaoundé for promotions, for education, ultimately for our citizenship. Even if many decried the steady erosion of our "rights" as states of equal status, no political movement, Anglophone conference (AAC I or AAC II), nor violent uprising ever was strong or sustained enough to resist or topple the annexationist regime. Many others, beneficiaries of Yaoundé's patronage, either took no notice or did not care. We passed from one who ruled for nearly two decades by emergency decree to another, still ruling into his 4th decade by decree, and then to war.

LRC can claim the levers of control: judiciary, education, media, and religion. They had used that power for extrajudicial killings, unlawful arrests, and imprisonment. The Nera 10, through Sisiku, the leader of the Ambazonia IG in exile were tricked into meeting for "negotiations with LRC" in the Nera Hotel, Abuja, captured and refouled, held incommunicado, and later tried in a military court. An estimated twenty thousand mostly young, unarmed "Anglophones," including hundreds of university students chanting "no more violence," were similarly rounded up and ferried into Francophone jails and torture chambers. Beyond the use of the judiciary as an instrument of terror, Biya's imposition of civil law in his NOSO regions that practiced common law was yet another form of violence over these six decades—from the dawn of our "bungled" independence in 1961 to the present.

They had used the lever of education to water down our education system and deny us opportunities. The average educated Anglophone youth who neither spoke good English nor good French was emblematic of the watered-down education at the hands of

Francophone teachers, themselves not fully conversant with English but teaching in English. They had used the media to sell their propaganda, and six decades later, when we asked only that our roads be fixed or that we need English and common law for our systems, they turned the guns on us and declared war.

CALL TO ACTION

Conflict Controls

What You Need to Know and What You Can Do

Ask yourself:

- What skills do I have to offer the world?

- How can I use those skills to help?

Whether you have great communication skills, engineering knowledge, or simply a desire to help, you can contribute to a cause. There are many categories of service that you can utilize your skills.

1. *Diplomacy and consultative process.* UN agencies, donors, NGOs, and governments all have processes to respond to the reality of conflict. Campaigns, letters to politicians, raising awareness, and fundraising are all part of this multifaceted process.

2. *Youth programs.* Although it is not only the youth who is affected by conflict, youth programs in particular are part of humanitarian programs. Issues that affect young people are front and center. A part of that is the creation of safe spaces, youth centers, or camps where children can play and receive the care, education, and safety they need.

3. *Data and research.* Unfortunately, there are many reasons why quantifying conflict is necessary. There are many

opportunities to contribute to the compilation and analysis of data surrounding conflict.

4. *Skills and training for refugees.* Providing language and skill training to those who have escaped conflict is essential to their transition. In addition, medical and dental care and psychological treatment/counseling might be required.

5. *Awareness.* The conflict is disproportionately felt in Cameroon. The Francophone is largely insulated. The war occurs in the NOSO regions. One of the most neglected part of the peace process is awareness. Because of the administrative burden, there is often not enough time or budget for marketing-type activities. Social media, thought leadership, and influencers are a vital part of this process. Any bit helps. Even word of mouth is helpful. Bring up the conflict to your friends and family. See what they know and don't know. You will be surprised how many intelligent and worldly people are unaware of the suffering out there. When people express their disgust for the humanitarian crisis, tell them about this book. And let them share it with others.

CHAPTER 9 :
FROM FEAR INTO ACTIVISM

Anonymity I So Dearly Desire

By the end of months of hospitalization—seven in total, with nine admissions and discharges—with my daughter and no expert able to confidently tell me she was going to be okay, I could only wonder what the future held for her and for us. As we came to the end of her more than eighteen months of hospitalization, I found myself caught between excitement and gloom, mulling over what lay ahead. After nearly three months of head-on fight with the administrative staff and some of the medical staff at Johns Hopkins not to prematurely discharge my daughter to her certain death, I finally came to a compromise. In fact, Praxie gave me the green light to arrive at that. She had grown weary of being prodded, pricked, the subject of countless medical studies, and examined in the hospital and wanted simply to go home. We had all agreed that over our cold, dead bodies would she be discharged into a nursing home after our difficult experience in one such homes in Columbia. We remembered the painful days spent in the nursing home, where there was only one nurse technician for almost ten to fifteen patients. It is only so much an adult immobile can hold his or her bladder!

Praxie still required full assistance for every activity of daily living. I could not do these by myself and often would ask her dad to assist or work with the nurse tech to care for Praxie. This day, at the nursing home, I called for assistance for Praxie to get her into a chair for the bathroom and for a bath. The nurse tech sympathetically and calmly pointed down the long hallway, saying,

"Ma'am, it's just me here. You see all those doors with the red light above the doorway? They all need help and have been calling before you. I will get to you, okay?"

I looked down the long corridor and noticed five red lights blinking above the doorways. Praxie's was the sixth. By the fifth day in this facility, my daughter's health had deteriorated. Normally, a cheerful person, in spite of being so sick, she had stopped talking, barely eaten, and developed a fever. I walked to the front nurses' station and calmly demanded a discharge and that an ambulance be called to take my daughter to the nearest hospital. I determined not to argue about what they needed to do at the moment. Any hospital will do, I reminded myself. All the while, our experience had showed only Johns Hopkins was equipped to deal with her health condition. From the nearest hospital, the next step will be that she will be medivacked to Johns Hopkins.

She was, again, readmitted to the hospital, and this time, her decline precipitated. I told her doctors that I would not, again, accept their recommendations for discharge unless she and I believed she had substantially recovered and was not being discharged mainly to make room for another high-paying patient. The lines were drawn between the bean counters and me.

When her final discharge date came, we, as a family, agreed she would be discharged to continue her medical care at home. We would make her home her private nursing home. Never again would we accept a nursing home. And so, in April 2018, after securing for her the same services she would have received in a nursing home, I agreed, and Praxie signed her discharge papers. She would receive doctor's visits, bedside nursing, specialty nursing, the four therapies that the hospital had provided (physical, recreational, psychological, and personal), and all the medical-grade equipment needed for her particular condition.

The hospital would not accept sending her home with the specialty lift they had bought specifically for Praxie. I dug in. I would not take her home unless a similar or like lift was available. How were we to move her? The decision took nearly a month for the higher-ups in the hospital to accept to send her home with this lifesaving equipment. In sat Cathy, the social worker at Johns Hopkins, as she printed out her service list and discharge planning plan. That was not enough. I insisted that she call every department that would provide those services and schedule their first day of service.

With all the names of agencies, phone numbers, and confirmed start dates of service and delivery of equipment secured, I returned and shared the good news with Praxie. Her eyes lit up. Finally, she was going home. We both hugged and cried. She was royally tired; it'd been nearly eighteen months of hospitalization. I had essentially lived in the hospital. The recliner, initially, was my bed. Later, the staff caved and brought in a bed and set it up at the far end of Praxie's room. She had been moved into a bigger room. They also brought us a minifridge. And I brought in a small Crockpot. This was our home. I would essentially be Praxie's stand-in nurse tech.

Some of the other long-term patients had become our extended families. We met in the common area, in the laundry, and in the kitchens, shared meals, cried on each other's shoulders, or just chatted away, forgetting for a moment the pangs of despair we felt watching our children battle a life-changing illness. There was Chris with a rare form of illness that left his spine unable to sit upright or use his limbs and was fed in bed and the young twenty-five-year-old lawyer, Kevin, who had recently graduated. I couldn't tell who was luckier: Chris, who, though not in pain, could not sit up or feed himself, or Kevin, whose arms and legs had to be amputated and who was blind because of a house fire. Chris had run in one too many times to rescue his parents. In the process, he had been badly burned. The intense fire had burned his corneas.

Once settled into our nursing routine at home, I began to feel the relief of not being the primary caregiver to Praxie. She had three caregivers, one full time and two part time. Two of them were young and good companions for Praxie. One, a student and same age as Praxie, shared her college experience. There was an unending, steady stream of providers in and out of the house. I was glad to know that, at any given time, there would be people who cared about Praxie near her. I still, though, could not sleep well, worrying. Praxie's room was in the lower level. The rest of the family's sleeping quarters were on the third level. The only egress/ingress was through our garage doors to the lower room, now a mini hospital with IV poles, physical therapy equipment, boxes of syringes and assorted medical supplies, bedside lift, hospital bed, adjustable bedside table, and fridge to hold thousands of dollars' worth of life-giving medications that streamed in every two weeks. There was no overnight aid. So, I decided to roll out the sleeping bed and spend the night with her in her basement room.

Through the nonprofit Affordable Resources for Independent Living (AFI), I made the case for help, and they provided most of the funding I needed to install a stair lift in the home. It would be a long time before Praxie had the strength to transfer from wheelchair to stair lift and make the ride to the family living space on the upper level, to sit alongside the family for a meal, or just to be around as we go about our lives on two feet. There were doors that were ADA-compliant, bathrooms, and ramps for a wheelchair. It was home, after all, far from the suffering that hospitals hold. I was grateful. I believe, too, Praxie was resigned but happy to be in her own environment. Soon, with her aides, Tavia and Nurse Arlene,

Praxie will turn her room into a purple haven where we all loved to congregate.

The phone calls to insurance for approvals, to coordinators and social workers for care plans that did not automatically get rejected, and to contractors to prioritize our work, went on for what seemed like decades. With each successive delay to bring Praxie's living space to ADA standards, I grew increasingly frightened that, in the event of a fire, we would not be able to quickly evacuate my daughter. And that day did come.

It was not a fire but a medical emergency. After her bath, I strapped her into her sit-to-stand lift and pushed the button, and she was raised from her torso to an erect position. Just as I was about to hit stop to wheel out of the bathroom, Praxie slumped into her lift, fainting. I called 911. They came in with the gurney. The challenge was how to get her wheeled out of the tight spaces, up a short flight of stairs, and out to the ambulance. The rescue squad/EMS was called, and four EMS resorted to carrying her out in her wheelchair. I resolved that all necessary ADA improvements would have to be my priority. She could not be a fire or medically trapped person in her home.

I did not sleep well upstairs. Praxie would make a lot of progress, and gradually, I began to sleep in my own bed and coming down only if she called at night for assistance. She also began to feel more independent in her state and did not worry anyone unless necessary for her ADL needs. Life was gradually normalizing. Praxie worked hard to bloom where she was planted.

The winds of the revolution had gathered enough steam. By 2018, no one knew if the Nera 10 were dead or alive, and the killings, refugees, and internally displaced persons (IDPs) were now being mentioned in some international circles. Magically, the number of deaths was fixed at three thousand and religiously reported by Human Rights Watch, International Crisis Group, and even UN's own statistics. I fought the urge to join in the resistance groups that were rapidly forming in the diaspora or those like the consortium, banned in Cameroon, but thriving elsewhere. I had my own internal war. Still, something in me wanted to lie low and keep my anonymity. I had heard stories from my mom that my dad's career was sidelined during the Ahidjo regime for embracing a Kwame Nkrumah ideology for a united socialist Africa free from colonial rule and fully in control of its political, social, military, and economic destinies. He was against neocolonialism, which was rapidly taking hold of the continent, even if colonizers preached independence of their territories. My dad was against the so-called reunification. My brother, too, had begun working with Fon Gorji Dinka in the '80s, serving as his chief of staff. In 1994, when President Biya changed the name of the country from the United Republic of Cameroon to LRC, the lawyer Fon Gorji Dinka and a few others concluded that this action was the final act of the French to attempt annexation, except for the Fon, French Cameroun had seceded from the union. Like Dinka, my brother had become persona non grata in Cameroon, and both were on Biya's list for extermination.

I feared participating in the fight against the injustices of Biya's regime, and now, I feared getting involved in the war that can only increase Biya's scrutiny of my family. I worried about that. I felt a great deal of internal conflict. Everything within me screamed out to stand up, be counted, or speak up against the genocidal war going on that directly affects me. My own family died because of the war, others jailed for peacefully protesting. My sister and husband were kidnapped by Amba Boys. Like many of citizens of NOSO, the subject for extortion. In Alabukam, my village just outside Bamenda town, several of my families fled as their homes were set ablaze. One cousin, homeless, sought refuge in Douala.

Every time I watched another young man being killed by Biya's BIR or learned of another young girl raped, a sudden flash of anger descended on me, and I was ready to speak up against such crimes and human rights violations. I would remind myself that I had more pressing concerns about my daughter's health to get involved. Perhaps God wanted it this way. I must stay here in this valley and listen to what all this meant. It was a difficult silence, one I would ultimately break.

Keep Quiet and Keep Your Head Low: Social Killings of Women and Others We Don't Like

While the war raged at home and the death toll rose, Cameroonians who had fled the stifling education and economic stagnation and harsh political climate to Europe, Great Britain, and the Americas, created another war front, the battlefield of social media. My fears about stepping into the diaspora war was well founded. One wrong statement or association could mean an edict to kill placed on your head or your family at home. I loved my largely anonymous role.

Over the years, I had cultivated several relationships outside the Cameroonian community to call on them quietly and speak to them about the war. My contacts at various embassies and missions meant I could reach some country leaders and plead our case. During the last elections, in one African country, I found myself at the high table in the party fundraising gala, and to my right was the president's public relations officer. He would be traveling in two days with the president back home. Here was my chance. I sang like a canary of the dangers for my people if other African countries did not intervene to stop Biya's war on Southern Cameroons. Could he arrange for me to meet with the president? That would not be possible, but the gentleman had heard an earful and wanted to help. He assured me he would speak to the boss. He advised that if I was part of a group, I should write to the president with a short background of the crisis and state the request. He promised to personally deliver it to him if an appointment could not be secured.

I had just, on Sunday, after the Saturday gala, reached out to my brother. Edwin was part of Gorji Dinka's RoA; I insisted that he write to the president about our plight, and I would make sure he got it. Long before the word *Ambazonia* was associated with a struggle for liberation from French Cameroun, Edwin fought as early as 1990 to make it mainstream. It was not taboo for what was conjured for Biya but outright rejected by our own as something foreign. Edwin served as the delegate general for North America and personal assistant to Fon Gorji Dinka, the first self-declared president of the RoA. Like most English-speaking Cameroonians, the country held little educational and economic prospects. There was little appetite in many to go to the French university to be lectured by unmotivated instructors and even less desire to live in squalor shanty rooms subsisting on less than a dollar per day, only to eventually spectacularly fail and give up. Or pass, graduate, and be jobless. Grades were bought and sold. It was the pervasion of education. For the NOSO student, an aberration. Many diehards persisted. A few bucked the system, embedded, succeeded or went elsewhere in search of greener pastures or form an anemic business middle class.

Edwin wrote the letter, and I quickly dispatched it by email to my contact. He came back with a few diplomatic suggestions, and we hurriedly tempered the language in the letter and resent it. Two days later, I received a call from the PRO. The letter was handed to the president, and while in flight, he read it. He asked a few questions but made no commitment. I was told if I could travel to the country, he would ensure that I had an audience with the president: a gamble. Again, I planned another African trip, this time with no appointment, just my contacts with the PRO and the now national communications director for the president. I had also come to understand through my interactions with others from the country that, unlike Cameroonians, they were not too big on formalities.

Their leaders did not hold themselves apart from their constituencies. Access, it appeared, was not so difficult as it was in Cameroon's political circles. I could believe that, if I was in the country, it would be indeed possible to secure an audience with the president to make our case. After all, I had just been given an honorary membership in his ruling party for my support in the diaspora.

The month I planned to take off work to travel, my contact called me to tell me a deadly mudslide just occurred. More than four hundred people were believed dead and buried under the mudslide and thousands internally displaced, their homes destroyed, or their neighborhoods deemed too unstable for habitation. He had lost some members of his family in the disaster. The entire country was in mourning, and humanitarian aid was sought to assist the survivors. My plans to travel now did not make sense. It could still be possible to travel, provided my trip was turned to a humanitarian visit from the United States. I actually contemplated heading a fundraiser. But how would I raise funds for victims in a country when my own community and several others at home were in dire need? In a few months, there would be presidential elections. On account of the mudslide and the threat of Ebola, elections were postponed for one year. I abandoned traveling until later.

The president lost the elections, ushering a new party into power. My contact in high places was no longer as influential. That was the sad case in Africa. A statesman at the pinnacle of political power, once out, began fighting to stay on as the flag bearer of his party. That focus meant there was little time to be a statesman whose office could be summoned for positive good in times of crisis on the continent. My once powerful friends who could help us were now, in the African sense, nobodies and fighting for their own survival. One friend who lived in the plush Potomac district, who was chauffeur driven, and whose children went to the best schools told me of the challenge in getting the incoming administration to give them enough time to vacate their diplomatic premises or even to find alternative places. It was the most brutal, rude, and discourteous transition I ever watched. The wife spent a busy two weeks packing up their lives and, at the drop of a dime, looking for an apartment to move into as they did not wish to return home all at once. The husband, as the diplomat, had to return.

My quiet efforts would pay off. I had introduced my brother to my contacts. He was more flexible and accepted their invitation to travel. My contact, Mr. Sesay, was true to his words and arranged for him to meet with the now ex-president. He arranged for a media interview, TV appearance, and a seminar on the war in Southern Cameroons to educate the population. It was broadcast nationwide. It was a small contribution given how little was known in Africa about our struggle, and those who claimed to know cited problems of marginalization and cultural and linguistic differences as the reasons for the war. The whitewashing was widespread.

Pressed Into Service

I lived inside Praxie's world for more than two years. The call came from a good family friend asking me if he had my permission to submit my name to the Sisiku Ayuk Tabe government, the president of Southern Cameroons, Ambazonia, a self-declared state of the UN-created Federal Republic of Cameroon. I simply asked, "Why me?" The answer was they needed a female. It would not be the last time I hear that as a reason. The truth was I considered it but was worried about such a role and the window dressing.

Again, I had a life, a daughter to care for, and my work. This was an opportunity to finally contribute to the war effort, and more so, in a role that could possibly bring out a rapid end to the war. At the same time, I was being asked to join Sisiku's government in exile. I had decided that I could no longer just sit by Praxie's side when I had read almost all the WhatsApp posting, followed eyewitness war accounts that made their social media rounds, and was thoroughly vexed.

I held a conversation. "I want to do something," I told her. "I can't just sit and watch this war from afar."

"Mommy, I will be okay. Do what you need to do."

I would go to Nigeria, visit the refugees, assess their needs, and once back home, work with any organization to bring assistance to those people. I asked around, and I learned of a local Nigerian NGO working directly with the refugees. I got hold of Pastor Eric and introduced myself. I shared with him my objectives. We struck up a relationship, and he kept me informed of what was happening with the refugees. I was even more convinced that my decision to travel to Nigeria was a good one and consistent with what I hoped to contribute to the revolution: human-to-human help.

I would do this initially by myself. But I would solicit help from only very close friends to make the trip possible and to bring along some aid with me, either in cash or in material. My GoFundMe fundraiser raised a paltry $800, $300 of which came from my dear sister, Eve. I also reached out and made contact with Sisiku's secretary general, Tassang. I told him of my plans, and he, too, was excited to meet me and at the chance of working together to assist the refugees. I told him I would let him know of my travel dates.

I fished out my passport and filled the online visa application for Nigeria. I saved it but never submitted it. I wanted to check on flights and get a good idea about when I would travel. Early the following week, I received a call from Sisiku. I was surprised. He said he had heard good things about me, and he hoped we could work together to free our homeland. His chief of staff had contacted me and included me in a strategic group to work with foreign interest groups to sell the Ambazonia revolutionary partnership. For their support, in concrete terms, a free Ambazonia would be a great partner for them. Our revolution was in dire need for money to fund its activities. We were endowed with resources, and Sisiku was ready to leverage them in the quest for freedom. If that meant brokering deals in exchange for future concessions in our resource-rich land, he was shopping. Though having never met the man, I was not entirely surprised he asked that I be contacted and connected to him. "He is certainly acting all presidential," I told myself.

I had received a phone call stating that the president wanted to speak with me. Would I be available for the call at around five o'clock after his meeting? At the end of our phone call, I mentioned to Sisiku that I had planned on visiting the refugees in Nigeria, and my trip was likely coming up soon. I just needed to submit my passport in for a visa. In fact, the passport lay by my nightstand as a reminder. Sisiku sounded pleased. He gave a second number and told me to use it to contact him immediately upon arriving in Nigeria, so we met for further discussions. For his part, he added, he had just received a particularly important an urgent call and would be cutting his stay short to return immediately to Abuja, Nigeria for a critical meeting. It would be just days from that conversation that the world would learn that Cameroon's notorious territorial minister accompanied by special forces military from

Yaoundé had flown into Nigeria. With the help of Nigeria's secret service and military, Sisiku Ayuk Tabe and nine members of his cabinet meeting in the Nera Hotel in Abuja had been arrested at gunpoint, blindfolded, thrown into a military jet, and flown to the dreaded military prison SED in Yaoundé. For the next eight months, Southern Cameroonians had no proof of life from what would be known as the Nera 10 abduction. It would take cries from human rights groups and unrelenting legal pressures from lawyers from Nigeria and the firebrand lawyer for the detainees, Barrister Fru John Soh to make the government bend. Eight months into their captivity, Barrister Soh was allowed access to meet with the Nera 10.

The following week, the news came as a thunderous shock throughout the diaspora. Sisiku and nine top aides meeting in the Nera Hotel in Abuja had been arrested, and no one knew where they were. That would be the news for nearly eight months. I looked at the passport lying on my bed stand and, in a moment, wondered what had held me back from submitting my visa application. I should have been in Lagos by now and likely Abuja, too, for a possible rendezvous with Sisiku. I could have met up with Sisiku by now. I certainly would have met up with Pastor Eric by now. There was something that held me back and slowed down my actions. I did not know that I would have been cajoled into meeting up with Sisiku's team, caught up in the dragnet, and be arrested, too. It was not too far-fetched that there was a small chance that I, too, could be languishing in Kondengui. The thought raised the hair on the back of my neck. Like the outspoken Cameroonian American Dr. Patrice Nganang—who was arrested by Biya's thugs, thrown in jail for criticizing the government, and released months later—the American Embassy would have vigorously protested my arrest, let alone for Nigeria to have allowed a refoulement, which would have been a diplomatic faux pas.

That day, I announced to my family and to those who had contributed that I had canceled my trip to Nigeria, as it was no longer safe to do so. Pastor Eric assured me that he had secured access to the refugees from the UN and that, for the most part, we would travel with their teams to visit the camps. That did little to assuage my fears. I told him I would have to postpone for another time.

But clearly, I could no longer hide under my cloak of anonymity for fear of being singled out for abduction, persecution by a ruthless regime, or derision from fellow Ambazonians. But still, I was at a loss about how to make something happen that settled my restless soul about the war 7,500 miles away in my hometown and all the villages in Biya's NOSO regions. Every possible action seemed frustratingly inadequate against the onslaught by the BIR.

I received another call from a family friend asking me if I could serve as a moderator for the All Southern Cameroons People's Congress (ASCPC) coming up. Again, that little voice told me, *No. Stay out and stay low. You do not need to put yourself out there like that.* He said I was the only nonpartisan and noncontroversial participant who could be the face of this meeting that the leaders, some of the armed groups fighting the BIR, now with daggers drawn, would support. In the end I accepted. If it meant bringing together all the factious leaders under one roof at the chance of collaborating to fight a common enemy, LRC, I would do it. On March 31, 2019, I moderated the ASCPC, whose brainchild was the now infamous Dr. Fontem. You have to realize that all leaders of this revolution, sooner or later, became infamous. You just must see it from a particular vantage point or be of a particular ideology.

At the conclusion was the formation of the now-defunct Southern Cameroons Liberation Council (SCLC), joining all the frontline leaders under one umbrella to speak on behalf of the Ambazonian people. They needed to speak to the world with one voice and one purpose and have one strategic direction. The SCLC would not get off the ground when the accusations and counteraccusations began. It would turn out that one key resolution of the ASCPC on negotiations without conditions for a separate nation had been conveniently—or inconveniently—deleted before widely publicizing the document. Before this leadership team could get going, bad blood ran through its veins. The finger pointed to Dr. Fontem.

I was approached by the State Department at the end of the first day. "I would like to meet with you sometime soon if you can find the time. Here is my card." I nodded in affirmation, looking down at the card, and made a mental note that it read "Cameroon Desk, State Department."

"Okay," I told myself, "so the United States is watching all this? Who else is in the room?" At the afternoon session, I looked more closely at one of the only two White people in the conference room. One of them was the White lady who had approached me during the break. Who were the others? I looked on with renewed interest. FBI? CIA? NSA? Of course, they would not be so obvious, right? They would look like us and blend in perfectly if they, in fact, came to the conference.

I purposely sat down next to him when I relinquished the podium to the next speaker. It was the Cameroonian next to him who reached out and handed me his card. "I am Otto. Nice to meet you." I smiled. The White guy also promptly handed me a card, smiling. "We came in from the UK. Great work there moderating." I thanked them both and stuffed the cards into my dress pocket.

I have this little thing where I insist that at least one piece of garment I wear during a conference must have a pocket. Great for my tissue when I break a sweat, phone, credit card, and license and came in handy for business cards and the occasional paper and pen to jot down my thoughts or capture notes. I hated to drag my Louis Vuittons—pun intended—around, only to give it its own seat or to place it on the ground. It would turn out that Mr. Otto would later be present in Geneva and later join the anti-SLP campaign. I would also learn that he was the grandson of Endeley and that his NGO had campaigned to lead the mediation effort when it was not possible to mediate alongside the European Institute for Peace (EIP) or be with the Swiss. It was rumored that the gentleman embellished a few things on his way to impress the Swiss to include him or his organization into the fold.

It was after my coming out party that I began to receive messages from numbers around the world I did not recognize. "We are dying in Kupe." "Doctor, we need your help." "You should fund our group; all we need is money to buy 'groundnuts and popcorn.'"

Another texted me on WhatsApp, "Hello, Doctor, my name is [he gave a pseudonym]. I am the commander here in Kupe. I will like to work with you on, Ground Zero, GZ. We need women because we can trust them. Right now, we cannot trust the men in the diaspora. Our hopes are pinned on you."

I feared that if I didn't respond, I might anger him. So, I politely told him I applaud the work and sacrifice he was doing. I pleaded that I didn't know him, and so I must decline. If he was genuine, I would do all I can to make sure the leaders do the right thing and support them. My role, if any, would be mainly diplomatic. It was outside my ability to engage with fighters.

When I got the call to join one of the frontline leaders on VOA, I was told it would be Rene Sadi, Biya's communication minister. I was prepared to take him on with everything I got. It would be my first live worldwide TV appearance. Though nervous, I made sure my game face was on. At the last moment, while we were in the green room, we were told the minister was unavoidably absent and that the ex-minister Elvis Ngole would be on instead. In a way, I was relieved. Yaoundé had clearly made a determination that I or my co-panelists were not consequential enough and sent their CPDM party chief instead, another NOSO son of the soil, to carry water for the regime.

Shaka Ssali, the host of *Straight Talk Africa*, gave the opening discussions to Ex-Minister Ngole. In his seven minutes, he lavished praises on his slave master, Mr. Biya, on the development he had made in his country on the implementation of the resolutions of the GND. He took pride in giving special status to Biya's NOSO. Cameroon was in a state of emergency, he crowed, and the world would soon bear witness. I would watch the program later; I smiled because as the minister poured profuse songs of praise of King Biya, the images that filled the screen were that of death, destruction, and an overall dilapidated country at the hand of his master. The audience must have wondered what lies were being told—shameless and baseless—by the speaker.

Shaka Ssali turned to me and asked if what the minister had just stated—GND implementation, particularly the law that had just passed granting special status to Biya's NOSO—were, indeed, good measures to bring the Anglophone crisis to an end. An avalanche can be triggered by a man's breath. A mountain spewing cataclysmic ash high into the sky begins with a tiny crack deep in its belly. My emotions boiled inside and threatened to erupt. In the coolest but firmest voice, I told the world how the construct called LRC was a contradiction of itself, a nation that cannot tell its authentic self from its make-believe form, one whose demons now plagued it for refusing the truth.

"My brother," I continued, "this history of convenience—simply a whitewashed history—can only go so far. There is not a country that is yours to believe that it is one and indivisible." I added, "as the evidence of gross human rights violations piles, Mr. Biya conceives solutions or pretends to solve them, all the while convincing the world that this is an internal crisis in his NOSO regions, minority grievances over marginalization."

I reminded the minister that la République's GND was designed for Mr. Biya to talk among his CPDM bigwigs on things that had nothing to do with the root causes of the war in Southern Cameroons that he declared in 2017. No bilingualism, diaspora integration, disarmament, judicial or educational reforms, decentralization, or cultural commission recommendations touched on the question of Southern Cameroons' statehood or equality and equity in the construct called Cameroon. He dropped off the program and could not be reconnected. That left me and my co-panelists more time to educate the world about our struggle.

CHAPTER 10:

ACTIVISM INTO MOBILIZATION AND DIPLOMACY

Where is our Roosevelt to Stand Up As One Man?
—1716, Movie

For the UN, Talk Is Cheap

I watched the dysfunction with the ACT and felt helpless. It was now clear that, as a team, there were power tussles, disrespect, and despair, mainly. If it was not my way, it would certainly be the highway. Supporters fell in line to support whatever their group member on the team said or did—no breaking ranks permitted. Within the ACT, it was loyalty first to the frontline group leader or group ideology and then, if expedient, to the ACT.

I watched one member sparing no effort in planning, appearing, and discussing with and on any media platforms that would invite him. I watched another group run a flawless TV platform that sometimes gathered five thousand online views, no small feat for running on a shoestring. One group carved its niche in the magazine and podcast business. Another on pure propaganda for dominance. Their weekly two-hour podcast broadcast on YouTube, SoundCloud, and their own website became a favorite for a cross section of Ambazonians and roundly applauded as a good journalistic piece. After all, its producer himself a career journalist. I looked forward to appearing on the other members' media platform on Zoom that took a less political twist on discussions.

Meanwhile, when these same personalities got together under the banner of the ACT, instead of shedding "party" affiliation and working together, they bickered ad nauseam. I felt helpless, and my voice was drowned in the testosterone-filled space. When I was not told to shut up, I was bullied to stop lecturing when I tried to call on reason and to debate issues, not personalities.

And so, in December, just after the UNSC meeting on the sixth, I created a favorability chart showing the statements and suggestions for a letter to a UNSC member. For all the top talents on the ACT, writing a one-page press statement or a letter invariably ended up in personal attacks, followed by resignations and more apathy. One member in a country with a twelve-hour difference had custody of the letterhead. When news broke and the ACT wanted to follow with a press statement, the top journalist in the ACT, who did not collaborate with another top journalist, crafted the statement. If anyone else crafted a statement, it gathered no traction, and if it did, it was scrapped in favor of one point of view. When the draft letter I suggested was revised and a new version was adopted by the ACT members, it languished and never was sent out to the UNSC members, even to those who had issued strong statements condemning Biya for failing to engage in the SLP.

Frustrated, I drafted another letter and appended my signature for each of the UNSC members. I was a stakeholder and victim. I was a NOSO. The war, by now, was a certifiable genocide coming from Dr. Gregory Stanton, Founder and President of Genocide Watch. The world was passive or duplicitous in condemnation or looking the other way as the number of the people killed in my village and others piled up. Young women fled into the Francophone cites and sold their bodies for a meal. Young men escaped Biya's BIR into the bushes and, at the first chance, ambushed the BIR so they can, in turn, point their AK-47s on the next contingent of military that dared to come back into their villages. Others simply fled into neighboring Nigeria into the highland areas of Cross River State, some returning back to the hot areas with weapons. Many took to South America and risked their lives crossing the Darian Gap: a death trap by all measures for asylum in America.

I did not expect to hear back from any one UNSC member after sending off my letters. But I heard back from Germany and incoming member state and Tunisia. They asked me to come in for a meeting. I would hear back from Russia, too. They were happy to hear what I had to say and what they can do. Some of my colleagues in the ACT politely excused themselves from accompanying me to New York to meet with Ambassador Shulz of Germany and Riad Ben Saliman of Tunisia. Frustrated, I called on my old friend, and we drove up at the crack of dawn to be in time for our ten o'clock meeting at the Tunisia Embassy.

To my dismay, HE Ben Saliman either knew little of what was going on in Cameroon or let on very little. He was sympathetic, though encouraging. Being an incoming UNSC member, he let me know there was little he could do unless at least nine or fifteen member states on the Security Council agreed to let an agenda item on Cameroon be tabled. He noted, to no surprise, that France would have to agree, even if the other nine members introduced an agenda on the war in Cameroon. The coffee was too strong, the conversation with the ambassador too light and friendly, that I grew weary trying desperately to call his attention to the growing number of people killed and displaced by the war. As a consolation, the gentleman placed his dainty teacup down and said, "I don't like the word *annexation*. Is Cameroon not exercising full control of its territory? Is separation the goal?"

I swallowed and recounted how, just this year, a new nation was on the brink of being born. "Bougainville," I reminded the diplomat, "signed a comprehensive peace agreement with Papua

New Guinea that had just expired, and the people of Bougainville just voted for an independent nation. Ours is a question far greater and more consequential than Bougainville, as LRC's borders were sealed at the date of their independence in 1960 and did not include the autonomous state of Southern Cameroons. We are seeking to redress a historical wrong where another African state, in clear violation, has annexed another in clear complicity with France and other interest partners." He concluded the meeting, promising me he would make quiet inquiries. He apologized that he did not know that the situation had gotten so bad. But he warned me not to keep my hopes up, as it was near herculean to get nine of the fifteen member states to agree on the issue of Cameroon and that I should not forget the power the permanent member state France played. I nodded, sad but not dejected. I still had the great nation of Germany to talk to. Hope sprung eternal.

My next meeting was delayed. The call from the ambassador's special assistant had come in while I was meeting with HE Ben Saliman, and I let the call go to my voice mail. Ambassador Shulz was delayed and can only meet me after two o'clock. What to do with all the time on a cold, freezing Manhattan Monday? Dr. Enongene and I walked to the German Embassy and planted ourselves in the lobby for some warmth. We would spend the next two hours each on our phones, on calls, surfing various social media sites, and occasionally, speaking to each other. I think we both recognized but did not openly admit that our first meeting with Tunisia, an African country, was less than sympathetic to our cause and that we were destined for the same in our next meeting with the German. I allowed only hopeful thoughts to come into my errant mind, pushing away any negativity. I had listened to the more than two-and-a-half hours of the UNSC meeting on Central Africa, during which more than 60 percent of the discussions had centered on the war in Cameroon, and I was hopeful.

HE Juergen Schulz had come out to not only condemn the fighting but also note that, despite Biya's GND, the situation had not yet improved. He had spoken the words I wished to hear, which was "We welcome the SLP by Switzerland." Was it Germany's Security Council mission to prevent conflict and uphold human rights and self-determination rights to freely choose sovereignty and determine one's statehood not consistent with the Ambazonian quest to restore its own sovereignty stolen through a failed decolonization process and through neocolonialism by French Cameroun and France? I was certain and confident in my diplomacy that Germany, having taken a stance in the Middle East to uphold the Jewish state's right to exist and to work with the conflict parties for the negotiated two-state solution, was the right partner for Ambazonians.

And so, I wrote a two-page brief and emailed it in advance of our scheduled January 13 meeting. The twenty-year-old-looking German lady, Theresa, was brought in and introduced as the expert for Africa at the embassy. I shook her hand and wondered how our destinies were in the hands of people and their policies.

"My ambassador," I began, "thank you for meeting with me and my colleague here." I looked up and noted that he appeared engaged, or was he just being polite? I opted for engaged and kept my upbeat and serious Emma tone, true to form. I began by thanking him for taking the strong and pragmatic position during the December 6, 2019, UNSC briefing calling on both the Republic of Cameroon and the separatist groups to fully engage in the Swiss-led peace initiative to comprehensively address the root causes of the conflict to find lasting solutions.

"What brings me here," I pressed on, "is the pressing need for the world to call for a cease-fire and to provide humanitarian assistance and protection to the growing crisis in Cameroon, now described as 'Rwanda in slow motion.'"

Without taking a breath, I reminded the German in front of me, "Germany and the people of Southern Cameroons shared a historical past that set the path that we find ourselves in today, and the international institutions that you now hold a seat in and the laws and policies you enact and uphold bind us in a common humanity, ensuring that injustice anywhere is redressed. I am here for the injustice that is unfolding in my homeland."

"For this," I added, "Germany is a natural partner for people of Southern Cameroons, who share the same principled pragmatism toward peace. And as such, Germany must use its considerable strength and voice on the global stage to bring a permanent, lasting solution to the war in Cameroon, a war that has only intensified in the last year and shows no signs of ending, a war that has left untold death and destruction in Southern Cameroons."

I am reminded of Amb. Christoph Heusgen's statement that "in the long run, we [Germany] can only overcome crises if we address their causes," in response to Germany's soft agenda focused on peace, justice, climate change, and partnership. Addressing the root causes to find solutions to a crisis in the world is strength. War-mongering is bound to fail.

The UN is giant talking and policy-making machine slow to take concrete action, slow to condemn members of its boys' club, and often more reactionary than preemptive in its dealings. They too often meet to take stock and quickly pass new international conventions that do not hold water. Going back in recent memory to the Helsinki Declaration, to the responsibility to protect, and to the "never again campaign," this body just seems incapable of being preemptive—totally inert, bloated, and dogged by special interests and complex geopolitical war games.

There had been no shortage of experts on the world stage warning that the war declared by Mr. Biya was "Rwanda-style genocide in slow motion," yet when the special representative and head of the United Nations Regional Office for Central Africa François L. Fall gave the opening remarks at the UNSC December 6, 2019, meeting, he lavished praise and support for President Biya on the situation in Cameroon for convening the largely failed the GND. As the highest-ranking UN member on Central Africa, Mr. Fall failed to acknowledge what President Biya already admitted to during the Paris conference, refusal to engage in the Swiss-led peace process, nor did he make mention of the root causes of the crisis. At this point, it had already been widely reported not only in Cameroon but also internationally that Biya's GND had failed in providing solutions and that they fully supported and called for third-party negotiations under the Swiss-led process. If not in a boys-only club, how can the unfolding genocide, dialogue among Biya's ruling party, or refusal to dialogue with the armed separatists be areas for praise at the highest levels of diplomacy, if not for the truism that nation-states do not have friends, just interests? It did not matter that, on June 2019, the NRC described the war in Ambazonia as "the world's most neglected displacement crisis," noting that, again, the international community had fallen asleep at the wheel when it came to preventing and stopping another Rwanda-style genocide in Africa.

By now, I could recite the heart-wrenching statistics in rapid succession:

- At the time of writing, more than ten thousand reported deaths since the start of hostilities

- Nearly million people displaced, the sixth largest population of displaced persons in the world

- More than four hundred villages burned to the ground

- Two million people in Southern Cameroons in immediate need for food, shelter, and security

- Eight out of ten school-age children in the affected region out of school

- Forty percent of health care facilities not functioning

- With an estimated two thousand in jails throughout the country, I reminded the ambassador that, on December 12, 2019, nine U.S. representatives wrote a letter to Mr. Biya noting that the vast majority of horrific acts of violence were committed by Cameroon's military and advising him that military action would not resolve the conflict. They again called for negotiations under the Swiss-led process. Failing that, the United States would consider further sanctions against Cameroon

And I tearfully pointed out that, on December 30, 2019, on Cameroon's Equinox TV program, the minister of territorial administration for Cameroon, Mr. Paul Atanga Nji, announced that "there is no humanitarian crisis in Cameroon" and that "the situation of the internally displaced is perfectly under control." Mr. Atanga Nji added that there were only 152,000 IDPs, of which 160,000 had received aid from his administration, a clear contradictory statement of his own fake statistics. As if his statements were not outlandish enough, the minister went on further to warn the UN's and its partner organizations' request for humanitarian assistance and funding as criminal enterprises were seeking to profit from the crisis in his country, who should cease "crying more than the bereaved." It was the whitewashing of crimes against humanity by the government.

On December 31, 2019, in his New Year's address to the nation, President Biya reiterated his resolve to continue with the war. And for good measure, the separatists announced a total lockdown of the territory beginning February 7, 2020, to ensure no election took place in the Anglophone areas. In response, on January 7, 2020, President Biya deployed thousands of additional troops to several towns and villages in Southern Cameroons to "protect" the citizens during the upcoming municipal elections on February 9, 2020. This can only mean further bloodshed on both sides, with civilians caught in the middle and an even greater humanitarian crisis.

"If the past is prologue," I concluded, "Germany should stand as a friend on our side. After all, I noted, in 2003, you brought the genocide in Darfur to the Security Council and subsequently moved the case to the ICC. Germany took a stance in the Middle East, holding historical responsibility for both parties to the conflict rights as freely expressed."

As a last-ditch plea, I looked at Mr. Shulz in his eye and said, "The question of an unresolved historical wrong, where the third option for outright independence for the former BSC as envisioned when UNGA no. 1608 was passed, will forever threaten the peace in this part of sub-Saharan Africa. As I mentioned, for every separatist fighter that President Biya's army kills, another will stand up to take his or her place. In this cycle of violence, our collective humanity is threatened in many ways, least of which is the full radicalization of the youths straight into the stronghold of the ISIS of West Africa's rank, further destabilizing sub-Sahara and the Gulf of Guinea. It is my hope and prayer that in looking up to Germany, through this outreach and appeal, the people of Southern Cameroons would soon find a true friend.

Germany's support for a UNSC agenda to end the war is a great first step. Germany's support to establish a commission to evaluate the crimes against humanity at the ICC is another great step.

Germany's support for protective humanitarian support is existential to the beleaguered people of Southern Cameroons." I concluded by saying that I was there not as part of any organized group. "But for the record, I want to end by noting that I joined the Swiss-led process as one of the only two women participants to date as an independent voice constituted as Ambazonian Coalition Team." And then I exhaled.

Like the Tunisian ambassador, I was treated with the utmost courtesy and dismissed with just the slightest of encouragement. Mr. Shulz said mildly, "Dr. Osong, I understand all that you are saying, and I sympathize greatly. My country is closely following the events in your country."

At this point, I wanted to correct him by stating, "Which country?" But decorum suggested that I had said my piece, that this was the signal our meeting had neared its end.

"Dr. Osong, all AU members are reluctant to bring up the concerns you have raised. We do not have the necessary majority to place Cameroon on the UNSC agenda. We have committed to support the SLP and hope that we can get to a peaceful settlement and a return to peace." What I heard was just the last sentence, and how I heard it was "peace within the construct of LRC." Call me naive in diplomatic machinations.

My fights ahead were many. I would return to Washington wondering how one could turn a country to see that their interests could be preserved or even made better within a free and sovereign Ambazonia endowed with all forms of natural resources. I did not have the answers. But I knew this not rocket science nor brain surgery.

Going It Alone

By the fourth year of the war in Ambazonia, it became increasingly obvious that we must court allies and chart our own path to Buea. The usual appeals to reason, lobbying from the U.S. Congress and the UN to national capitals, had done well to raise awareness that something bad was going on in that part of Gulf of Guinea. Many people appeared completely out of their league on the knowledge about this part. Or many wrongly said they had heard about the marginalization of English people in Cameroon and sympathized with us. This latter category of people annoyed me the most. It was better for me to learn they had no freaking idea what was going on in Cameroon, and for this, I can take my time and educate them on the pernicious annexationist actions perpetuated on us. But for those who instinctively sympathized for our marginalization and pledged they, too, would join in the campaign, I was infuriated because they did more harm than good to us. There is no country in the world without a minority population who decries one form of marginalization or another. For that, our problem was situated squarely as an internal problem, for which any one of Mr. Biya's creative solutions would do.

Nigeria, the dominant regional actor, had its own secessionist movement. It had played the role of allowing for the refoulement of the Nera 10. Some have said Nigeria actively participated because an illegal government sought refuge within its borders with a friendly nation. How did they support us and not give aid and comfort to their own troubles to flare up? The United States had taken a few practical and concrete actions to signal to Yaoundé its displeasure with Mr. Biya and had written through its Congress several stern letters calling for an end to the violence and for the regime to engage fully in the SLP. LRC knew that the removal from AGOA and the reduction of military aid to fight against Boko Haram were just opening acts of the type of international pressure it stood to get.

The United States had not gone far enough, as it turned inward under a nationalist president: Trump, focusing mainly on domestic issues—issues that aligned with its security and trade concerns. Cameroon was a far cry from their minds.

As for China, the resource-rich Africa in miniature was too lucrative. As they salivated about what next to gobble up and haul back in the form of our resources, China was busy buying up everything it can and burying the country under unsustainable debt. LRC was an important trade partner, a great source for raw material, and a dumping place for manufactured goods. In international relations, Cameroon was all too important African states China needs in its corner when votes mattered.

Britain had talked a good game. They, like the UN and the United States, had held the obligatory "purging of conscience" parliamentary session—a catharsis of sorts to decry the atrocities they were now aware was going on. For good measure, theirs was an impassioned two-hour session, ending with a mixed bag of recommendations that no one took on to implement.

Successive speakers would stage their support in some form of dialogue, the SLP dialogue, and even the GND dialogue. They would declare that only some form of redress up to and including a close-knit federation could ever possibly work given the deep-rooted animosities between the French and the English. And others would note that the sovereignty of their former trust territory was botched, and they can undo the past, but they must deal with the realities, which are peace and security. Mme Theresa May, would obligatory accept mildly, concur slightly, and placate her members that the Great Britain was doing everything it can to ensure that the violence would end, that the territorial integrity of the country would be preserved, and that they would commit to its return to social integration and peace. This was the code phrase for "this is an internal matter, and we are actively monitoring events." Did the world not monitor events under Hitler, too?

As for the French, textbooks had been written about their complicity in the genocidal war going on in Ambazonia as elsewhere in Africa. In an interview granted to JDV TV, the new ambassador to LRC could not have been clearer. When asked how he believed the crisis in the NOSO would be resolved, he calmly noted the merits of the GND and lamented the lack of participation of hard-line secessionists. For him, if only they could have attended, all would be well today. Unfortunately, these hard-liners continued to attack LRC armed forces. He happily announced that, today, thanks to France's and LRC pacification efforts, the Southwest had returned to normalcy and that only the Northwest was a problem, which also would be calmed.

When asked if he was satisfied with Biya's response so far, the gentleman replied that they (France) were merely an observation. "France," he reminded the reporter, "had just one ambition, peace, and security, and we will do all we can to accompany LRC to achieve these objectives."

As for how far France would go to assist LRC in achieving these objectives and resolve the crisis in the NOSO, Mr. Guilhou replied, "France is staying out of the internal affairs of LRC. They have been told by LRC that they do not want any external party or mediator to interfere in the internal affairs of their country." To the Swiss, LRC told another story of interest to engage.

If there was one thing to say here, it was that France had been consistent. They practiced what their outrage representative Mr. Nadot called *chaise vide* during the December 2019 UNSC hearings on CAR. By staying out of their chairs, out of the chambers, they would not be on record to have said no to the SLP when nine out of the fifteen members strongly endorsed it.

Never Swissers

Never Swissers are the collective of groups, pundits, opinionated strongmen adamantly against any form of process by the Swiss. From the armed group, ADF, led by Dr. Cho Ayaba, to the Sisiku's IG wing and the women's groups that support him as their leader, support for a SLP can only come from persons or groups who are dishonest, imbeciles, shady, nincompoop.

Ever since the Swiss begged, cajoled, or egged on in complicity by Yaoundé for some of the armed groups to come together to form a coalition in preparation for talks with LRC, Ambazonians have remained divided on the issue. Some see nothing but the outsourcing of a peace process to the Swiss NGO, HD, as indication enough not to take it seriously. Ambazonians, in particular activists of the brand of Mark Bareta, Eric Tataw, Tapan Ivo, all complicit in the hyperfragmentation for pushing one conspiracy over another and for being the go-to information source for many, have found new careers and a large loyal following on social media to spin out every form of conspiracy about a shadowy, opaque process going on in Geneva.

On December 6, 2020, at 8,679th meeting of the UNSC, eight of the fifteen members states called for a cessation of hostilities and for both the government of President Biya and the separatists to fully engage in the Swiss-led process and dialogue without conditions. It should be noted that UNSC members stated that the GND had failed at providing solutions and that third-party negotiations should be pursued. For his part, the UN Regional Office for Central Africa special representative François Lounceny Fall, reporting on the situation in Cameroon, offered flourishing support for the efforts at peace by Biya for the recommendations from the GND he was already implementing. He did not acknowledge what President Biya himself already admitted to during the Paris conference a few months earlier on the Swiss-led Peace Process, nor any other root causes for the crisis. The international posturing was well underway, aimed at keeping the status quo.

Each international mention of the Swiss-led mediation breathed new life in the process and hope. Ambazonians preferred the hope, and some rejected the process, preferring to call it the Swiss-led negotiations. Each mention drew even more condemnation from within the Ambazonian ranks hell-bent on criticizing the process or leading the talking point that the Swiss process did not exist or was dead. Live Facebook shows with thousands tuned in were held to debunk its existence or to critique its weaknesses. Like with the divisions of Ambazonian leadership, the people were divided between love and hatred for all things Swiss. Adherent were derided and even threatened.

A few things remain indisputable, though, that has largely flown under the radar in the incessant chatter, noise, and threats from the hyperfragmented Ambazonian populace, activists, frontline groups, and surrogates. First, President Biya has categorically refused to end hostilities or to address the root causes of the crisis, showing his unwillingness to end the war. Any solution to stem the humanitarian crisis can only be temporary at best unless the international community steps in and compel Mr. Biya to dialogue with the separatists. That the Swiss-led process offered a modicum of hope and was slowly being swept aside in favor of strongmanism, outright military victory, make the "ground hot" agenda.

Next, it seems totally oblivious that a clear framework proposed by the international community is unanimous in their support for peace through third-party negotiations without conditions, addressing the root causes. But that is only in public statements. President Biya continues to hold the unrealistic belief that he can win a war against the separatists. For every Ambazonian commander killed on the ground, another takes his place, ensuring another long and needless war of untold suffering. This is an opportunity to push both sides to come to the table as, in fact, war can only guarantee losers. A swift negotiated settlement in the long run is best for all and for the region. It would be a half-hearted engagement for the armed groups, and a diplomatic cat-and-mouse game for LRC, neither outrightly refusing the SLP nor faithfully engaging in it.

The incessant chatter ignores to take stock that, while talking peace or delaying in fully embracing the only peace process available, President Biya continues to deploy its military into the villages, in hopes of breaking the separatists' resolve and gaining ground while doing so. And they killed thousands and displaced many more civilians, who took refuge in the bushes or across the Mungo, where often they become indentured. Sadly, while the strongest support for an independent Southern Cameroons comes from the diaspora, it seems to be hurling toward its destruction.

The impact of the conflict is disproportionately felt, contributing to problems of statistics, communications, coherence, and participation on the ground. Those in the French part, who do not see the carnage of the war, believe in palliative solutions. Mum on the SLP. Those whose lives have been irrevocably changed by the war, wanting lasting solutions. Though largely fragmented, the people of Southern Cameroons are tough and resilient and determined to carry on with the defense of their territory.

LRC believes it can win militarily. History is not on LRC's side. LRC believes this is an internal issue to be left for Biya. Whether it is today's Libya, The Democratic Republic Congo, South Africa, or Cote D'Ivoire, these conflicts were eventually resolved outside the country because both sides needed a trusted third party outside theater of war to resolve the crisis. The SLP offered this possibility. LRC and some Ambazonians take a different approach.

There needs to be genuine, credible, mediated third-party talks. SLP is critically important. It is a format where both sides have to sit down without predetermined outcomes. There are too many demands, and that is an obstacle. Negotiations is about finding solutions. Negotiations are in secret. How do we have justice if we are not talking? There are hard-liners who are working to make sure there is no negotiation. We need to call LRC's bluff. We are giving LRC an out as long as we call for negotiations with conditions.

"We need women's participation at the SLP," I was told by one of the frontline leaders who had met the Swiss when I received a call in early September 2019. "Your name has come up as someone we should bring into the process. I hope you will consider it. I need to know your response so I can give your name to the coordinator to begin preparations for travel to the next preparatory session in Geneva." The meeting was slated for September 19–23, 2019, in Geneva. I had less than two weeks to decide. Although I was afraid for myself and my family, at this point, while it lingered in the back of my mind, I knew I could not say no at the chance to push—at the international level—what I had been doing stateside, for a quick end to the war and at a chance to negotiate our freedom from the clutches of Cameroon and France.

I would come on to the SLP, provided I joined one of the three armed separatist groups or the other movements to show I had a constituent. This was not up for debate. I had asked for a meeting so that I could ask and understand what was going on in Geneva. We met at the Royal Farms Cafe, and I fired off the questions I had. "Who were the groups already committed? What other country is involved?"

Is this another ploy to trap us in a hotel and refoul us back to LRC to stand trial for sedition, state terrorism? How do I know I am safe? I thought but did not voice my greatest worry.

If I accepted like my brother, I would forever give up the chance to go back and visit my ancestral home to commune with my family, holiday, and bask in the sunbaked, dusty, potholed streets of Azire, as long as the regime was in place. I had read about and spoken to others who were arrested as they deplaned in Douala and taken into custody for questioning. If they carried an American passport, they were released and put on a flight back to America. If they were Cameroonians known to be active in the struggle, their fate was not obvious. If I accepted, I would have to live with that fact—a real fact—that I would never return to that part of the world I still called home. The thought saddened me. I agreed to go to Switzerland as an observer.

The call to service was stronger than my deepest fears of self-exile from all that my childhood held, my ancestral home. The call came just days after I gave my consent that I would participate and improve the gender balance of the SLP in Geneva. But what exactly was the balance sought? Fifty-fifty? I would only learn that upon arrival.

I arrived in Montreux, Switzerland, on the morning of September 20. There were others traveling, and we were all on the same flight. We met up with the taximan in the arrival hall. He was holding up placards with our names. There was Dr. Sako and his bodyguard, serving as the president after Sisiku Ayuk Tabe was kidnapped in Nera Hotel in Nigeria alongside nine others and sentenced to life for acts of terror against the state of Cameroon, were on the same flight. We arrived at the hotel Fairmont Le Montreux Palace in the late afternoon. I took a quick shower and was escorted to the underground conference room of the vast hotel to meet the rest of the attendees who had come in a day earlier.

There were three guards stationed outside the conference room. Sako had flown in with his own bodyguard. He wore a dark suit and tie and completed the look with dark sunshades. Now there were four guards just outside the double doors to the conference. One let you in and out of the room. One manned the large glass doors, which I later learned led up a steep flight of stairs to the road aboveground. The third stood at the end of the long, winding tunnel that led back to the base of the hotel some 1,500 feet underground. They all wore black suits and dark glasses. Like the guards at Saint Peter's Square in Rome, they stood immobile throughout the day, one moving only to open and close the door behind him as we entered and exit for personal breaks.

My initial fears grew. Was there really a chance that what had occurred in the Nera Hotel in Nigeria could again happen here? Did President Biya's tentacles go that far? *Yes*, the voice in my head replied. *Did you forget Geneva is Biya's second home?* My suspicions and fear wore off as the day wore on.

With the Swiss negotiation news making its round in the social media, an even fiercer battle between various frontline groups emerges, making internal coalescing even more difficult. Instead of constituting a team that will hurdle to forecast likely scenarios in what is potentially a historic negotiation between French Cameroun and English Cameroon, the groups put out even more videos, audios, and analyses of how funds were embezzled in an already balkanized environment that has, since March, seen their leader in prison fire his deputy and the entire bloated cabinet on social media replacing it with another. Both are acting interim president of the future state of Ambazonia—or the Federal RoA or the RoA, depending on which camp you find yourself in, for one seems to have no convincing reason for the other.

Were the Swiss a Neutral, Independent, Impartial Mediator?

I had heard enough on the Swiss-led peace process. We are not ready for negotiations. We must go in only from the position of strength, that is, we must win on the ground. We do not hold enough territory, we can't defend our demands, and we are fragmented and confused. We should be focused and fund GZ.

As for the Swiss, they are not to be trusted. Who is funding the Swiss, and why is an NGO the mediator? Some interesting comments are why these frontline movements are so eager to go talk to a White man but will not talk to their own brothers. For this later part, I am all for talking to one's brother and don't see the white-man relevance. Others decry the Swiss's lack of independence and neutrality because of their interest in LRC. At the same time that the Swiss announced they would mediate in the crisis, their government was actively competing for the management of the Douala Port in LRC. Glencore have been at the forefront in the buying and selling of oil concessions in the Rio del Rey. SLP detractors cite all these and conclude the Swiss are in the service of LRC as their ally. They are compromised and should never have been accepted as the mediator. There are other countries willing to mediate like Norway, Belgium, and the almighty USA, who have offered, but the Swiss are blocking them. The ACT members were too eager and jumped into accepting the first chance they got, and that was a sign of weakness for want to begin negotiations they cried.

The accusations could be overlooked. But how does one counter when the mediator is believed to have infiltrated your side to the extent of taking your ground commanders into foreign countries to persuade them to drop their arms and sign up for LRC's DDR program? The lines were now drawn. The depths of despair were growing. On one side, the cry was that, by staying away, we were essentially validating Biya's declaration that he had no one to negotiate with.

For fifty-eight years, no country stepped in to mediate between the Ambazonians and LRC. Now that one such process was in place, some claimed the refusal was like looking a gift horse in the mouth without having an alternative. This was irresponsible, and those pushing for the Swiss to step aside were tragically irresponsible and reckless. Were they really aware of the grave consequences of their actions to the people?

Those who claimed that some level of readiness on the war theater translated to strength on the negotiating table, though right, failed to understand that it is never too early to make peace—the time for peace is always now and not in the future to spare innocent lives. When LRC declared war on us, we were not ready. Our sons, daughters, and men fought with guns, machetes, and their bare hands, fending away LRC's deadly BIR. We weren't ready, yet we continued to fight till now. If we were not ready for war, we must be ready for peace.

And yes, one had to look only at Glencore to begin to hold a similar sentiment on trust and interests. In 2017 the president of Glencore's local taxes alone were so large that the city council had to be given advance notice to prepare to receive millions of dollars in tax revenue. The windfall was promptly used to lower the taxes for each person in the already affluent Swiss canton. As philanthropy is never far from the minds of the privileged whose wealth is gotten by the backs of Africans and the poor, the canton in Switzerland voted to take 2 percent of their windfall to support the poor children in Africa. I wonder how many of the residents of the canton knew that the Glencore president's wealth was gotten from the resources of Ambazonia in the Rio del Rey, Gulf of Guinea, and that none of the benefits of oil went to the impoverished children in Ndian or Bakassi. I wondered if, had they known this little fact, they would return all the money to those poor children and vote in their cantor against the exploitative practices of their country and of Glencore. Among all the accusations against the Swiss, the one I found hard to defend was their interests and how they may or may not influence their impartiality, neutrality, and independence. The Douala terminal was hotly contested by the Swiss Federation. Their chocolate industry is largely from the cocoa fields in Cameroon NOSO and West Africa. I could argue that countries do not have friends, just interests, and all countries in the world engage in bilateral relationships fueled by their interests. As for Switzerland being the second home of Mr. Biya, the proof is that, in 2019 after several days of protests in front of the InterContinental Hotel, where Biya was hold up for his usual sojourn, the Swiss parliament, exasperated, voted to consider him persona non grata. Their security resources were being strained, normal life was disrupted by this one president, and they were having nothing with it. For that, the Swiss showed that they can stand on their own without Mr. Biya.

As for other countries willing to mediate and for the Swiss refusing to engage in multi-mediation, I am less sympathetic. For their part, the Swiss have suggested that multi-party mediation often lends itself to forum shopping among members of the same side and creates unnecessary work and could be detrimental to the process. They are aware that, once the process gets underway, countries will send their special envoys or observers to the process, ensuring that it is fair and remains credible. I am willing to accept this explanation, although I, too, will prefer that one other country be part of the mediation team. Many are not privy to the fact that other NGOs who were interested in the process but were evaluated and ruled out by the initial set of frontline movements were those promoting the narrative of multi-party mediation. One consultant had aligned himself with a European mediator and was later found to have plagiarized himself was rejected.

Why were we here? While I didn't want to believe that my sex was singularly the reason, I sat in this room across from two other women, one who later quit in frustration just months after the meeting in Montreux, and ten men representing their groups and armed rebels in what was now dubbed "ground zero"—NOSO. They commanded rag-tagged armies against Biya's dreaded BIR. They wield machetes and dane guns, mostly. Conflict, left unattended, only matures. They bought arms or smuggled them for defense from ground one, Nigeria, into the country. They recorded videos to brag or for propaganda or to share their victories. They were both an elixir and the debasement of our collective humanity. The BIR created their own videos of terror, showing persons digging their graves at gun points and then cut-out to heaps of dead bodies. Either way, it was clear that it was still unsettling being there among all these men. I had waded into a testosterone-filled agenda—life and death, war and peace. They joked, but their language was deadly—literally. Whether the others knew it or not, admission was based on unconditional support for a free and independent Southern Cameroons, Ambazonia. Nothing would please me more.

I am not a *seconde classe*. I now understand my history. I am now a Cameroonian American because there is little chance for a girl like me with no Uncle Steeple in the French system to give me a lift. I want a free and independent Ambazonia for all the right historical and legal reasons. Why ask for less than your worth? I aim for the stars first. If I settle for the moon, it will not be because of lack of trying to be all that I can be or to get all that is due and coming to me. I prefer doing so peacefully. Biya prefers war. And now, I must fight for peace but a peace based on justice, not acquiescence, fear, appeasement, or patronage. If doing so means that I must liaise with those who have taken up arms, then I must fight even more to end the hostilities.

What I did not bargain for was that the SLP that gave hope in some quarters energized derision, divisiveness and sadly, instead, a reversal of any forward momentum toward peace. The massive, peaceful rallies were now mostly online vitriolic fights on our side. Add the Swiss to it. On ground zero, the body count climbed daily. The end was far from sight. We were a pariah for some, hope for others. No good deed goes unpunished.

The Swiss opened by telling us that the objective we must have was to build an Ambazonian platform for negotiations and that they brought us here to create the space for the various factions to speak to one another and collaborate as talks on talks were eminent. In fact, the Swiss said that this could happen as early as December 2019. My heart raced a little. I flushed and let the thought sink in. I wanted to run out and tell someone. Finally, we would get our chance to look Mr. Biya in the eye and tell him our terms of separation. And that, my friend, were the claims, as straightforward as they can get. "Mr. Biya, you never acquired us through conquest—in war, we entered into a confederation with your already independent nation. Your borders were fixed at the time of your independence and are inviolable. You left the federation through your government's illegal referendum of 1972 and your unilateral decree of 1984, reverting the name of the confederations from the United Republic of Cameroon back to LRC, as named in the 1960 independence." I would gleefully let Mr. Biya know that I hated to disappoint him. "Our problems are not rooted in linguistic differences. They are not a problem of being marginalized over your fifty-eight years of tyranny. Neither do we have a problem of lack of regional balance." I was hearing those statements; I fancied schooling Mr. Biya on causal effects and side effects. No illusion, though, that I would be in a room with Biya or his acolytes. Nonetheless, an exciting ideal. The Swiss warned that the risk we faced was for the world to grow tired and turn against us or begin to call us terrorists. Other groups were invited but had declined. Major activists had been invited, but one activist now in exile cited immigration concerns and grave fears that this, too, can be another ruse to bring the Ambazonian leadership in one place and arrest and ferry them back to LRC torture chambers at the SED. They feared that they, too, would suffer the fate Sisiku, and his Nera friends suffered.

Ah, I get it. Preparation for negotiations really means mediating to address the humanitarian crisis. The UN session at Montreux cited the deteriorating security and humanitarian concerns in Cameroon, and as the direct interlocutor for Antonio Guterres, they were here to tell us that since our armed groups on the ground also participated in causing the crisis, the leaders of those groups in the room must also propose solutions to end the crisis. I blinked and looked at the leader—authoritative, fending sympathy for our cause—and her message did not escape me. *So, how do I propose a solution to the war we are mainly defending ourselves from total annihilation? Is she asking that the armed groups should put down their weapons; declare a cease-fire; sign up for the demobilization, disarmament, and reintegration (DDR) camps; and ask Biya for pardon?*

I glanced around the room to see if there would be a response from the group leaders. None came. I lowered myself back into my chair, took a sip of my eau frizzante (carbonated water), and picked up a grape from the thoroughly warmed-up fruit platter that I had hurriedly grabbed and placed in front of me since seven o'clock. "We needed to move from activism to political mobilization," I heard from across the room. We heard situation reports from various international actors, both in the country and outside on the humanitarian situation and the political landscape. Next step was a structure for collaboration and preparation for participation in negotiations. We were told the latter was imminent. We needed to create a platform that can work to build up a negotiation team. Get it.

Deadly Sin of Negotiations

But before that, we needed to learn what other revolutionary groups did that was successful or deadly. For this, we listened to the six deadly sins of negotiations. The first sin struck me as particularly appropriate. The frontline movements, by 2019, were not fragmented. They were hyperfragmented and at one another's throats, least of which was the great divide over accepting Switzerland as a mediator. The first self-declared president, Sisiku, was sitting in Biya's gulag, Kondengui prison, with nine of his cabinet members. Dr. Sako, some preferring to deridely call him Pastor Sako, who had been elevated by his cabinet as interim president, was not accepted by Sisiku. The two were not on speaking terms. Sisiku supporters saw the move as usurpation. Sako supported the claim that no person should be allowed to run a country, even a fictitious one, from the enemy's jail cell. Many broke for or against these men. The women's group did not help as each lined up behind their favored man leader.

On the eve of the first ever Arria-formula meeting on the deteriorating humanitarian situation in the two regions, Sisiku fired Sako as his interim president and fired off a letter to the UN and other notable organizations around the West, announcing the formation of his new cabinet members. He nominated a certain Dabney Yerima as his vice president and began holding cabinet meetings from jail. Sako would be in the room as we were told of the unreality trap sin. What was our negotiation team's position, and if at all it existed at this early engagement phase, did they reflect the reality on the ground—the power balance? It was clear for me that they did not. But was ATC not much weaker than the apartheid regime in Southern Africa? What was going for the ATC was its strong national support. The war in Syria that began in 2010 resulted in tens of thousands killed. A joint team headed by the late Kofi Annan was formed to negotiate with the Assad regime. Syrians in the diaspora formed numerous groups, but these groups lacked the support from the Syrians on the ground, and that led to confusion and strain on their goals. No one group could claim military, political, and even economic support from the people. It was now five years since the start of the war. We continued to suffer from the unreality sin.

It was now three o'clock on day two on jet-lagged territory. We had all hurdled around the fake fire just outside the restaurant, bathing in the glow of our comrade, Abdukarim, who came from ground zero. He had inside information and warned that we must work smart, or we would all sink. The French, Biya, and the Swiss were not to be taken lightly, and they were not on our side. We must not give in.

The Ambazonians may be accused of overreaching, but this sin is like one of the Ten Commandments. It has not yet been broken. When independence movements reject solutions, sometimes they lose the support of key actors, opening the way to be defeated by the government forces. That was the case with the Tamil Tigers of Sri Lanka, who withdrew from the 2003 Norwegian peace process. Ambazonians cannot be blamed for overreaching. If anything, the newer Swissers blame those involved with the process for reaching too far by accepting a country that they cry is not neutral.

We can be blamed for breaking the next commandment of being unstrategic and letting our small egos edge out and undermine the bigger issue of liberation from French domination in our land. Just as we have often heard the more powerful Israelis say, they do not have a partner to negotiate with for peace; so, too, Biya has announced to the world that he does not know with whom to negotiate. Ambazonians have made power struggles and tussle a primordial fixation over winning the hearts and minds of the people or consolidating interests and position so key actors in the international community can take them seriously. That has yet to happen. The balkanization on the Ambazonian side and the failure to be strategic five years into a deadly war have ensured that the negotiations do not occur from the SLP. They fought the process, mistaking it for the negotiations.

For its part, the Biya government—using surrogates, accomplices, favorite sons and daughters, and paid civil servants—ferments differences. The international community increasingly believes the government narrative as true. Some have decried the formation of an IG as distracting from the strategic goal of liberation. The resources are plundered due to mismanagement that otherwise should have gone to buy arms and equip the ground zero forces. There is bad blood still running for where nearly $1 million from a successful drive dubbed "My Trip to Buea" went.

It is easy to say that the "I have arrived" deadly sin is and was committed. This sin plays out within the coalition where an IG does not see itself subordinate to a coalition and vice versa, leaving even the country willing to mediate, scratching its head about who to look to for information. In the end, each movement deals almost unilaterally with the mediator. LRC capitalizes. No one can say Ambazonians have not done much to bring along their own stakeholders. What you can accuse them of is whether they have brought along all stakeholders. There is a critical mass on ground zero, who religiously follows the directives coming from the IG. Take the case of the Monday ghost town and lockdowns. The populations stay home every Monday as a show of civil disobedience against the Biya regime. The IG locks down the entire territory to protest atrocities by the BIR. The majority of millions of NOSO inhabitants respect the call and stay home.

Timing has not been one of the sins to worry about. You can say that was a problem for the Scots who, in 2014, called for a referendum to secede from Great Britain. They needed more time to bring their constituents to warm up to leaving behind their queen. That vote lost narrowly. That, too, was the case in Quebec.

It is easy to speak of the sins, and there are plenty on our side. It is equally easy to talk about how to avoid them. The reality is no two conflicts are the same. What was successful in eastern Europe was that groups were able to bridge their divides, transcend their differences, promise to collaborate on a common vision, and agree that, once independence was gained, only then would they dispute their differences. For the moment, they all agreed on a structure and process to prosecute the war they faced. Simple? It is easy to speak of avoiding the ground zero, diaspora dichotomy. This simple understanding is perhaps an Achilles' heel and a deadly trap that, if it persists, will ensure negotiations never occur. LRC banks on widening this dichotomy. For starters, there are active campaigns to arrest or cajole fighters, others arrested and taken into DDR camps. The next day was focused on how and why political platform is important. What to call it, how to describe it, procedures, membership, officials, decision-making style, internal and external communications, and the stuff of organizing are often described as sausage-making. We were told we needed a constitution, a charter, and communications modalities. We needed to adopt a negotiation mandate, agree to it, work on the negotiation team, and start outreach work in ground zero, the diaspora, in the international, political, humanitarian, media, and prisoner and displaced populations. Talks, they said, were imminent.

I can't speak for the others, but my heart was thumping. It was all too much to take, mind you, not the organizational piece but the negotiation part. I had taught conflict studies at the postgraduate levels and was familiar with the concepts. Here, I was dealing with it in reality and had no clue about what to do.

Our next stop on all things capacity-building was the obligatory SWOT analysis. While some claimed we had unity of purpose, I wondered just how true. I glanced at the box that read "threats" and read the words *fragmented, multiple incoherent voices, federalism, Kamto, Biya's GND, war fatigue, lack of support*, and *military escalation* on both sides. Were these threats linked back to our unity of purpose holding up?

Ambazonians are still unsure about a freedom and liberation fight. There are those flag-carrying, anthem-singing people who believe they are in a fight for restoration. What exactly does that mean? Independence, sovereignty, self-determination? Restoration is a return to 1961's two states in a federal republic, arguably a division yet still a construct called Cameroon, with a seat at the UN as it is today. Those fighting may not be in this camp. They want a country that is now called the RoA or the Federal RoA, depending on who is the leader.

My eyes were drawn to the scribbles on the whiteboard that read "weaknesses." Beyond the lack of media reach for the movements gathered there, the words *fragmentation* and *incoherence* showed up again. We were happy to show opportunities for a new country, willingness for talks, and the growing international attention. Clearly, there was work to do. The threats and our weaknesses clearly stated so. For the coalition that would go on to be called ACT, it needed someone with broad constituent appeal easily accepted across all movements and with the right temperament, mindset, and judiciousness to manage military, political, and diplomatic fronts. But was that necessarily true? Such a leader will never be named nor identified. Group fight for dominance trumped ACT's raison d'etre.

At the end of the fourth day, the ACT was born, with eight out of the eleven groups who showed up signing in a statement giving their mandate for the Swiss to mediate to end the war. The Fon Gorji Dinka RoA and Milan Atam's Southern Cameroons Congress of the People (SCCOP) walked out. One weakness was now on full display. The newly formed ACT could not get unanimity on unity of purpose and on a coherent voice for independence. It could not agree on someone to head its affairs from its inception. It could not agree on a charter, a united front. It was bogged and dogged by the very weaknesses it had just SWOT analyzed from the very beginning. It would not surmount them years later. Was LRC winning?

By now, I was increasingly getting nervous about my role as an ACT member. It did not help that there was subtle bullying going on. One woman unceremoniously bowed out. It was no secret that she was disliked for being a supporter of the Sisiku camp. In fact, comments on the online workspace on WhatsApp from some frontline groups openly called her a spy. The ACT members had agreed post-Montreux to submit the names of one other representative to be on board and join the coalition. For those with armed wings, they would have two additional representatives on the ACT. She had committed the cardinal sin of submitting IG under Sisiku's brother, who was a member of her AIPC group. It would take what seemed like two dozen reminders to get him included in the forum. Once on board and part of the online forum, it did not help that he never uttered a word nor participated in meetings. I often wondered why he signed on if he had nothing to contribute, at least in kind, to the group, if nothing else.

My role within the ACT made me nervous. I had no professional or personal experience to speak of on matters of diplomacy. I had taught conflict management for nearly ten years, both on the undergraduate and the graduate levels, and can rattle off half a dozen conflict-handling strategies and models. I understood how to carry out conflict-mapping, negotiations, and mediation and had studied and read my students' analyses on various case studies around the world. The truth was the more modern conflicts were not necessarily in the academic textbooks that formed part of my curriculum development. I was heavy on theory and light on practice.

One thing I had going for me was I grew up watching my brother from the tender age of twenty-one work with the father of the Ambazonian revolutions, HRH Fon Gorji Dinka. I knew that there was a deep-seated anger in the DNA of every child born in that region. I grew up knowing there was always an uneasy calm in the two regions and unspoken worry that we were not of the French mold. For those now on two opposite sides, many Francophones did not see themselves as agents of oppression nor their silence as complicit. They were beneficiaries of our resources, even those at the lowest rung of society, and like many of our own brothers and sisters, had an interest in continuing the status quo. Their historical basis for understanding the injustices was strong. It was the truth they knew.

As I contemplated what I possibly could bring to this new role as a diplomat for peace, I would often be gripped by fear. I worried that all the complaints against the process would become mine and the ACT members' to carry. It did not help that after AIPC member, a lady, quit ACT, I felt an even greater sense of loneliness in a man's world. I was heaped with platitudes as I told to shut up or bullied. I was even called an enabler and threatened. I was told I was a show-off, an impostor, and a know-it-all and should quit trying so hard. By the way, which constituency did I represent? When I thought about the burden that the twenty-one men and two women carried, I wondered if I was the only one feeling overwhelmed or fearful and optimistic about the future. I had no illusions that I or any of the quarrelsome men would be the key negotiator, yet the thought that I was in the process of making history humbled me. When I looked around, the men all appeared arrogant, defiant, and inflexible to any and all advances either from other frontline groups or from goodwill peace ambassadors or just helpful criticism. It was ice-cold fighting or idle chat and camaraderie.

As the months grew, I became more measured and somewhat less engaged. I picked a handful of people I could bounce ideas with; we worked behind the scenes, and I would let one or suggest another to bring up the idea. I did not step in or lean in; I shrunk and leaned out. In a stretch of one month, I contemplated dropping out of the AIPC member. I was good at being an advocate for things I found interesting or good. Perhaps I was not cut out for such acrimony, such a consequential job, or even the rancor and the threats. I did not.

It became clear that I could throw in the towel, but I would still wake up to hundreds of images of dead bodies, mainly in and around my place of birth in the northwest region. We were taking the brunt of the war and genocide. Our villages lay in ruins, and many of my family were displaced or living in utter terror. This was pervasive and getting bleak each day all around the NOSO areas. When I get worn out, I don't speak out; I write. So, I wrote a long note for the boys in the ACT, letting them know that what was going on was not sustainable. The ACT was on its last gasp of air. The bullying, the fighting, the one-way-or-the-highway approach, the strong group identification, and lack of flexibility were the doom of the ACT. We might as well pack up, accept defeat, and go home. We were not helping anything.

Upon returning from Montreux, I was filled with excitement and the can-do spirit. I believed everyone would jump on board and that the ACT would be the biggest collection of grassroots and diaspora groups to take on Mr. Biya. Who would not want to speed up the negotiation process, and who would give up the chance to be part of making history to create a new country?

I began to accept TV interviews on the crisis or the Anglophone problem in Cameroon or on the SLP. At first, I was quite reluctant. When I received the invitation to appear on VOA's *Straight Talk Africa*, I resisted. I asked so many questions that the host had to call me to assure me this was not the torture chamber. You see, my problem was not articulating the nature of the crisis nor opining on what was going on in Cameroon and here in the diaspora. My fears were the over looming threats from Mr. Biya, including kidnaping in foreign lands. I also was afraid for my family, many of whom still lived in Cameroon.

I was equally afraid of reprisals from family members who were CPDM supporters and fought to keep the status quo. They had become persona non grata in our village, and when they ventured out to campaign or to further Mr. Biya's agenda of assimilation, they came in armored cars and a contingent of armed BIR men, clothed in bulletproof vests. They held rallies with tight security and a pre-vetted crowd of cheering locals, and if they could not get enough locals to accept the 1,000 CFA ($200) honorarium, they ferried in Francophone citizens from the neighboring region, all too glad to keep their one and indivisible Cameroon intact. Every now and again, the Amba Boys would attack such crowds or wait until the BIR retreated and seek revenge on anyone they identified as having participated. It became clear, in family settings, not all things were discussed. Even their homes and vehicles were burned, or they were kidnapped for ransom or killed. I feared these relatives in high places more than renditions tendencies. They fought to keep their paymaster and did not bat an eye if that meant killing over fifteen thousand civilians, including the Amba Boys defending their territory.

For the Ambazonian Coalition, Conflict Lingers

The ACT's deadliest sin was having the temerity to speak of negotiating on behalf of Ambazonians even within the context of a nascent peace process. How dare those freaks and non-leaders assume that they held the balance of power or legitimacy or full representation to call themselves the coalition for dialogue? Other coalitions for negotiations, like the CDNs, would soon form, to the great delight of the never Swissers. Hyperfragmentation continued.

No one ever doubted that there were no mechanisms in place for anyone to seek the consent of the Ambazonian people. The fighters and their group leaders were the de facto party at any negotiations. No one knew what would satisfy never Swissers sufficiently to gain their consent. If three major groups—Dr. Cho Ayaba's, AGovC, Milan's, SCCOP, and Fon Gorji Ndinka's RoA—held out the process, was that sufficient to torpedo an engagement with the Swiss? Are the groups engaged in the SLP considered broad-based enough to move a process forward? Only LRC stood to gain from such polarization.

Clearly, there was a need to continue to build as broad a coalition as possible, improve on trust deficit issues, and become more transparent and judicious with resources and to Ambazonians. From the get-go, there were no expectations of good intentions on both sides. Suspicion on everything was the norm. No one doubted that broad-based participation was best and would ultimately yield better outcomes than a fragmented party to a negotiation. No one, it seemed, was ready, willing, or able to do the heavy lifting. It was a free fall and open season for social killings, mainly.

Never Swissers decried the fact that Switzerland was the only mediator. They conveniently forgot both sides needed to agree on multi-mediation. They would often cite other conflicts around the world with multiple mediators or with contact groups. The case of South Sudan and the Intergovernmental Authority on Development (IGAD) was a natural go-to on why we must be the same. The ACT submitted a letter to the Swiss agreeing to mediation. Where was a similar letter from LRC giving a mandate to mediate? This could only mean bad things for never Swissers. "We are not desperate," they said.

For starters, they argued that, for the Swiss to mediate, they must first recognize us as a state and quit referring to us as the

NOSO regions of Cameroon. That can only mean the Swiss cannot be trusted. For those now formed as the ACT, the Swiss cannot be trusted for canvassing and speaking with groups outside the ACT. No group can be contacted unless they accepted the ACT as the platform. They cited the lack of guarantors as another reason the process was flawed but forgot to see parties had just signed up and that there was not mediation yet, let alone negotiations, to speak of. Guarantors was a matter for later.

Never Swissers held legitimate and seriously hubristic, if not funny, questions and comments. "Why should we trust the Swiss given Biya's second home is in Geneva? The sit-tight president Biya spends more time in Geneva with his family and closest collaborators than in his palace in Etoudi, Yaoundé. Can the Swiss be trusted given they are one-third French and neighbors to France, our archenemy and colonizer? Why did the ACT rush in to accept the first offer to mediate? Why not America? Why were the European Institute for Peace and its partner, Pave the Way Foundation, booted out of mediating for us when they were the more trusted party?" This, they claimed, was a major distraction from prosecuting the war on ground zero. We must reject it.

By the end of September, just after the commitment to the Swiss to mediate, Biya launched his GND. The holding pattern by LRC had begun and would persist without any movement toward talks. A law would soon be passed and signed, giving Biya's NOSO a special status. This would further balkanize ground zero.

There is no diplomacy without secrecy. Ambazonians must embrace the peace process with all its attendant principles—flexible, informal, delicate, and private. There is time for a global discussion about mediation and negotiation. Unfortunately, our wrangling costs lives as the process slides further onto the rocks. Wars are fought to cause the other side to agree. LRC knows this.

Best Practices and Our Deadliest Sins

A string of experts offered us their version of our struggle and best practices they believed would help us structure our negotiating platform, build support and participation, and adequately prepare for future talks. We were schooled on the six deadly sins of negotiation. First, Ambazonians should avoid the unreality trap decoded as daring to hold positions that does not reflect the underlying power balance. LRC was bigger, stronger, and proving deadlier than we could be to date. I kept my eyes fixed on the Swiss diplomat and wondered how in the world the ANC of Madiba Mandela and Winnie did it against the apartheid regime in South Africa.

We were warned that the Syrian War was the bloodiest Middle Eastern war of our time that killed over one hundred thousand people and crushed rebel groups eventually, and the goal to unseat Assad failed. The failure was because diaspora groups rushed in to fund and support factions and nationalist groups, while the Syrians at home did not feel supported. This created friction and confusion. No one group could boast of military, electoral, or political power large enough to tip the balance of power.

Hmmm. At this moment, I again scanned the room, looking for some aha moment. Were these some of our deadly sins? I saw none, only a quiet and controlled classroom of students. This time, I did not reach for my *eau frizzante*. I got up for a quick personal break. The door could only be opened from outside by the guards. I pulled and wiggled the doorknob to signal that someone needed to be let out; the huge and creaking mahogany door swung open, and the dark-spectacled Swiss guard stepped aside, making way for me to pass. I walked across the twenty-foot foyer, past Sako's personal bodyguard, and up four flights of stairs into the ladies' room. It wasn't really a bathroom break for me, though I took a leak; it was more of a mental break to stay awake and clear my head. I longed to speak to someone, anyone. After all, no one knew I was here except my husband. My phone was not with me. Bummer. At the start of each session, you surrendered your phone to the HD worker at the corner of the room until you needed it and took it outside. I had forgotten to take mine on my way out. I returned to the session and sat down.

"Overreaching and overplaying our hand in negotiations was another deadly sin," the Swiss diplomat said. We were reminded that, in 2003, the Tamil Tigers of Sri Lanka overreached withdrawing from the Norwegian peace process. They were later crushed. The Serb rebellions in Croatia rejected every solution offered, and the government was able to defeat them. What was our lesson for the day? Was it that the dynamics within a movement pushed the negotiator to extreme positions? No surprises here. No one had offered us anything to refuse yet.

Was advocating for our freedom an extreme position? So far Biya must now see that a war, like most in the works, does not end in a clear-cut victory and that, like in 1918 in the defeat of Germany, the winners take all and share the spoils as they did in carving up Africa among themselves. Precisely, the need was to address the root causes between LRC and us. Extreme positions are not what make failed negotiations. Negotiations that do not address the root causes can only lead to an indecisive war or the reoccurrence of wars.

Was our side strategic enough? Avoiding the strategic trap was another deadly sin, and boy, did we meet and surpass this one sin. First, I saw that the international interests in Cameroun did not overlay Ambazonian interests—at least not at this point. To be candid, all their interests undermined our issues. I had said a lot about that in the section "In Service to the French." Mr. Biya, like successive Israeli presidents, sounded to the world that they did not have a partner to negotiate with; meanwhile, the problem was really that of a power struggle, not a strategic goal. The old cold-war lines align unapologetically on each side of the long-running Israeli-Palestinian conflict. For Ambazonians, the entire international community played a wait-and-see game, deferring to French hegemony, a permanent Security Council member to pressure his best student, Biya, into more palliative care solutions. The hope was something was bound to stick, the Anglophones would grow tired, and the separatists would all be captured or killed.

Another shoe seemed to fit. But this time, it was almost five o'clock, and we had one hour for a sit-down lunch. I was jet-lagged and unable to keep my eyes open. I stood up, walked to the wall, and listened. While these lectures were getting interesting, my mind, when awake, returned to "We anticipate talks on talks by the end of year." This was seductive. Many had been exiled, jailed, captured, tortured, maimed, killed, or exiled from LRC for daring to ask for less in a system that pitted them as second-class minority. Here, some fellows were told they should prepare for negotiations. Perhaps this is what was leaked, setting off the never Swissers in a tizzer. Who are they to negotiate? Many fumed. No one bothered to recall that this was just the capacity-building phase in preparation for talks or that the gathering of armed groups and their leaders needed schooling on mediation and negotiations.

I listened on. Our pluralism, our rugged collectivism, and our long enslavement lasting sic decades in a culture that pitted one against the other, was highly centralized, and was state-run, lacking in trust and knee high in spirit of scarcity and depravity in a country teeming with rich resources under and above the ground. Like the curse of black gold, our pluralism was our strength and our nadir.

I counted ten different frontline group leaders or their surrogates seated in the large conference room. These movements were used by LRC to ensure that no talks would ever happen or, if they did, succeed. It was the art of war, as Sun Zu wrote hundreds of years ago. To win in war, ensure that you sow discord in your enemy's ranks. LRC had mastered the art of encouraging differences without distinctions, and they were "winning fatly" as the activists liked to say. To make the sin deadlier, the poison added was playing favorites. The government contacted a leader of the group to encourage them that they can work with them toward peace. In the meantime, another acted as a benevolent informant, leaking this guild to the masses. Now the leader, who believed he was on a path to bring rapid peace, was now viewed as a sellout by the other groups. Their armed groups on the ground were now pitched against one another. Instead of fighting LRC, they turned their guns against one another. The case of Guzang, Batibo, and Bui where armed groups engaged in tit-for-tat was plentiful.

Are Ambazonians reaching in to snatch defeat from the jaws of success? Can we afford to be complacent or to think we own and govern a country, or can we not engage in the SLP for a cacophony of reasons, some of which may be valid and others mere speculations? Can any one group or a combination afford to move ahead without bringing along their stakeholders? Hmmm. The trouble with stakeholders is that, for Ambazonians, it is their tribe. By this, I mean those who support me for my sake, not for what I believe in. In our hyperfragmentation, we have splint in a dizzying array of every diminishing faction.

As I walked back to sit down for the closing of this lecture, I wondered whether the critical Mass of 2016 that rallied with peace branches throughout Ambazonia, chanting, "Ambazonia rising to fall no more," and the five thousand Ambazonians in the diaspora who gathered in the fall outside the UN, chanting, "Biya, you go kill, we tire," had since dissipated. Did we need a critical mass that can agree on one big idea whose momentum couldn't be stopped, not by Biya's BIR guns and certainly not by the vicissitudes of the international community saying one thing and failing to stand behind their own words?

Not to mention that we snatched defeat. I wondered how all the free media, charismatic activists, and political pundits are not now doing the same friend-on-friend killing, only this time words actually lead to target killings of those considered not part of the tribe. The IRA–Sinn Fein Good Friday Agreement are some examples.

Did I hear that our deadly sin is failure to launch at the right time? The Federal RoA was declared on October 1, 2017, by Sisiku Ayuk Tabe from a hotel room in New York City. He would later return to his work in Nigeria, and shortly, at the meeting with nine other members of his newly formed government, they were abducted and flown to LRC to stand trial. They are now serving life sentences. Then there is the RoA, led by the exiled Fon Gorji Dinka, who has relegated the reins to his son. And then there is AGovC, headed by the recalcitrant, Mandela wannabe Cho Ayaba. Did Ambazonians not only launch what some now call an internet country, an imaginary country, too soon? The case of the Quebecois came to mind, where they pressed for secession from Canada but were roundly defeated and the ideas almost relegated to the back burner. When the vote came up, many voters stayed home or stayed out.

Many now say we should have waited to have state recognition from other nations who, in turn, can host a government in exile. But we didn't. On the power of our argument, not the power of the gun, Mr. Ayuk Tabe declared to the world that Ambazonia was now a country. When he was arrested, Dr. Sako stepped in as interim president and, till today, continues to draw both praise and the wrath of Ambazonians from those who buy into this deadly sin, those who believe he scammed them out of $800,000, My Trip to Buea monies collected to fund the revolution, or other groups simply gunning to bring him down and elevate their own standing as the leader of the imaginary country, more like the only leader with the authority to sit in Geneva and negotiate. Not only is our sin failure to launch at the right time, but our sins are also in ensuring that our fragmented independence movement, LRC, wins as they fan and encourage these differences and play favorites, unbeknownst to these factions they pit against one another.

Is the Middle of the Road the Surest Path?

I was not naive, in thinking ours was an outlier case that will go down in the annals of history as the worst-case study for how not to prosecute and defend a war and negotiate an end to a conflict. For my comfort, somewhere in the string of speakers, one mentioned, to my sadness, how our war was considered a low-level conflict. Translation: it had not achieved the level of death and displacement to be taken seriously by the UN. For now, the measures taken were consistent with these types of conflict.

Croatia had experienced divisiveness both militarily and politically, but they managed to bridge the divide between the extremes and did this by talking frequently to all sides and holding joint meetings. They seemed to learn early on that you can't fight a war and successfully run a country democratically. And so, they resolved that they would only dispute their differences once they secured their independence. They were clear about what divided and what united them.

I have sometimes heard the mantra "Until we reach Buea." This is more a rhetoric than a way for Ambazonian frontline groups. On one hand, the likes of Dr. Sako as president of one group are treated as democracies where the citizens have the right to free speech, right to freedom of information, and right to share, leak, or sabotage state wartime secrets. Then there are those who constitute secret meetings to discuss wartime strategies and their supporters who see this as the prevue of those on the frontlines and their handlers.

When the White man left the room, we quarreled to the point of exhaustion and breakdown. The assignment was to work in close session to agree on a structure and a leadership. The Swiss said, the next meeting, they would engage with the leadership as it would not be necessary to fly every participant to Geneva or wherever they chose to hold the next secret meeting. Hell broke loose.

You can fault Mr. Biya for many things, but one thing you can't hold him accountable for is his complete lack of charisma and penchant to shy away from the public. He is, after all, the world's most absent president, preferring to spend most of his time on the InterContinental Hotel in Switzerland. In his now famous public gaff, the painfully awkward Biya sat with other world personalities at the 2019 Paris Peace Forum. He had just returned from reporting to Mr. Macron, the French president, about the success of his GND. Emboldened, he felt that being seen more in public would send the signal to the world that he was firmly in control of his fiefdom. And so, uncharacteristically, he accepted to participate in a talk show on peace in front of the world.

Mo Ibraham, the moderator, asked him about the crisis in his country. To the shock of the world, Mr. Biya—after fumbling for what felt like an eternity with his earpiece and microphone—began to say there were some terrorists who wished to break up his country. And to school his audience, he announced that his country was under Germany, and unfortunately, it was divided between the French and the British. For his part since becoming president, he had tried and failed to assimilate the Southern Cameroonians into the French part. Because of this failure, he continued, he had accorded them a *status speciale.*

We had, again, been reminded of the force of our arguments. Mr. Biya laid claim to a country, German Kamerun, that no longer existed. For his arguments to hold, he would have to take back parts of his one and indivisible Kamerun not only from Ambazonia but also from parts of Chad, CAR, and Niger. Did Mr. Biya forget that his country ratified the AU Constitutive Act on the inviolability of borders or the UN charter on territoriality? Mr. Biya's sad display of ignorance, while pitiful, was equally laughable. I could only imagine one of the countries in the Middle East laying claim to its neighbors on account of having been part of the Ottoman Empire. What an imperialistic dream, except we are in the yoke of LRC and dying each day, literally and figuratively. Biya finally accepted the root causes of the crisis he started. In more than one hundred years, since the Treaty of Versailles, Central Europe was redrawn, Africa was redrawn, and in four years, LRC wished to redraw a part of Africa back to the Treaty of Versailles.

On ACT and Navigating the Quicksand of Frontline Armed Group

LRC had its negotiators ready. "Hurry up and constitute yourselves," we were told. Talks on talks were expected to begin by the end of the year. That was what the Swiss/HD staffers told us. It was powerful, invigorating, and exciting to hear those words. After all, the ten frontline groups, I and another independent participant to the SLP were there for one reason alone, and that was to press for negotiations to begin as soon as possible so that not only the war but also our ultimate freedom and independence can be achieved. It must have been hearing that Ambazonians needed to begin preparations to hold their first face-to-face talks by the end of December 2019 that pushed the groups of frontline leaders to hastily meet at the end of the Montreux, Geneva, meeting to form the ACT. The ACT members would return and continue to bring in other frontline groups' leaders, create a coalition that had its governing instruments, set up its technical teams, and lead negotiators to deal with LRC.

The Swiss warned that the risk we faced was the world growing tired and turning against us or beginning to call us terrorist. Other groups were invited but had declined. Major activists had been invited, but one activist, now in exile, cited immigration concerns and grave fears that this, too, can be another ruse to bring the Ambazonian leadership in one place and arrest and ferry them back to LRC torture chambers at the SED. They feared they, too, would suffer the fate of Sisiku and his Nera friends. But who and what was the ACT, and why was it so loved and so hated?

The ACT came into existence at the end of a meeting in Montreux with the SLP HD in 2019. It was made up of Ambazonian movements, organizations, self-defense groups, and independent people representing equity-seeking groups. Their mission statement was to find lasting, just, and permanent peace in the war in Ambazonia. To that end, the ACT would explore, exploit, and prosecute her engagement to restore the former UN trust territory of Southern Cameroons, aka Ambazonia. In this group, the mere mention of a French word earned you the title of an enabler, and the mention of any type of reconciliation was resoundingly rejected as a trap for federalists to step in and take over the process. The dominant voice led to these charges, and surrogates followed in lockstep, denouncing and refusing any attempt by parties to bring both sides to collaborate on the SLP.

The fact was that leaders of various frontline groups were contacted by the Swiss, inviting them to a meeting, and those who accepted found themselves in front of international actors purporting to bring peace to Cameroon and solve the problems in the NOSO regions. By the fourth meeting, a faction of leaders had written a twenty-four-point letter to the Swiss, demanding that, until and unless the conditions were met, they would not accept the Swiss to mediate. The remaining groups pressed ahead and continued to meet and engage with the Swiss. To listen to the international community on the SLP was to believe that, indeed, the war had gotten to a point that intervention in this form of mediation was needed, and the Swiss were just the kind of neutral, independent, and impartial country to take on the role.

The ACT was supposed to work with all like-minded independence groups for the full recognition of Ambazonia as a nation among nations in the world. That mission to build, strengthen, manage, and prepare an Ambazonian-centric negotiation platform comprising a diverse cross section of Ambazonian frontline movements and civil society actors committed to a peaceful, permanent solution to the war in Ambazonia was hard to come by. It could not link nor politically mobilize any broad-based consultation with the people. By the middle of 2020, less than nine months after its introduction to the world with fanfare, credibility, collaboration, messaging, and trust were largely in short supply. It seemed the team was teetering on the brink of collapse.

For those who loved the ACT, they entrusted all their hopes and dreams on the real and palpable chance that Ambazonians are a people entitled to rights to statehood through negotiations that will come to be. They were the pragmatists who were dragged in and chose to see nor hear no evil and certainly went to bat for all anti-ACTors on social media. They could not care less about the curses levied on those who called themselves ACT members; neither did they care if those characters, as some referred to them, were the actual negotiators or not. No one actually knew what the process was, so much so that speculations that negotiations had begun actually took hold, even if detractors screamed that LRC had not even given their mandate.

A UNSC December meeting on CAR, during which nearly half the time was dedicated on the Anglophone crisis, became my motivator. I spent weeks writing to each member of the UNSC that had said anything slightly favorable to our cause. I would sneak to the coffee room downstairs from work to make phone calls. I called every listed number until I spoke to a human. I left countless voice and email messages. Germany, Tunisia, Russia, and Ghana were pleasantly understanding on the phone. I was invited to meet with the ambassadors of Germany and Tunisia. I never heard from the United States. I would not be daunted, and I cannot give up.

Someone was bound to see that talk is cheap and that actually moving the mammoth called the UN was needed to take concrete actions and stop the empty words.

I set out to convince all those holding out against the SLP. In my pleas to the head of the South African group, I reminded him of Mr. Biya's statement in September 2019 just before his famous GND, during which he stated that the world was pressuring him to dialogue with the secessionists. "There's need for peace through dialogue. But there is no one to dialogue with," he continued.

"He has looked around, and there is no one to negotiate with, pointing to our balkanization, fragmentation, and incoherence. Are we going to prove him right?" I asked. My impassioned pleas were, "Our shared goal is to free Ambazonia, and that is far greater than our group differences. We must organize for a common good—for our suffering people."

I was determined to convince all the holdouts against the SLP. I reminded Sisiku's Dabney that we had done a great job as activists. But what we needed now was not activism but political mobilization. We needed to build our institutional capacity, a strong organization that included the willing coalition committed to pressing Mr. Biya to a negotiated settlement. The activists' voices had grown, as was their following. Ambazonians listened to them and repeated their every work.

Just as they were becoming a force to reckon with, the once formidable crusaders for a free and independent Ambazonia turned into platforms for dead threats, fighting between the frontline groups and channels to buy fighters on the ground and pitch one against the other. Each accused the other of being the villain. It seemed that they had broken a sacred oath taken to be the mouthpiece of the grassroots, pepping them up and rallying the troops to continue, persist in the revolutions, and heap mental and spiritual demonization of the right enemy—LRC. Sadly, it had turned into a fight to the death among activists, frontline groups, and leaders. Scores were settled in plain sight; phone conversions secretly recorded were being aired on podcasts, TV programs, and Facebook to show who was lying and who was telling the truth. For the activists, their stock-in trade was conspiracies, threats, and counterthreats. Each one had its loyal followers, ready to screenshot, record, and analyze the jobs on all social media platforms, ensuring that their views go viral as fast as possible.

Each day, I wondered just how this form of activism was doing to the revolution. It seemed that what happened on the battlefield was now only secondary to the scores that had to be settled in full display before the camera and to the world. Was activism not for general mobilization where perhaps, organically, a strong leadership could emerge? I wondered how a leadership made of activists, each with its tribe and each peddling a particular brand of social killing, can be looked on as the leadership of a revolution. Who would the international community engage with? What we needed was institutional recognition that we are the party at the table backed by grassroots and diaspora constituencies from whom we took our direction.

As the activists' voices grew louder and deadlier, they, too, took on the teardown of the ACT. Detractors of the ACT now had a bully pulpit from where to rain down and tear down the SLP and dissolve the ACT. And they found many willing activists to do so. I sensed that with the vitriol oozing from the activists, growing louder and being repeated by more and more people on GZ, the international community would become reluctant to risk their reputation or their institutional recognition to those they didn't trust or those they had disdain for. The lack of stable leadership was hurting the revolution. But most Ambazonians saw the infighting as their biggest concern to stop on one side, and for others, it was a great thing to partake in. How would the international community know that peace and justice can be secured if they saw a people quick to spin off conspiracies that did nothing for their own cause?

Those willing to go alone with the SLP complained that the process was too opaque. For this, I would argue that these incessant complaints were because the quiet diplomacy-deprived Facebook activists and WhatsApp generals of information to spin out of context and into conspiracies. I could not understand why the process needed to be carried out in the market. Was mediation not a flexible, private, delicate process, mainly? How many knew that, before the Arria-formula meeting in May 2019, a handful of organizations and people had quietly lobbied for the UN to hear the brother had fought for that nation. They would remain relatively unknown to successive decades of children as their peers acquiesced to the French domination of the Anglophones. They would give up their fight for independence for a semblance of multi-partism. They would give their language and their legal systems for a prostituted French education and for civil law. Ultimately, they served as fodder for the successive regimes, from Ahidjo to Biya, to tell the world, "Look, my country is democratic. We have a multi-party, elections are free, and the opposition participates in national affairs at all levels of government and society. The problems in your regions are no different from that of the people in the north, east, and southern parts of my country." As I looked back, it seemed like our own people decried the SLP and sought to discredit not only the Swiss but also those of us who participated, and the endorsement of the process grew less. In the months leading up to the Montreux meeting, all international bodies could be heard endorsing the SLP. There would be Twitter announcements, press statements by the Swiss, and newspaper and TV shows dedicated entirely to it. Ambazonians pounded their fist and raised their voices to Mr. Biya, letting him know that the end of his tyranny on the people of Ambazonia had come. He would be crushed at the negotiation table. From Muslim scholars to opposition parties in LRC, the lineup of pundits was a mile long. In the diaspora, frontline leaders were filling the airwaves on Al Jazeera, VOA, BBC Africa, and ABC Amba TV. Our pride, for now, being counted among the contenders in an existential fight, was clearly on display. It would be repeatedly reported that the negotiations were imminent and that Mr. Biya had consented to participate in the mediation. All that was needed was for a date to be set for a talk on talk to begin, and that, too, was just in a matter of months. The HD was concerned about the Ambazonian fragmentation and told us we needed to hurry up and get up to speed with building a strong coalition and closing up the widening gaps of discord among the groups.

The AU, UN, and others all endorsed the SLP through various means. It was still unclear what role Canada played. Were they, as we were told, the funders? I would make the argument that it didn't matter whether all these countries were deceiving us, and if so, what harm was there in testing the waters and going along to see what we can exploit from their deceit? Was staying away to our advantage? Did the diaspora not hold the international community's attention through protest, lobbying, and letter-writing campaigns, eventually bringing a peace initiative to the war in Sudan?

CHAPTER 11:
PLEA FOR THE FUTURE

Will Posterity Forgive? What Will Our Legacy Be?

Posterity will not forgive our generation if we do not correct the historical and legal wrongs we suffer. We are yet to find our Roosevelt who will make us stand up as one man. War knows no friend.

The year 1776 was a fine one. When the congressman from South Carolina took to the hall and requested that James Adams remove "the offending passage from your declaration," calling for independence of America from Great Britain, Adams responded, "We would be committing the offense we are rebelling against. And if we give in to this, posterity will never forget us." Was that hubris, was it bolstering, was it the price they had and continued to pay in blood for their freedom? They would not know until all the votes were counted. Their own brothers from the South preferred allegiance to the king.

The gentleman from South Carolina threatened to "bury now and forever the dreams of independence." The federalists and the obstructionists threaten to bury our dreams. If we give in on this issue, posterity will never forgive us. Posterity may not think of us as demigods; even if we will long have departed this earth and not hear a thing about our past actions, we must look past our flaws and seek creative, albeit contentious, ways to work. There is optimism, and there is no shortage, too, of heartbreaks and dejection. The death toll keeps rising.

Against all odds, many declared a nation. This was the case in 1776, much more than a generous God would have ever allowed.

The world had passed resolutions in support of peace and for sanctions on perpetrators of human rights violations. We have a slipping peace process—not dead, not non-existent—but a process for all that it portends. But for posterity to judge, we must first be on deck and working for our independence.

We have seen many within the Biya government, including our own brothers and sisters, taking up roles aimed solely at frustrating our every effort to be heard and to negotiate. Many within Biya's side are adamantly against any talks and believe in military victory. Others like James Wilson are ambivalent, unsure where their fortunes lie—a free, untethered Ambazonia or a one and indivisible Cameroon with special status given to a once separate but equal partner? They straddle the fence and neither prevent nor foster a change in the war. They are largely happy with the status quo. If there is to be a referendum, will it prevent our independence? Will there be just another person who so richly deserves anonymity, or who will be brave enough to stand up for the righting of historical wrongs? For Jefferson, revolutions come into this world like bastard children—half improvised, half compromised. Our side is providing the compromise. And it is left to a few brave souls to furnish the rest. Perhaps, as with the Congress of 1776, we need mutual security and protection and propose that no person be allowed in our territory if they do not attach their name to our fight for independence as we are about to the brave the storm in a skiff made of paper, and how it shall end nobody knows. For LRC, we are all seditionists and treasonous. By speaking up against the almighty Biya, we have signed up for the gallows to be hanged. Ambazonians are braving the storm and very unsure how it will end. We are not backing out now. For if we do not hang together, we shall most assuredly be hanged separately.

The crisis had opened old fault lines. It had accentuated all the traditional lies the White man had implanted in us in the earlier part of our own coming into the globalized world that we now had retooled, rebranded, reinforced, and reused as tools of self-oppression. No one people or nation should have so many ways to self-abuse, self-label, or self-divide.

The once autonomous state, geographically called the UN former trust territory of the BSC, will, one day, be its own nation. It will be in a new form—for good—in the world. That form may well be an autonomous state in relation to its French neighbor; it might well be in the form of an independent nation. Whatever form it takes, you will be in that world as a citizen or as a global citizen connected near and far by a common humanity. The question, then, will be yours to answer. "Did I contribute to alleviate human suffering, advance peace, or advocate for justice?"

Give War a Chance; Give Peace Process a Chance

When it comes to Africa and its own version of tribal wars, the global north throws out their political playbook. The majority stood by during the period from 1939 to 1944, waiting for a consensus— for the majority to take action. We were left years later decrying the slaughter, the genocide of six million of our fellow human beings, just because they were Jews at the hands of Nazis in Germany. The majority stood by again, unable and unwilling to take a decisive action in 1984.

And then there was the Rwanda genocide. Thankfully, the United States, under the Clinton administration, quickly intervened in 1999 to end the genocide against the Kosovars led by the Serbian president, Slobodan Milosevic. This occurred not before five hundred villages had been burned down and nearly one million Albanian Muslims became refugees in the surrounding countries.

The world is willing, again, to stand by and stand back as Biya and his BIR army wipe out thousands of Southern Cameroonians. It is called nonintervention in the internal affairs of a state and respect for their sovereign rights.

There is one school of thought among conflict experts, and that is to give war a chance. It is insidious to think in such terms but a theory, nonetheless. Some call it conflict ripeness. Why not let the war drag on and get a more decisive victory before diving headlong into mediation in hopes of achieving some compromise, only to see the parties to a conflict balk at a deal and return to fighting because they believe in winning outright? This has been the intention of the belligerents in the Cameroon war. The AGovC, the faction of armed groups fighting against Biya's BIR army, sees no value in peace talks when it has not captured and held territory from LRC. Biya's war ministers believe with their dominant military position that they can secure an all-out victory. No one is a loser at this time in the conflict landscape, and some peace advocates think little can be achieved until both see a lose-lose proposition in their actions. For our collective humanity, posterity will not forget nor forgive.

No Peace Until We All Experience Justice

Let us agree on the basics. Peace is serenity of spirit. It can be acquired through sheer willpower as it can be enforced through fiat. It is an ephemeral state when not emanating from and supported by just systems, processes, and institutions. This means that, for there to be peace, conflict must be resolved and injustices addressed. To resolve any conflict, certain ingredients must be considered. What is the framework? Is there international support for resolving the conflict? What are the geopolitical interests? Is there a willingness to end the conflict? Who controls the environment, and can it be controlled, with truth as the central piece of the talks? Who are the parties, and is there parity at the table?

Justice is fleeting in a crisis whose impacts are largely unevenly experienced. Further complicating the prospect are the problems of communication and participation and reasons for fighting each other. The assimilation, as perverse as it has been over six decades, is one reason from variously antithetical viewpoints. Those in favor of peace hates the Ambazonian Amba Boys for disturbing their peaceful coexistence with their brothers across the Mungo. Those in favor of Ambazonia suspect all peace processes as yoking them to Yaoundé, which they wish to break away from. Some just want this to go away and to return to their lives. This is the tension between both sides. For their part, Ambazonians are tough but fragmented and not cohesive in their positions. Biya's inner circle is also fragmented, with its own extremist wing believing outright victory is certain, even if it means genocide.

Both sides still think in terms of winning against the other. LRC continues to send its military into the NOSO to kill or capture. The commanders of the Ambazonian fighters tell the world they must capture and hold territory; they must be a contender on the ground, win the war, and force the enemy to come to the negotiation table. Both sides are winners believing in a military solution. Each side kills but forgets that when one commander is killed, another comes up to replace him.

Way Forward

Give me freedom or give me death. Our history is like the Titanic. Everyone saw it sail—those on the docks who read the news and heard the announcers trumpet its historical voyage. Then the deep blue sea swallowed it, burying its treasures. Divers struggled throughout the decades to bring the wreckage up from the sea. A generation has wised up and refused to allow the Titanic to lie obscure in the annals of the sea. They speak of freedom and are now willing to die for it—but not the kind of freedom in the BLM movements that swept across the globe when a knee to the neck killed George Floyd. It is sovereignty.

Ambazonians throw around words like *sovereignty, self-determination, IG, mediation and negotiation, activism,* and *political mobilization.* We must learn to build and cross the bridge to freedom. For now, there is no confidence, no expectations of good intentions from key actors, be it in the international community or within the Ambazonian groups. We say that we are a people suffering oppression. We are an independence movement—for our freedom and liberation. We cry that we are subject to international law, charters, resolutions, and principles, like all other former colonies. From these, the world prefers to look away. Our stories, sometimes confused, are born out of the effects of years of subjugation and assimilations. So, we cry that we did not dissolve the federation of 1961; LRC dissolved it and later walked away, leaving us free, except the world is unwilling to help usher us into the club of nations.

We need to show we are pragmatic people willing to engage other parties in search of ways to end a war, even one we did not start. This includes consolidating the myriad of groups and their heads, consolidate our position, and create a mechanism to deal with the world, which finally is listening but unwilling to act to save us. We need to shore up our capacities. This will have to be piecemeal, a slug. We need to build legitimate institutions with a common agenda on what we call ground zero, where actors reinforce the credibility of other actions, not put them through the meat grinder of social killings and real killings.

Southern Cameroons has suffered, first through successive White imperialistic incursions, from slavery and slave trade to settled Whites, staying on as colonial masters, and later through colonial administrators, all-knowing and powerful, directing and managing our affairs to self-governance. Did animals govern us before they invaded? Procedurally, we suffered the indignities of being told we cannot walk, and we were too illiterate and dependent to be among the membership of nations. And for that, our choices were made for us. The people went to the polls to confirm what was now our freely expressed wish—to gain independence by joining an already independent nation. We suffered another indignity at the ballot box at the hands of a conniving Ahidjo who exploited the unsophisticated populace's ability to see that the results of a referendum—in which 75 percent were already in favor—was going in their favor no matter what the 25 percent did.

Morally, we suffered exclusion at the hands of the French majority ruling over us. Never good enough to be president or to hold any top offices in a country, we were forced to accept ourselves as one and indivisible and as brothers. Culturally, an imperialistic French loomed large over us, imposing through policies from its puppet regime in Yaoundé economic, military, and social exploits. We have read about our national reserves, gotten mainly from our resources, deposited in the French central bank in Paris. If Ambazonians hold these grievances with a sense of righteous indignation and of the right to go on our own, it is because of the sense of injustice we feel and have felt for six decades. For some, the solutions are clear. For others, any solutions outside that of a strongman focus is the unraveling of the Francafrique.

War, death, destruction—that is the landscape now in my homeland. The end is far from sight. Peace is illusive. Justice is given only an obligatory window dressing in the corridors of power in the construct dubbed as Cameroon and outside the grand saloons of the UN and AU. The Amba Boys fight on. The BIR deployments increase. We are not looking to shore up the political, judicial, or parliamentary systems in LRC. For that, French Cameroun must contend with the likes of Maurice Kamto of the MRC, decrying a stolen presidential win. Ours is an international problem warranting international solutions for just and lasting peace. We are not for truth and reconciliation commissions. Our search is for the dignity of our people, rights, and claims to the soil.

Prayers Are Not Enough

In the case of the Anglophone crisis in Cameroon, a few things can be seen as levers to move toward finding lasting solutions. First, Cameroon is predominantly Christian, with nearly 55.5 percent of the 26 million inhabitants identifying as Catholics. These Catholics love their pope. Pope Francis, bishops, and clergy are officers with great decision-making abilities and intervention skills. So do the Musli, Presbyterians, and Evangelists. The faithful of the population is most likely to accept the intervention of the church to solve their problems. This authority can be marshaled to good use to end the suffering of the people.

The clearest sense of community is religion. For good or bad, the saying that religion is the opiate of the masses is clearly true in LRC. The church and the state are intricately intertwined, making it difficult to get the masses to think beyond the religious lens. Everything is to be prayed about, to be left for God to fix, or to be the work of an angry God. There is a growing disappointment with the church. They are believed to be nonpartisan, to be neutral. Today, they are believed to parrot the voices from Yaoundé. The elite class, also considered the leaders, know that they, too, must get anointed and become religious if they are to be taken seriously, for only through prayers can anything happen to them and for them.

We all pray with a great deal of conviction for a peaceful land we call our own. No one in their right mind quarrels with peace.

Biya and his acolytes speak peace but do not mean peace as we all know it. He just wants to gain a little more control, today, to reassert himself and his policy of claim on Southern Cameroons. He speaks of peace with his international friends with one purpose: to buy time to complete the annexationist agenda. He speaks of peace as master of a captured people, and we cannot make peace with dictators. We cannot make peace absent justice.

The Vatican secretary of state paid a high-level state visit to Cameroon. It was believed that this was mainly a religious visit for the laying of the pallium on the archbishop of Bamenda. Under my newly formed organization, Women for Permanent Peace and Justice (WPPJ), I penned a letter to the secretary of state of the Vatican. We also launched a campaign titled "Petition: Pope Francis, call Mr. Biya of Cameroon to end the war and engage in third-party-mediated talks." I contacted friends within the Catholic church, and one agreed to hand-deliver the signed petition. The petition garnered over one thousand signatures, which was hand-delivered to the pope's secretary of state upon arriving in Cameroon. The petition is open and can be found here: https://www.change.org/p/ petition-pope-to-call-president-biya-of-cameroon-to-end-the-warengage-in-3rd-party-mediated-talks.

This was the case when the Vatican intervened in Venezuela, a Latin American country. Beyond Africa, Catholicism is highest in Latin American countries, boasting 425 million Catholics, about 40 percent of the world's total Catholic population. Moreover, Pope Francis hails from Argentina—in Latin America—and has intervened to bring peace to the region.

It is my expressed opinion that any state affair worth a "holy visit" needs to:

- publicly support the current mediation effort and call for the full participation of Mr. Biya;

- liaise with Switzerland and, if necessary, agree to convene under the Vatican's auspices;

- at minimum, request both parties' proposed solutions, hearing from both sides and doing so through intermediaries;

- secure a full agreement to end hostilities from the government, its military, and the armed groups engaging in atrocities.

Cardinal Pietro's visit is greatly welcome, but prayers without actions consistent with the intent of the prayer are dead faith. It perhaps gives hope to not only the never Swissers—those categorically opposed to Switzerland as a mediator for reasons this author will not opine—but also the millions caught up between the military forces and the armed groups in Biya's NOSO.

You Will Walk Again

Just as the clouds will move without pushing, even in bending, the truth will prevail. Ambazonia will bloody well walk without being tethered to you. Praxie bloody well is fighting to get back on her feet. And back on, she will. I see the improvements, sheer force of will, resilience, determination as she pushes, leans forward, and with a little help here, a little tug there she summons every fiber of her body and bring her 5 foot, 6 inch frame to the upright on her crutches. Still determined, she lifts one leg—drags it if she must across the bare floor, and then the other; one step, then another. It is victory. The tears have long since dried up when I contemplate her struggles with life debilitating challenges. In their place, my eyes light up, my smiles bright for each success, each triumph to beat the odds lifts my spirit, builds my character to be still and know God's will at work could be like watching water boil, slow, imperceptible at times; seen only with the eyes of one faithful to a higher spirit, not with one seeing with human eyes. A child can indeed teach a mother. I am a believer in the ancient wisdom that, when the student is a reader, the teacher will appear. Perseverance, grace, and love were the central themes in the schooling I received from a child I thought I would teach until I die.

Today, I question my birth nationality and no longer hold any allegiance to a one and indivisible Cameroon, which, until the breakout of the war, was my country of origin. I cannot return to Cameroon. I fear I will be arrested or, worse, killed for the crime of sedition or for offering support to what the government calls "terrorists." Biya and his dreaded army, the BIR, make no distinction between advocating for justice and fighting with arms for the same. If you are not with them, you must be the enemy.

In 2019, I founded WPPJ, a gathering of women wanting *permanent* peace and justice. The emphasis is on permanent, and justice is what animates our agenda. Recall that I talked about women's focus on issues of welfare of victims and peace. In Cameroon, peace means not agitating the order of things. There is peace in Cameroon if you go along to get along—the peace of churches or the peace of the graveyard. Dissent, however, just is treasonous. A trip to Cameroon's Kondengui prison is filled with rapidly emaciating faces of men and women who have uttered one defiant word against Biya—the sit-tight kingpin, the head of state himself—or his acolytes.

As founder of WPPJ, in the first ever public event I hosted, nearly five hundred participants joined in from all over the world to listen to seven women from Colombia, Indonesia, South Sudan, Sudan, Europe, and the United States recount their own freedom and liberation struggles and the lessons learned. I could have had participants register and leave their emails.

It is nearly five years since the first gunship helicopter rained bullets on peaceful protesters in my hometown. Despite many cries from Cameroonians and a few other activists, the war is largely not reported by mainstream media. This book is one way not to look away from the ignorance of half-truth, a whitewashed past, and now the dark clouds of war encircling my birthplace. I am caught up, just like 25 percent of the people who are awakening to their truths, facing their stateless spirit, searching for an anchor.

I frequently speak on TV and other social media platforms about my experiences, the lessons I have learned along the way, and how others can benefit or use my suggestions to make a difference. My daughter is blossoming where she is planted. She teaches me each day what conflict-inspired living really means.

While troubled by the killings each day, most coming from my hometown and its environs, I am more centered on advocating for those facing the barrel of the gun and being a couch warrior is not consistent with my principles of life lived through the storms. I have learned to engage and enroll friends along the journey who know more than I do about war and peace, dealing with the challenges of working, caring for a sick family member, or dealing with disabilities. That has meant that I have to accept responsibility for dealing with the conflict, no matter its nature, and committing to doing something about it, however small. Shaking off my fears means I have to be answerable first to myself and to those around me—family, work, society—recognizing that I hold within me the power, control, and requisite management to be counted on.

Just as the clouds will move without pushing, even in bending, the truth will prevail. Ambazonia will bloody well walk without being tethered.

ACKNOWLEDGMENTS

A s in life, first experiences leave indelible impressions on our lives in the most profound of ways. Though I have written extensively for myself and for others, this book is my first widely published work, and the fruits of which I share today would not have been possible without the counsel, support, and love of many along the way.

The prolific defender and champion of a truly free and democratic Africa, the famed Professor PLO LUMUMBA, left a strong impression on me the very first time I was in his company, and I sought him out for his endorsement of my work. I am grateful he found my work worthy to pen his name in the foreword. And for that, I thank him immensely.

Dr. Sébastien Nadot, a French member of parliament, will strike many as an unusual partner and advocate for justice and for peace in Cameroon, but he stands as the few lone voices on the international arena, calling for meaningful participation of his country, France, in peace talks to end years of carnage and decades of neo-colonization in Africa. I am indebted to you for your continued candor on the issues and support to me.

Though I offered a place of special gratitude to my daughter, Praxie, whom I often lovingly call "Bubbles" for her bubbly free-spirited character, I wish to again express my sincere thanks to her for allowing me the freedom and support to write about the life-affirming and life-defining struggles we both endured; a story that opened my heart to embrace my own struggles about engaging conflict and staying on the sidelines, about character and the inertia born of fear and ultimately about war and the search for just peace. Praxie's boundless love, courage, and confidence through the years of long rehabilitative treatments showed me as the prolific writer and motivational speaker, Wayne Dyer often says that "no one knows enough to be a pessimist," and that courage requires that we rid ourselves of the neat little device called blaming. For a daughter, you became my teacher. Thank you.

I owe my very existence to a courageous, humble woman I am honored to call "Mami." Again, while herself the product of an era that saw no value in the educated girl child, she moved heaven and earth for me to ascend the highest levels of my educational pursuits. For that, I dedicate this book to her.

For Nadine and Stephan Miya, my other two children. Your lives are just beginning. It is my hope that someday you and your children live in a world free from wars and that, through my words, you are encouraged to live conflict-inspired, stepping into your own truths and owning them. Your voices matter. And the world waits. Thank you both for your encouragements when I felt discouraged along the way.

Thank you, Gerald, my husband of over three decades, for your early appraisal of the manuscript.

To Emma Leslie, Dr. Pauline Riak, Maria De Rosa, Professor Lenox Hinds, Dr. John Fobanjong, Beth Lyons, Rev. Father Nyuykongmo, and Rev. Father Niba, I am forever grateful for your early reviews of my work.

I wish to thank Jenny and my editing team, many working behind the scenes, for their keen attention to details. I am grateful to you for ensuring there were no obvious gaffs in the text. After staring at my own words for so long, I needed help with crossing my t's and dotting my i's. For my readers, I pray you pardon what may have been missed.

ABOUT THE AUTHOR

Dr. Emma M. Osong is one of America's notable advocates and leading voices, striving for permanent peace and justice in Southern Cameroons-Ambazonia war. She is an author, educator, speaker, and peace advocate. Dr. Osong is a prominent aerospace engineer and the founder of WPPJ. She's featured in Voice of America, Equinox TV, Obsessed Hub, ABC Amba, NRC Media, and more. While Emma uses her speaking platform to educate people, corporations, not-for-profit organizations, and international development sectors on conflict and social justice leadership, she is also a sought-after transformational speaker and leadership expert. At the core of her teachings is addressing human transformation instead of change, living a conflict-inspired life, and using a step-by-step system that generates actionable personal, group, or organizational results. Dr. Emma is available for speaking engagements, personal coaching, and op-eds.

My Philosophy

My entire world crumbled at once. At the same time that my birth country devolved into a deadly conflict, and my daughter was told she would never walk again. For many years, I watched conflict from the sidelines. Suddenly, I was in the thick of it, and I had a choice. I could let conflict destroy me, or I could let it inspire me. Once I overcame my personal adversity and crushing fear of speaking the truth about the "Anglophone" crisis in Cameroon (because of the high visibility of those who speak out), I knew I had to help others do the same. Writing a book about my struggles was only the beginning. As you know, there is a limit to how many pages a book can hold. The lessons I have learned from this journey called life are innumerable. My book is merely a snapshot of the learning experiences that I wish to share.

Albert Einstein said, "Wisdom is not a product of schooling but of the lifelong attempt to acquire it." As part of my lifelong journey to acquire wisdom, I've developed a philosophy to keep myself present, to step into my truth and own it, and be energized in conflict. I welcome everyone to live conflict-inspired. In addition to the lessons found in my book, I've prepared a personal and group program to help you adopt my conflict-inspired philosophy. Here's a sneak peek of my easy step-by-step, done-for-you program:

- Define your CEO of Me Inc. mission and vision.

- Identify your goals.

- Pinpoint conflict areas that hold you back and how to be conflict-inspired.

- Improve your relationships, releasing your power to be REAL (real, responsible, engaged, acting in focused service, and loyal).

If you're struggling to turn your pain into positive action, you can book a session to get unstuck. I also welcome you to contact me with questions or suggestions or simply to say hello.

Made in the USA
Middletown, DE
12 January 2022

57623231R00186